THE KNOWLEDGE MAP ASSISTING ASSESSMENT SYSTEM

BASED ON ACCUMULATING AND VISUALIZING TACIT KNOWLEDGE OF TEACHERS

CHIEN-YUAN SU

ZHEJIANG UNIVERSITY PRESS
浙江大学出版社

Preface

The purpose of this book is to design and implement an on-line intelligent assessment system to assist teachers of primary schools in test item construction and performance assessment. As we know, knowledge maps have nodes and links, nodes as key concepts and links as relationships between key concepts. It is as a visual-architecture of knowledge domain that facilitates the users to examine the knowledge on a global scale and from different views (Eppler, 2001). From the knowledge map presentation, the teacher can recognize the important courses, assessment concepts and the relationships between them. This assessment system we designed will harness technologies from knowledge map, domain concept energy appraisal, Bloom's Taxonomy, automatic item recommendation, and dynamic item difficulty adapting. Wherein, an attempt was made to automatically build an assessment domain knowledge map from capturing teacher's implicit assessment knowledge by using knowledge acquisition techniques.

The assessment system development seems to be divided into three stages in this book.The major work of the first stage is to establish an assessment system prototype **(Knowledge Map Assisted Assessment System)**, and the establishment of domain concept hierarchy for a targeted domain by analyzing several editions of teaching materials and the creation of an item bank, into which test items collected from different sources are put. A test item classification mechanism will also be built to automatically figure out the relationship between test items and teaching objective, domain concepts, and Bloom's Taxonomy in course units.

Collected test items, before putting in the bank, will all be analyzed by the mechanism automatically. The second stage focuses on the web-based IKMAAS (The Internet-based Knowledge Map Assisted Assessment System), and investigating how to create a knowledge map with energy appraisal of domain concepts under specific course units and, based on which, an evaluation system is designed and implemented. Based on the achievements of the first two stages, the IKMAAS system will feature automatic item recommendation based on clustering similar assessment preferences, dynamic item difficulty adapting, item discrimination, and learning objective classification.Teachers can flexibly adjust or modify an auto generated examination paper according to their teaching needs and with the help of knowledge map with energy appraisal.

In this book, system usage records, questionnaires and interview responses were used for evaluating the usability of the methodology and the satisfaction of using the IKMAAS. The results indicate the potential of the methodology, as each of the teachers agreed that the visualized assessment knowledge helped them to comprehend easily the proportions of concepts they intended to test and helped them to notice clearly concepts that they may have ignored. The promising results confirm the feasibility of the methodology and the system in helping teachers compile their educational assessments easily and precisely. The results of the evaluations were also used to improve the assessment system to make it more effective and efficient. All of the methodology and technologies employed by the IKMAAS are well developed and are domain independent, which makes it highly flexible and able to transfer from one course subject domain to another. Furthermore, the results of this book showed the potential of using knowledge maps and knowledge accumulating methodologies within the pedagogical paradigm.

This book is organized into fifteen chapters. Chapter 1 introduces the background and motivation why we want to explore these topics, and describes our goals and contributions to this assessment system we developed. The relevant literature introductions accompanied by background information is reviewed in the next several chapters.

Apparently, the role of assessment in the classroom will be introduced in Chapter 2, it described assessment implications, and several assessment types such as summative and formative assessment, and emphasized the importance of classroom assessment that teachers constructed. In Chapter 3, we illustrate the relationship between course concepts and assessment items, and describe several assessment criteria, such as the difficulty and the identification of items, and Bloom's cognitive taxonomy. The existing computer assisted assessment system or tools are introduced in Chapter 4; in Chapter 5, it introduced the implicit assessment knowledge of teachers; knowledge and its management, knowledge representation and visualization are introduced in Chapters 6 and 7. We separately illustrate the definition of explicit and tacit knowledge, and introduce several different knowledge's representations and visualization ways. Knowledge maps and several types are described in Chapter 8; several item categorization technologies are described in Chapter 9. Teacher clustering, and personalization and item recommendation were being described in Chapters 10 and 11. From the beginning of Chapter12, we introduced the Knowledge Map Assisted Assessment System (KMAAS) prototype that we designed. The IKMAAS, and a specification of a recommendation mechanism on IKMAAS are described in Chapters 13 and 14. In these chapters, a detailed description illustrated their architecture and several designed modules are shown, as well as how to prove their efforts and to help teachers conduct their assessment through the system assistance. Finally, several conclusions and future work are offered in the last chapter.

Acknowledgements

Throughout the development and writing of this book, I would like to thank all my advisors, colleagues and friends who gave so freely of their time and advice. First, I particularly thank my advisor Tzone-I Wang, who served in the department of engineering science, National Cheng Kung University (NCKU), Taiwan, China. He provides the highest quality research environment for me and supports me to immerse in the academic atmosphere. And then I'd like to thank Chiung-Hui Chiu, she is my advisor in my master period. She led me into the academic field, and guide me to turn towards the academic road. And extra thanks Tieh-Hsiung Wu, the former president of Tainan University, which was a scholar who lets people respected. He always concern me and often give me encouragement, when I feel depressed. In addition, thanks to juniors in LINA Laboratory, Jimmy Chang, Pei-Chi Chang, and Chieh-Pei Chu, who made many contributions for system development, and all the participated teachers who have directly and indirectly contributed to this book through their comments, experiences and participation in assessment activities. I would also like to express my appreciation to the following colleagues in the Institute of Educational Technology of Zhejiang University, they include Jianping Zhang, Yan Li, Yuqing Guo, all of whom have provided encouragement, advice and support. And finally, I would like to special thanks to my family, especially to my mother, Mei-Ci Chen and my sister, Chiu-Hsia Su, who encourage and give me the greatest spiritual support.

CHAPTER 1 Introduction

Knowledge maps have nodes and links, nodes as key concepts and links as relationships between key concepts. From a map, the teacher can recognize the important course and assessment concepts and the relationships between them. In this book, we integrate knowledge map into the educational assessment, and develop an assessment system to assist primary teachers to arrange their classroom assessment. In this chapter, we described the background and motivation why to explore these topics and described the goals and contributions. Finally, the organizations of this book are described in the last section.

1.1 Background and Motivation

Computers and information technology have advanced rapidly in recent years and are now widely used by educators to facilitate teaching and learning (Chou & Liu, 2005; Goodison, 2002). However, these technologies have also had a significant impact on educational settings and educational assessment. Many research studies carried out on the issue of computer use in educational assessment have agreed that computer aided assessment activities are much more effective. Allowing for enhanced innovation in testing and assessment (Bonham, Beichner, Titus & Martin, 2000), computer technology significantly improves the assessment process for all stakeholders, including teachers, students and administrators (McDonald, 2002). Computerized testing and assessments have become a promising alternative to traditional paper-and-pencil assessments because computer-based assessment results are immediate, unbiased and accurate.

Other benefits of computer-based assessments include enhanced feedback, decreased economic costs of manual data input, convenient individualized administration and improved test security. Given that the computer has the ability to do all of the routine work involved in test administration, computer-based assessment is proving to be extremely beneficial within the field of education (Barak & Rafaeli, 2004; Kveton, Jelinek, Voboril & Klimusova, 2007).

A considerable amount of research has evaluated the systems and software tools designed for creating educational assessments and satisfying specific test environment needs, such as assisting educators with the construction of assessments, providing data analysis tools for exercises or tests, assessing student performance at various levels, giving quick diagnostic feedback, allowing random test-item arrangement and improving the convenience and efficiency of computerized test administration (Conole & Warburton, 2005; Huang, Lin & Cheng, 2009; Nuntiyagul, Naruedomkul, Cercone &Wongsawang, 2008). According to our observations, computer-assisted assessment tools have become increasingly indispensable to instructors in primary and secondary education (He & Tymms, 2005). In Taiwan, China, many of the commercial assessment systems and assessment software tools developed by textbook publishers have been designed to assist educators in creating and managing tests in the primary and secondary education environments. Instructors generally use these tools to harness freely shared item banks and to select, arrange, edit and administer the assessments.

In this context, generating good assessments depends on both the subjective appropriateness of the test items and on the way the assessment is constructed (Hwang, Chu, Yin & Lin, 2008). Some researchers argue that to select appropriate test items, educators must consider multiple criteria, such as the expected time needed to answer individual items, the number of test items to include, the specified distribution of course concepts to be learned and the expected degree of difficulty of the test (Chamoso & Ca'ceres, 2009). However, other researchers contend that these test item criteria are inefficient and fail to meet the multiple assessment requirements simultaneously (Yin, Chang, Hwang, Hwang & Chan, 2006). For example, when instructors create assessments applying the aforementioned criteria, they run the risk of not properly balancing concepts, levels of difficulty, and relationships between item development and content due either to ignorance or subjectivity (Panjaburee, Hwang, Triampo & Shih, 2010). In addition, instructors may encounter difficulties in determining the number of concepts to be assessed in comparison to the number of test items, or as a result of neglecting key points in the curriculum, they may assess course concepts disproportionately in their assessments (Su & Wang, 2010). The reasons for such problems are twofold. First, even veteran teachers may forget to assess certain important concepts without a visual overview of the distribution of the concepts covered by the test items. Second, novice teachers, without much assessment experience, may not appreciate the relative importance of concepts to be tested and may fail to arrange the test items with a proper ratio reflected the relative importance of the concepts. Consequently, many teachers feel discomfort with the quality of their own assessments and believe that they need assistance in constructing appropriate assessments (Frey, Petersen, Edwards, Pedrotti & Peyton, 2005). The first critical step in the assessment development process must be to determine the proper concept-item proportion (Yin, et al., 2006). Yang and Chan (2008) have indicated that a multi-expert approach is a more effective means of recognizing and rejecting incorrect solutions and suggestions compared to a single-expert approach. Moreover, information and knowledge reuse minimizes the need to refer explicitly to past projects, reduces the time and cost involved in solving problems, and improves the quality of solutions during the construction of assessments (Lin, Wang & Tserng, 2006). Several enabling activities should be performed to help attain the eventual goal of experience and knowledge reuse, such as preserving and managing experience and knowledge; capturing, modelling, storing, retrieving, adapting, evaluating and maintaining restated activities; and creating assessments that promote knowledge acquisition, sharing and application so as to achieve innovation (Lin, et al., 2006). The knowledge acquired through the collaboration of teachers regarding the relative importance of and the relationships between course concepts should be an effective tool for helping inexperienced teachers, especially when experienced teachers cooperate to combine their assessment knowledge and experience into a single knowledge base (Nevin, Thousand & Villa, 2009; Panjaburee, et al., 2010). When captured knowledge is reused and shared among teachers, it can enhance the construction process and decrease the time and cost of problem-solving, while improving the quality of the solutions. Novice teachers can then employ valuable assessment knowledge taken from multiple expert teachers to determine a more accurate distribution of concepts to be assessed through the selection of appropriate test items.

Although the sharing of assessment experience and knowledge does not guarantee effective teaching, it promotes the development of a knowledge base for assessment that is more applicable to 21st century educational assessment settings. Assessment enhancement depends largely on how teachers make sense of sharing their experiences, their perceptions of how suitable the experiences of others are to new teaching contexts and how they adjust their own teaching practices to meet the perceived demands of new contexts (So, Pow & Hung, 2009). However, most assessment project-related problems, solutions, experiences and expertise reside with and are confronted by the teacher during the assessment construction phase. This implicit knowledge is usually abstract and unstructured and is normally not documented or stored in any system database. Capturing this implicit assessment knowledge and transforming it into a form of explicit knowledge is important for the preservation of such abstract implicit assessment knowledge, as well as for the management of such knowledge.

In addition, researchers have shown that offering overview supports by providing access to relevant information greatly assists people in making decisions, solving problems, and avoiding disorientation problems (Edwards & Hardman, 1999; Thomas, 2009). Visual representations are forms of metacognition that graphically display the thinking process (Costa & Garmston, 2002), which is helpful as such visual methods are able to externalize and elicit the abstract structure of knowledge (Jacobson & Archodidou, 2000). Thus, graphic tools or map presentations can be used to create overview supports, restructure content, and deepen or elaborate upon the knowledge of a subject (Zumbach, 2009). The various forms of maps can facilitate information searches within a domain (Chen, 2008). Knowledge maps, for example, provide a graphical representation of the relationships among concepts, thus ensuring that specific aspects of knowledge are more easily understandable (Speel, Shadbolt, Vries, Dam & O' hara, 1999), thereby aiding in the acquisition of explicit information or tacit knowledge by illustrating how knowledge flows throughout an organization (Grey, 1999). Not only can knowledge map outline where important gaps in receiving knowledge exist, but they have been used in the formulation of recommendations to support a series of related research projects and workshops. The briefing sheets of an individual knowledge map are meant to serve as quick snapshots of information in key areas related to the use of ICTs in education (Trucano, 2005). Certain researchers, such as Pirnay-Dummer and Ifenthaler (2010), build "SMD technology", which is based on the mental model theory and graph theory. SMD technology uses (a) graphical representations, such as concept maps, and (b) natural language expressions to analyze the individual processes in persons when solving complex problems at single quantitative measures and standardized representations for qualitative analysis and feedback.

A knowledge map is generally a representation of "knowledge about knowledge" rather than of knowledge itself (Eppler, 2001). It basically helps to detect the sources of knowledge and their structure by representing the elements and structural links of application domains. Knowledge maps with visual representation (using circles, images connected by lines) conceptualize hierarchies of data, information and linkages. A knowledge map is a technique that increasing efficiency of an explaining associations of knowledge bodies with the purpose of managing knowledge in an organization by creating similar content associations (Watthananon & Mingkhwan, 2012). Knowledge mapping is used to organize knowledge in a database so that users can find what they need in a convenient and easy way. In the sense that the knowledge map is a knowledge representation that reveals underlying relationships of the knowledge sources, a map metaphor is used for a spatial display. Knowledge maps can be used as primary references for knowledge acquisition, as adjunct aids to text processing or as retrieval cues, which serve as scaffolds or supports to cognitive processing as they can reduce cognitive load, enhance representation of relationships among complex constructs, provide support for students whose verbal skills are weak, and serve as important props for communicating shared knowledge (O'Donnell, Dansereau & Hall, 2002). Therefore, knowledge maps can save teacher's considerable effort by outlining the distribution of concepts weights, thereby facilitating the teacher's ability to recall and comprehend the distribution of concept weights from a knowledge map. The knowledge map provides a framework for visualizing assessment knowledge that can be easily examined, refined and shared by knowledge teachers, they are as blueprints to help teachers to find useful assessment knowledge, and this facilitation is especially beneficial for novice teachers.

In this book, we propose an assessment system called the Knowledge Map Assisting Assessment System (KMAAS) and upgrade KMAAS into the Internet-based KMAAS, which captures the teachers' assessment knowledge and integrates knowledge maps to assist primary school teachers in creating assessments. This system also clusters the teachers' assessment knowledge and then recommends the most suitable candidate test items based on the individual teacher's personal assessment preferences.

1.2 Goals and Contributions

As previously mentioned, this book proposes several methodologies for accumulating teachers' tacit knowledge of specific courses when they are compiling their assessments, by using an implicit knowledge extraction mechanism. The methodology visualizes the accumulated knowledge, using knowledge maps, which shows the overall importance distribution of course concepts and the closeness of these concepts, to help teachers construct their assessments. Teachers may refer to these maps as they adjust balance among concepts in an assessment by creating test items or by selecting from item banks appropriate test items, recommended by a teacher-cluster-based collaborative filtering mechanism that stays within the individual teacher's assessment preference.

The goals of this book are threefold. The first purpose of our study is to integrate knowledge maps into educational assessments and build an assessment prototype system, the Knowledge Map Assisting Assessment System (KMAAS), to assist primary school teachers in constructing assessments. The KMAAS harnesses a number of technologies, including course concept extraction, knowledge maps, natural language processing, item categorization, and item retrieval. KMAAS not only automatically performs concept extractions from course materials, analyses their relative importance, and classifies collected test items to establish their associations with the concepts, but it also automatically constructs real-time updated knowledge maps with a weight appraisal of concepts for creating effective assessments. This part of the study extracts important keywords from textbooks, teaching materials, and test items and uses them as the "nodes" to represent learning concepts in knowledge maps. The "concept weights" are a set of important values weighted within the curriculum. The terms that directly indicate course topics are considered to play a more important role in assessments (Song, Wenyin, Gu, Quan & Hao, 2011). These topics are given a higher weight by multiplying their original weight with a coefficient larger than 1. The KMAAS helps teachers analyze and reorganize their own collections of test sheets and test items and provides a search method for retrieving concept-associated test items from an item bank. Teachers may refer to an automatically constructed knowledge map with concrete weights that show the relative importance of course concepts and their interrelationships in the specified testing range, or they may refer to another knowledge map that shows the current proportion of concepts embedded in the items on a test sheet that is updated in real time when test items are rearranged. All of their assessments, which implicitly contain their valuable knowledge and experience, are kept in the test sheet bank. This sheet bank is a preliminary assessment knowledge base for sharing among teachers. One critical issue is how to define and implement a methodology to extract and integrate teacher assessment knowledge and experience further, as well as how to visualize and share this knowledge.

A secondary purpose of this book is to propose a knowledge accumulation and sharing methodology to capture and manage teachers' assessment knowledge as they compile assessments to benefit their future assessment work. This methodology is realized in the KMAAS as a knowledge management framework that acquires and converts teachers' assessment knowledge and allows it to be shared among other teachers, thereby assisting them in their assessment tasks. The revised Internet-based KMAAS operates in two phases. In the first phase, KMAAS automatically extracts and compiles teachers' knowledge on assessment tasks and specific subjects based on their item-selecting records. In the second phase, KMAAS calculates and transforms item and course concept probability distribution into knowledge maps that displays the teachers' accumulated assessment knowledge. These visual overviews constructed and presented in the framework are used for item-selection assistance that supports teachers in their compilation of assessments.

The last goal is to propose an item-recommendation mechanism that supplies suitable candidate items according to the teachers' personal assessment preferences, thereby helping teachers to select items and thus decrease the amount of time spent on selecting items when they viewed numerous items from the item bank on IKMAAS. We first clustered teacher groups using the collected assessment data on IKMAAS and subsequently integrated a cluster-based collaborative filtering recommendation approach. When the teacher begins to construct an assessment, IKMAAS, via the item recommendation mechanism, shows items sorted first by the teacher group based on similar preferences that conform to his/her need, thereby allowing teachers to quickly search the appropriate items.

1.3 Organization of This Book

The remainder of this book is organized into several chapters. The relevant introductions accompanied by background information is reviewed in the next several chapters. Apparently, the role of assessment in the classroom will introduced in Chapter 2. And several of previous literature studies on the relationship between course concepts and assessment items; the existing computer assisted assessment system or tools; the implicit assessment knowledge of teachers; knowledge management and an overview of knowledge maps, test item categorization; teacher clustering and item recommendation will be described in Chapters 2 to 11 in this book. Chapters 12 and 13, provides several introductions about the knowledge map assisted assessment system that we designed. The architecture of KMAAS and IKMAAS and its component implementations are described in these two chapters. In addition, the practicality of the proposed methodology and designed system is demonstrated through experimental study presented in. In Chapter 14, we propose an innovative, personalized item-recommendation that automatically adapts to the similar clustered groups of teachers' assessment interests and preferences. The proposed method described how to cluster teachers' assessment knowledge, and how to proceed with the personalized item recommendation, and the evaluated results for the effectiveness of the item-recommendation via experiments are respectively presented in this chapter. Finally, some conclusions and future work are offered in the last chapter.

CHAPTER 2 The Role of Assessment in Classroom

This Chapter introduced the definition of educational assessment, and different types of educational assessment such as Formative and Summative evaluations, as well as Preliminary evaluations and Diagnostic evaluations, we would also illustrate their implication, difference and application in the educational assessment.

In many researches, the term measurement, assessment, and evaluation are often used interchangeably in education (Oosterhof, 2003). The differences among these terms are not absolute. The distinction between measurement and evaluation is the easiest to establish. In education, measurements are concerned with establishing the characteristics of individuals or groups of individuals, usually students. Evaluation, however, combines our measures with other information to establish the desirability and importance of what we have observed. Evaluation is the outcome of measurement after value has been added.

By way of contrast, given the recent use of the general term "assessment", it is important to clarify what is meant by "classroom assessment." (McMillan & Workman, 1998). According to Cizek (Cizek, 1997), there are four definitions of assessment. The term can refer to formats for gathering information, such as using a portfolio or performance assessment. Some see assessment as referring to a new attitude toward the way students are tested away from standardized multiple choice. The term has come to represent a new ethos of empowerment to hold students and schools accountable. Finally, assessment can refer to a new process of gathering, synthesizing, and using information, one that is similar to what doctors and psychologists use when diagnosing and treating patients. These connotations suggest a much broader definition than what is typically conveyed when using the term "test." Airasian (1997) defines assessment as the "collection, synthesis, and interpretation of information to aid the teacher in decision making" (Airasian & Russell, 2001). Assessment is often used as a stylistic alternative to measurement, and it generally has broader connotations than does measurement. Were measurement limited to assigning numbers to attributes, assessment might be thought of as combining of qualitative and quantitative attributes. Assessment and instruction have a reciprocal relationship. Assessment is determined by the curriculum and on the other hand, assessment has a strong effect on what is taught and how it is taught (Pellegrino, Chudowsky & Glaser, 2001). In general, assessment and its interface with curriculum, teaching and learning has always been a significant component of classroom practice. In this book, we mainly used the assessment to represent the classroom assessment which the teacher arranges to evaluate their classroom students.

Effective assessment plays a significant role in appropriately placing students, diagnosing learning problems and progress, improving and enriching teaching practices, as well as achieving and maintaining academic standards. Following (Popham, 2000), we consider assessment as "a process by which educators use the students' responses to specially created or naturally occurring stimuli in order to make inferences about students' knowledge, skills, or affective status." These inferences can lead to decisions with respect to individual students, complete classes or schools, or to the educational system as a whole.

Teaching, which includes the use of student assessment, is most effective when these powerful contextual forces are aligned with what the teacher is doing in the classroom. For example, when the curriculum and your instruction are aligned with state standards, it's likely that students will achieve well on state tests. When the teaching and assessment are aligned to what we know about how students learn, achievement and motivation are enhanced. Essentially, there are a number of powerful influences now that affect everything you do in the classroom, including assessment, and understanding these factors is essential in developing and using effective assessment. Figure 2.1 emphasizes their impact on classroom assessment (Oosterhof, 2003).

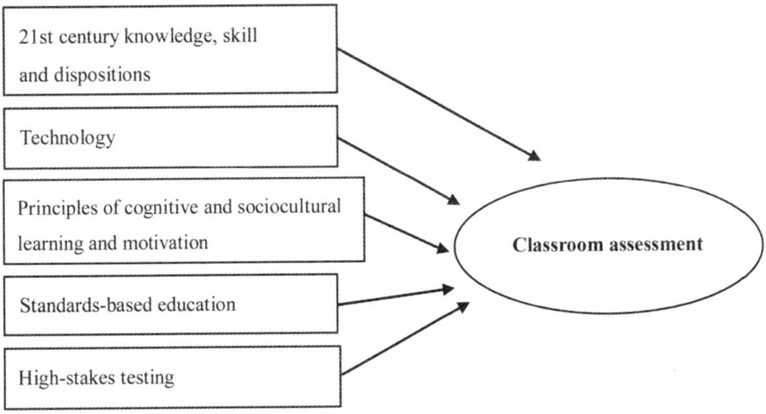

Figure 2.1 Significant factors influencing classroom assessment

Classroom assessment is in these complex environments that teachers must make some of their most important decisions about what and how students have learned. Accurate and appropriate student assessment provide the information to help teachers make better decisions. In the classroom context, then, classroom assessment is gathering, interpreting, and using evidence of student learning and motivation to support teacher decision making in a variety of ways (Maclellan, 2004):

• Diagnosing of student strengths, weaknesses, misunderstanding, and learning errors.

• Monitoring of student effort and progress toward proficiency.

• Documenting student learning.

• Improving student learning, motivation, and 21st century skills and dispositions.

- Assigning grades.
- Providing feedback to parents.

In general, assessment has different strategies according to its purposes. Usually these assessments are meant for certification or accountability purposes. The two main distinctions in this regard are Scriven's differentiation of summative and formative assessment (Scriven, 1966).**Summative assessment** is performed at the end of specific learning activity; and used to judge the student progression and also to discriminate between them based on the results obtained (Bransford, Brown & Cocking, 2000; Learn, 2000). Summative assessment refers to the assessment that occurs at the end of a school year, a particular course or program. Contrary to summative assessment, **formative assessment** is part of the learning process; this assessment is used to give feedback to both students and teachers in order to guide their efforts toward achieving the goals of the learning process. Where, formative assessment is done during a program or at its beginning. This assessment primarily informs teachers about their students' learning process, though it can also inform the students themselves. Mostly, the results are intended to adapt the program to the students' needs. Additionally, according to the teaching phases that occur before, during, and after instruction is aligned with three major types of classroom assessment (Chap-man & King, 2009): pre-assessment, formative assessment, and summative assessment. They extra defined that pre-assessment is what you will do before instruction to ascertain students' knowledge, attitude, and interests. This information is then used as starting point for designing instruction. Other researchers take into consideration apart the above two main basic types, and added several other types of assessment such as: diagnostic assessment, adaptive assessments, forward-looking assessment, self-assessment, and performance-based assessment (Reed, 2006).

Relevant insights and relationships about different assessment type are described as follows. Bloom, Madaus & Hastings(1981) proposed that assessment is used to facilitate formative, summative and diagnostic evaluations. Oosterhof (2003) add a fourth role: preliminary evaluations. Figure 2.2 illustrates the relationship among the four evaluative roles of classroom assessment. Preliminary evaluations feed into formative evaluations. Formative evaluations occur during instruction and are based on frequent assessments. Diagnostic evaluations are concerned with problems that might be or, more typically, already are preventing students from learning. Summative evaluations follow instruction. As indicated in Figure 2.2, preliminary, formative, and diagnostic evaluations depend mostly on informal assessments. These evaluations require measures of student performance that are highly responsive to immediate situations. They require assessments that can occur without a pause in instruction. Summative evaluations, in contrast, require the more controlled measures provided by formal assessments. Summative evaluations do not depend on the spontaneous and responsive characteristics of informal assessment.

(1) Preliminary evaluations

Occur during the first days of school and provide a basis for expectations throughout the school year. They are obtained mainly through a teacher's spontaneous informal observations and oral questions and are concerned with student's skills, attitudes, and physical characteristics. These evaluations are basically the same as those you establish whenever you meet new people. They happen naturally, and they are essential to guide our interactions with others and with students. When preliminary evaluations involve general or overall assessment of student's knowledge and attitudes, non-referenced interpretations are required. Their general assessments of what students know or what their attitudes are involve domains too broad for criterion-reference interpretations. As always when norm-referenced interpretations are used, it is important to identify your norm group. Are you comparing the new students with each other, with previous students when they were new, with previous students at the end of last year, or possibly with what you consider to be ideal students? Each reference may be appropriate, but it is import to recognize what comparison group is. A student may be his or her own norm group. During preliminary evaluations, you often establish what is reasonable or typical for individual students. This norm becomes useful for interpreting later performance. Assessment leading to preliminary evaluations may be criterion-referenced instead of, or as well as, norm-referenced. Is a student a loner? Does he volunteer ideas or ask questions? Does he know what is meant by electrolysis? Each of these can be a well-defined domain. Each is a domain that can be used to describe what a student can and cannot too. Each can also be norm-referenced when used to describe what is reasonable or typical.

(2) Formative evaluations

Occur during instruction. They establish whether students have achieved sufficient mastery of skills and whether further work with these skills is appropriate. Formative evaluations are also concerned with the attitudes students are developing. The purpose of formative evaluations is to determine what adjustment to the present learning environment should be made. Formative evaluations are based primarily on continuous informal assessment, such as listening to what students say, using oral questions to probe comprehension, and watching students' facial expressions and other behaviors. Formative evaluations are also based on formally developed assessments such as quizzes, seat work, homework, and group projects. Most assessments that occur in the classroom lead to formative evaluations (Maclellan, 2004).

(3) Summative evaluations

Occur at the conclusion of instruction, such as at the end of a unit or the end of the year. Summative evaluations are used to certify student achievement and assign end-of-term grades. They serve as the basis for promoting and sometimes for grouping students. Summative evaluations also help determine whether instructional strategies should be changed before the next school year. Unlike in formative evaluations, the role that assessment plays within summative evaluations is not to establish student proficiency with each skill, but instead to provide an overview of achievement across a number of skills. With summative evaluations, each skill might be measured by just one test item, which is not enough to establish with confidence proficiency with individual skills. Often, only a sampling of skills are tested. Summative evaluations are based on formal assessments.

(4) Diagnostic evaluations

Occur before or, more typically, during instruction. Diagnostic evaluations are concerned with skills and other characteristics that are prerequisite to the current instruction or that enable the achievement of instructional objectives. During instruction, Diagnostic evaluations are used to establish underlying causes for a student's failing to learn a skill.

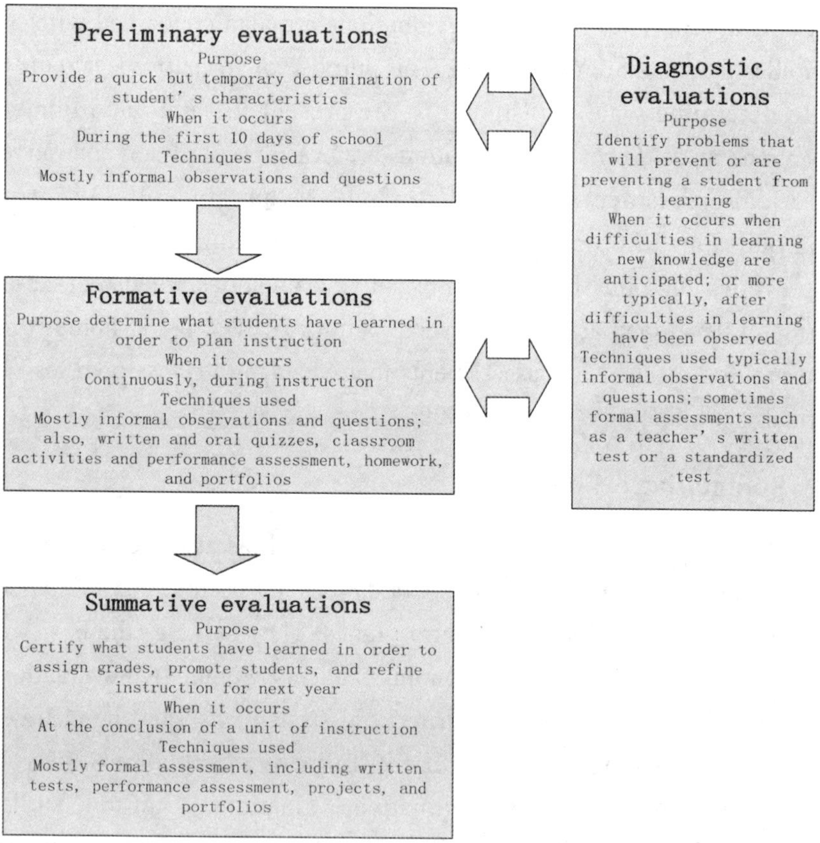

Figure 2.2 Four roles of classroom assessment (Oosterhof, 2003)

When used before instruction, diagnostic evaluations try to anticipate conditions that will negatively affect learning. In both cases, the role of measurement is to assess a student's performance in specific prerequisite skills not typically taught in the present classroom setting. Diagnostic evaluations are based mostly on informal assessments, although formal measures, such as standardized tests, are sometimes used.

Different assessment scenarios require different technological conditions, so one-single solution cannot optimally serve every possible assessment need. Teaching and learning in a modern society extend well beyond formal schooling, and even in traditional educational settings, there are diverse forms of assessment, which require technologies adapted to the actual needs. Different technological problems have to be solved when computers are used to administer high-stakes, large-scale, nationally or regionally representative assessments under standardized conditions, as well as low-stakes, formative, diagnostic assessment in a classroom environment under diverse school conditions (Csapó, Ainley, Bennett, Latour & Law, 2012).

CHAPTER 3 Assessment, Course Concepts and Items

Educational assessment is a common way to evaluate students' learning performance (Noorbehbahani & Kardan, 2011). Classroom teachers generally use this way to realize how well they taught and how well students learned at the end of instruction (Black & Wiliam, 1998). In this chapter, we introduced, "assessment", "course concept" and "item", and further described their relationship in the educational assessment. In addition, we introduced several assessment criteria such as item difficulty, item discrimination and Bloom's Taxonomy.

Researchers analyzed the relationships among assessments of teaching and learning (Bowden, Bowden & Marton, 1998; Brown & Glasner, 1999). It was found that in addition to its constructive role in evaluating student learning outcomes and teaching quality, assessment also provided a powerful tool to improve teaching and learning effectiveness (Brown, Bull & Pendlebury, 2013). In general, typical educational assessment makes use of preselected measurements, norm-referenced standardized tests, for example, to measure and evaluate the educational quality of students, instructors, classes, institutions and the educational system as a whole. Effective and efficient assessment is significant in properly placing students, diagnosing problems and progress in learning, improving and enriching teacher's performance, evolving curriculum, as well as achieving and maintaining academic standards (Huang, He & Davidson-Shivers, 2011).

In order to develop better assessments, classroom teachers are usually required to consider their teaching contents covered course knowledge. Some researchers argue that the notion of course *concept* can be regarded as an atomic unit of knowledge (Chang, Chiu, Lin & Heh, 2003). Novak & Gowin (1984) defined a concept as a designated label of regularity in events or objects. That means a concept is a representation of something that could be used as an atomic unit of knowledge pieces. Integrated knowledge is created by forming connections among concepts (Hsu, Kuo, Chang & Heh, 2002). Instruction in schools is intended to teach concepts (Novak, 1979). Each course unit is made up of a certain number of concepts, and each concept has its own size and its own special importance in the course material. In 2006, Agarwal, Edwards & Perez-Quinone proposed that a course can be organized as a graph with concept as nodes and interrelationships as edges, when selecting test items, some general principles should be followed. Each item should relate to a specific course concept so that a correct answer implies knowledge of that concept. Also, test items should cater to varied knowledge levels. A number of studies have been conducted related to course concepts and assessment questions. For example, Smith, Wood & Knight (2008) designed an assessment tool recently to assess central course concepts in genetics and diagnose misconceptions or preconceptions. The created assessments were taken by more than 600 students at three institutions. This tool can be used by genetics instructors to measure students' learning gains as well as to identify strengths and weaknesses in teaching approaches for specific concepts. Huang and colleagues proposed to incorporate the intelligent diagnosis and assessment tool into an open software e-learning platform developed for programming language courses (Huang, Chen, Luo, Chen & Chuang, 2008). This study applies the corresponding relation of the concepts and questions to explore the degree of student familiarization with the concepts, according to students' assessment records. Their experiments were conducted in two introductory-undergraduate programming courses examining the effectiveness of the proposed diagnosis and assessment tools. Also, Hwang, Tseng and Hwang (2008) propose a novel approach for constructing concept-effect relationships, diagnosing learning problems, and providing personalized learning suggestions for Science and Mathematics courses, based on students' current tests and historical assessment records. It has been shown that a clear and strong relationship exists between course concepts and test items. Thus, by determining concept weights for course materials and understanding the relationship between these course concepts and test items in advance can provide important information for supporting teachers when they construct educational assessments. It can also help teachers to know which concepts need further focus or remedial instruction.

Moreover, as we know, a variety of assessment criteria have been proposed for educational assessment (Brown et al., 2013). The most commonly assessment criteria were used to analyze the difficulty index and discrimination index of each item.

(1) The difficulty index

Teachers produce a difficulty index for a test item by calculating the proportion of students in class who got an item correct. (The name of this index is counterintuitive, as one actually gets a measure of how easy the item is, not the difficulty of the item.) The larger the proportion, the more students who have learned the content measured by the item. First scoring of the whole test for all students is done, then students would be ranked based on their total score. The bottom third is taken as low achievers and upper third as high achievers. The difficulty index is calculated as percentage of the total number of correct responses to the test item. It is calculated using the formula $P = (H+L)/2 \times 100\%$, where P is the item difficulty index, p_H is the percentage that the number of students answering the item correctly in the high achieving group, p_L is the percentage that the number of students answering the item correctly in the low achieving group and N is the total number of students in two groups. An item is considered difficult when the difficulty index value is less than 30% and considered easy when the index is more than 70% and the value between

30% - 70% is acceptable (between 50% - 60% are ideal). Item difficulty can range from 0.0 (none of the students answered the item correctly) to 1.0 (all of the students answered the item correctly). Experts recommend that the average level of difficulty for a four-option multiple choice test should be between 60% and 80%; an average level of difficulty within this range can be obtained, of course, when the difficulty of individual items falls outside of this range. If an item has a low difficulty value, say, less than 25%, the item may have been miskeyed.

(2) The discrimination index

The index of discrimination is a useful measure of item quality whenever the purpose of a test is to produce a spread of scores, reflecting differences in student achievement. It is a measure of an item's ability to discriminate between those who scored high on the total test and those who scored low. The item discrimination index measures the differences between the percentages of students in the upper group with that of the lower group who obtained the correct response. Though there are several steps in its calculation, once computed, this index can be interpreted as an indication of the extent to which overall knowledge of the content area or mastery of the skills is related to the response to an item. Perhaps the most crucial validity standard for a test item is that whether a student got an item correct or not is due to their level of knowledge or ability and not due to something else such as chance or test bias. The discrimination index was calculated using the formula $D = P_H - P_L$. P_H is the percentage that the number of students answering the item correctly in the high achieving group, P_L is percertage that the the number of students answering the item correctly in the low achieving group. Items with a discrimination index between 25% - 35% are considered good, those with indices more than 35% are excellent, between 20% - 24% are acceptable and below 20% are poor. The value of a positive point-biserial discrimination index can range between 0 and 1; the closer the value is to 1, the better the discrimination. (The value of a negative point-biserial discrimination index can range between - 1 and 0, but positive values are desirable). Item discrimination is greatly influenced by item difficulty. Items with a difficulty of either 0 or 1 will always have a discrimination index of 0, and item discrimination is maximized when item difficulty is close to 50%. As a general rule, point-biserial values of 20% and above are considered to be desirable.

Consequently, a variety of exercises which assess the different assessment objectives' levels should be applied. With the superior capabilities in people cognition analysis, Bloom's Taxonomy developed by Bloom and his colleagues in 1956 (Anderson, Krathwohl & Bloom, 2001). It is widely applied in many approaches for educational assessment (Bergendahl & Tibell, 2005; Burgess, 2005; Choren, Blois & Fuks, 1998). It identifies six levels: knowledge (information, such as simple recall and recognition, specific facts, principles, trends, criteria, and ways of organizing events), comprehension (understanding/interpretation/ paraphrasing information without necessarily applying this information to new situations and without fully understanding the implications of this knowledge), application (use of an abstract concept in a specific but previously unused situation or of principles to concrete situations), analysis (clarification/ decomposition or breaking a concept or communication into its component pars), synthesis (creation of new patterns or structure, or

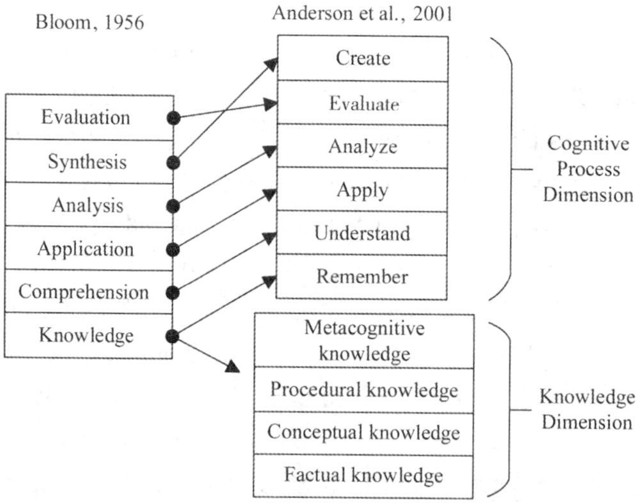

Figure 3.1 Comparison of Bloom's Taxonomy and Anderson's revision

putting elements together into a cohesive whole) and evaluation (making a judgment about the value of products or processes for a given purpose) within the cognitive domain (Bloom, Engelhart, Furst, Hill & Krathwohl, 1956; Bloom & Krathwohl, 1956), from the lowest recognition or recalling of facts to the high order thinking. Following Bloom's Taxonomy, Anderson et al. revise Bloom's Taxonomy and also identify four knowledge types associated with each cognitive process (factual knowledge, conceptual knowledge, procedural knowledge and metacognitive knowledge) (Anderson et al., 2001) as shown as in the Figure 3.1.

Further, a table of specification is a two-way chart which described the topics to be covered by a test and the numbers of items which will be associated with each topic. Examination specifications show "test balance". The construction of the examination specification is an adaptation of a previous model (Heard, Nicol & Heath, 1997) based on Bloom's Taxonomy of educational objectives. It enables the designer to subdivide the examination into topics (y-axis) and relate each topic to the level of learning (x-axis). The topics reflect learning outcomes of the module. The question numbers in each topic are shown and their subtotals calculated for each level of learning. The total number of items in each topic and the total number of items for each level of learning indicate "test balance". The purpose of the examination specification is to enable academics to reflect on the "balance" of the examination before design begins. Examination specifications would be accompanied by definitions of the levels of learning. They are also accompanied by a suggested list of associated "action verbs" (Heard et al., 1997) that can be used in the stem of the items and which are synonymous with the six levels of learning. Objective test items should be realistic, up-to-date and unambiguous (see Table 3.1).

Therefore, teachers can make a deeper evaluation of student performance, instead of only checking their grades. Furthermore, according to analysis results, teachers can evaluate their teaching strategies, modify and develop the curriculum and classroom activities to raise the student cognition levels, i.e., to enhance student learning outcomes (Bergendahl & Tibell, 2005; He, 2006)

Table 3.1 Cognitive domain levels and descriptive verbs

ACTION VERBS APPROPRIATE FOR EACH LEVEL OF BLOOM'S/ ANDERSON & KRATHWOHL'S TAXONOMY (Cognitive Domain)

Remember	Understand	Apply	Analyze	Evaluate	Create
Define	Choose	Apply	Analyze	Appraise	Arrange
Identify	Cite	Demonstrate	Appraise	Assess	Assemble
List	examples	Dramatize	Calculate	Choose	Collect
Name	of	Employ	Categorize	Compare	Compose
Recall	Demonstrate	Generalize	Compare	Critique	Construct
Recognize	use of	Illustrate	Conclude	Estimate	Create
Record	Describe	Interpret	Contrast	Evaluate	Design
Relate	Determine	Operate	Correlate	Judge	Develop
Repeat	Differentiate	Operationalize	Criticize	Measure	Formulate
Underline	between	Practice	Deduce	Rate	Manage
	Discriminate	Relate	Debate	Revise	Modify
	Discuss	Schedule	Detect	Score	Organize
	Explain	Shop	Determine	Select	Plan
	Express	Use	Develop	Validate	Prepare
	Give in own	Utilize	Diagram	Value	Produce
	words	Initiate	Differentiate	Test	Propose
	Identify		Distinguish		Predict
	Interpret		Draw		Reconstruct
	Locate		conclusions		Set-up
	Pick		Estimate		Synthesize
	Report		Evaluate		Systematize
	Restate		Examine		Devise
	Review		Experiment		
	Recognize		Identify		
	Select		Infer		
	Tell		Inspect		
	Translate		Inventory		
	Respond		Predict		
	Practice		Question		
	Simulates		Relate		
			Solve		
			Test		
			Diagnose		

CHAPTER 4 Computer-Assisted Assessment System and Tools

Information Technology may significantly affect educational assessment along a number of dimensions. It improves the traditional assessment environment, and help teachers and students include reducing the cost of test distribution and administration, providing instant feedback and automated scoring, offering adaptive testing, collecting data on testing processes, or presenting test items with multimedia to measure complex skills and understanding (Kuo & Wu, 2013). In this chapter, we described the advantage of computer-based assessments, and introduced some computer assisted assessment system and tools.

Currently, Computer-based technologies have highly influenced how and what students learn in school (Roschelle, Pea, Hoadley, Gordin & Means, 2000) and have also changed the assessment. It improves the precision of detecting the actual values of the observed variables and the efficiency of collecting and processing information, as well as it also enables the sophisticated analysis of the available data, supports decision-making and provides rapid feedback for participants and stakeholders. Technology helps to detect and record the psychomotor, cognitive and affective characteristics of students and the social contexts of teaching and learning processes alike (Csapó, Ainlcy, Bennett, Latour & law, 2012). In which, one of the major opportunities that ICT-based assessment provides is a rich and natural working environment for students to work on complex tasks. An ICT environment makes it possible to present tasks that cannot be presented to students through a conventional paper-and-pencil format (Barak & Rafaeli, 2004). This is so as the computer can interactively carry out simulations in which different, but related values are dynamically linked. These computer simulations of problem situations are considered to be a rich and highly promising genre of ICT-based assessment (Burkhardt & Pead, 2003) by which skills and processes that are difficult to document using traditional tests can be assessed (Pellegrino et al., 2001).These advantages also include real time data collection, reducing the cost of test distribution and administration, providing instant feedback and automated scoring, individualized learning and teaching assessment, offering distributed and interactive assessment, collecting data from testing processes, expert (intelligent) system analysis of teaching and learning curves and styles or presenting test items with multimedia to measure complex skills and understanding (Kuo & Wu, 2013). Bennett thought that technology can be used to improve assessment in at least two major ways: by changing the business of assessment and by changing the substance of the assessment itself (Bennett, 2004). The use of technology in assessment may also play a crucial role in informing curriculum reform and pedagogical innovation, particularly in areas of specific domains in which technology has become crucial to the learning.

Most classifications in the literature showed two kinds of computer-based assessment: computer-based assessments and computerized adaptive tests (CATs)(López-Cuadrado, Pérez, Vadillo & Gutiérrez, 2010). The former refer to the use of computers in assessment administration and scoring, and they are often used interchangeably with computerized fixed tests (Parshall, 2002), and the latter determines and gives the next question based on the learner's response. At present, some web-based assessment systems or authoring tools were developed to facilitate the educational assessment construction and administration for the classroom teachers (Ashton, Beevers, Korabinski & Youngson, 2006; He & Tymms, 2005; Su & Wang, 2010; Wang, Su & Hsieh, 2011). As is known, most classroom teachers have chosen to use assessment authoring tools or system to construct classroom assessment manually in the primary or secondary educational fields in Taiwan, China. They take responsibility to dominate the assessment arrangement and administer their assessment tasks. However, in e-assessment platforms, most common assessment services only provide a medium for teachers to take a test and cannot offer meaningful functions to them usually (Huang, Lin & Cheng, 2009; Su & Wang, 2010). Therefore, to provide beneficial assessment functions or mechanism is very urgent and important for assisting teacher assessment tasks.

4.1 Computer-Based Assessment (CBA) and Computer-Assisted Assessment (CAA)

The application of computers in the assessment or evaluation has been very popular. One of the major opportunities that ICT-based assessment provides is a rich and natural working environment for students to work on complex tasks. The advantages of computer-based assessments over conventional paper-based testing have been identified. These advantages include reducing the cost of test distribution and administration, providing instant feedback and automated scoring, offering adaptive testing, collecting data on testing processes, and presenting test items with multimedia to measure complex skills and understanding (Bridgeman, 2009; He & Tymms, 2005; Kozma, 2009). In addition, computer-based assessments allow adaptive testing, diagnose students' learning progress based on their responses, and offer individualized support that is not possible with paper-based assessments so that assessment activities could closely tie to classroom instruction (Brown, Hinze & Pellegrino, 2008).

From the application point of view in educational assessment, they can be distinguished as **Computer-Based Assessment (CBA)** and **Computer-Assisted Assessment (CAA)** which are often used interchangeably and somewhat inconsistently. CBA can be understood as the interaction between the student and computer during the assessment process. In such assessment, the test delivery and feedback provision are done by the computer. Where CAA is more general, it covers the whole process of assessment involving test marking, analysis and reporting. Additionally, e-assessment is not only applicable for individuals, but is also used for groups. Assessment of groups, also referred to collaborative assessment, is used to assess the participation of individuals in group work and their behavior of how they collaborate with each other to solve problems (Reimann & Zumbach, 2003). Besides, According to the nature of the users' response, some people defined that e-assessment systems can be classified the test items fixed response systems and free response systems. Fixed response systems which also referred to as *objective* forces the user to have a fixed response by selecting an answer from a pre-prepared list of solution alternatives. Where, in the free response systems *non-objective,* unanticipated answers formulate the user's response. In such type of systems skills like programming, essays writing and Meta skills are assessed rather than fact or knowledge assessment which represents the main domain of the first type. Additionally, portfolios can also be used to assess learning outcomes. Moreover, portfolios represent the highest point of students' learning, what they collect, assemble and reflect on samples are represented in their portfolios.

Specifically, Al-Smadi & Gütl (2008) are proposing a flexible e-assessment system which may include some characteristics:

- Flexible design to be used as a stand-alone service or to be easily integrated with existing systems.
- User-friendly interfaces for both students and educators where a user interaction and online submission of solution and evaluation can be done.
- Assessment environment for various learning and assessment settings, which supports guided as well as self-directed learning.
- Management and (semi-)automatic support over the entire assessment lifecycle (exercises creation, storage and compilation of assessments, as well as assessment performance, grading and

feedback provision).

- Rubrics design and implementation interfaces to allow the educators to design their own rubrics based on learning objectives to assess learners' performance against a set of criteria.
- Support of various educational objectives and subjects by using various tool sets which, for example, enables automatic exercise generation or selection, automatic grading and feedback provision.
- Results analysis and feedback provision (immediately or timely) of the current state of user knowledge and metacognitive skills for both educators and learners and also for adapting course activities and learning contents based on users' models.
- Standard-conform information and services to be easily sharable, reusable and exchangeable. This will include the test questions, answers and students' results, rather than any other required services.
- And finally, security and privacy where a secure logon of users based on pre-defined levels of access, and also users' authentication based on machine (domain users) or by usernames/passwords.

As Pirnay-Dummer & Ifenthaler (2010) supposed, the assessment systems need to accomplish specific requirements, such as (a) adaptability to different subject domains, (b) flexibility for experimental and instructional settings, (c) management of huge amounts of data, (d) rapid analysis of specific data, (e) immediate feedback to learners and educators, and (f) generation of automated reports of results (Pirnay-Dummer & Ifenthaler, 2010).

4.2 Existing Computer-Assisted Assessment Systems

In fact, the e-assessment systems or tools could reduce the efforts needed in grading, marking, recording, analyzing and other time-consuming examination related operations(He, 2006). Also, they allow a test to be attempted anywhere, anytime through the use of commonly used web browsers (Chetty, 2000; Kinnersley, Mayhew & Hinton, 2001; Ko & Cheng, 2008). At here, we examine and collect some existing and related

Computer-Assisted Assessment systems as follows.

(1) Web-based Portfolio Assessment System

Chang, Tseng and Lou (2012) explored the consistency and difference of teacher-, student self-, and peer-assessment in the context of Web-based portfolio assessment. Participants were 72 senior high school students enrolled in a computer application course. Through the assessment system, the students created and inspected portfolios, and assessed themselves and their peers. Three teachers reviewed portfolios and evaluated learning performance.

(2) The Graduated Prompting Assessment Module of the WATA System (GPAM-WATA)

Wang (2011) adopted the Graduated Prompting Assessment Module of the WATA system (GPAM-WATA) and applied it to remedial teaching in junior high school mathematics. In GPAM-WATA, when examinees fail to answer items correctly, they obtain instructional prompts (IPs) in a graduated way. Ninety-six junior high school seventh graders from three different classes participated in this research. The results indicate that compared with other groups, performing remedial teaching using GPAM-WATA is significantly more effective. The IPs in GPAM-WATA is effective in remedial teaching, not only for those students most lacking in mathematical problem-solving knowledge, but for all students.

(3) A Computer-Assisted Design, Analysis, and Testing System (CADATS)

He and Tymms (2005) presented a Computer-Assisted Design, Analysis and Testing System (CADATS) that primary and secondary schools and other test organizations can use to undertake computer-assisted assessment. Specifically, the system makes it easier to create items and databases, and to design and conduct computer-based tests. It also allows the user to diagnostically analyze students' performance at individual, group (class) and school levels to identify curriculum areas where students are under performing.

(4) Practicing, Reflecting and Revising with WATA System

Wang, Wang, and Huang (2008) proposed the "Practicing, Reflecting and Revising with WATA system (P2R-WATA) Assessment Literacy Development Model" for improving pre-service teachers' assessment literacy. The WATA system offers personalized learning resources and opportunities for pre-service teachers to assemble tests and administer them to students online. This system facilitates testing and item analysis, enabling pre-service teachers to review test statistical information and to revise test items with item analyses. Sixty pre-service teachers participated in this study. The research results indicate that pre-service teachers using P2R-WATA Assessment Literacy Development Model more effectively improving their assessment knowledge and perspectives.

(5) The Personalized Assessment System Based on Learner Knowledge and Objectives

Lazarinis, Green and Pearson (2010) presented an adaptive Web testing system where testing procedure adaptation relies on the performance, prior knowledge, and goals and preferences of the test participants. The paper discusses the adaptive assessment tool's utility, presenting the authoring process where educators utilized different adaptive rules to create a number of summative and formative assessments.

(6) The Assessment System Based on Particle Swarm Optimization

Huang, Lin and Chen (2009) developed and implemented another adaptive testing system. This system can support several assessment functions and different devices. Moreover, the researchers apply particle-swarm optimization (PSO), a novel approach that alleviates computational complexity and resolves the problem of item exposure. While developing the system, they embedded a formative evaluation into an integral part of the design methodology used to improve the system. These evaluations indicated that the system provides adaptive testing for different devices and supports versatile assessment functions. The system can estimate the students' ability reliably and validly and conduct an adaptive test efficiently. The PSO approach alleviated the system's computational complexity. With this approach, the test-item selection procedure becomes efficient, and the average best fitness values are very close to the optimal solutions.

(7) Questions Sharing and Interactive Assignments System (QSIA)

Rafaeli, Barak, Dan-Gur and Toch (2004) proposed a Web-based and Web-distributed system named QSIA (Questions Sharing and Interactive Assignments), an environment for learning, assessing and knowledge sharing. QSIA offers a unified infrastructure for developing, collecting, managing and sharing knowledge items. QSIA enhances collaboration in authoring via online recommendations and generates communities of teachers and learners. Moreover, QSIA fosters individual learning and might promote high-order thinking skills among its users.

(8) Interactive Test Item System (ITIS)

Koong & Wu (2010) proposed a visual-item authoring system, called the Interactive Test Item System (ITIS), and developed an auto-grading exam. Meanwhile, they constructed an item-sharing website based on Web 2.0, which allows users to exchange the created interactive item templates, interactive items, and interactive test sheet. An online visual authoring item editor has made it possible to create items by click and select, drag and drop, link, or parameter setting. Multimedia such as text, image, audio, and animation can be added, deleted or set to the desired animated effect to integrate into an interactive item. It also supports on-line interactive testing and auto-grading.

(9) A Testing and Diagnostic Systems Based on the Concept-Effect Model

Panjaburee, Hwang, Triampo and Shih (2010) proposed an innovative approach to eliciting and integrating test item-concept relationship weightings from multiple experts. Based on the proposed approach, they implemented a testing and diagnostic system. According to results from four groups of students using learning suggestions provided by different models, the learning performance of the students who received learning suggestions by applying the innovative approach was significantly better than for those receiving guidance based on the original model.

(10) A Progressively-Focused Self- and Peer-Assessment System (PFSPA)

Sung, Chang Chiou and Hou (2005) proposed a new approach to implementing self-and peer-assessment, named the Progressively-Focused Self-and Peer-Assessment system (PFSPA). PFSPA emphasizes the integrated and recurring nature of self-assessment activities, observation, peer assessment and peer interactions. It focuses on the increasingly sharp contrast in work quality during activities. This increases the learners' sense of quality and awareness about making judgments. The PFSPA procedure seeks a balance between thoroughly evaluating works and the economy of time allocation.

Besides, some developed computer learning systems are used for Computer-Based Assessment and item analysis. For example, a web-based learning systems adopted Bloom's Taxonomy as the framework for individualized learner assessment (Peat, 2000) and automatic quiz generation and correction (Choren et al., 1998). Additionally, a new question style that uses computer graphics to implement high level questions from Bloom's Taxonomy was proposed by Baniulis & Rĕklaitis (2002). In addition,Oliver, Dobele, Greber & Roberts (2004) proposed a grading system to assign a Bloom Rating for a course test, which indicated the cognitive difficulty of that specific test. The proposed Bloom Rating was applied in six IT (Information Technology) courses, with the conclusion that some entry-level programming courses were more difficult to teach than advanced programming courses. Another example was Scott's application of Bloom's Taxonomy in computer science exams in order to verify the students' understanding of course materials (Scott, 2003).

Unfortunately, many existing systems are designed for higher education organizations (Conole & Warburton, 2005). They only pay limited attention to primary and secondary education (He & Tymms, 2005), especially to help primary and secondary teachers produce educational assessments.

CHAPTER 5 Implicit Assessment Knowledge of Teachers

Assessments, embedded with teachers' implicit domain knowledge, play an important role in evaluating learners' comprehension of a subject.It follows from what has been said that valuable implicit assessment knowledge and experience are definitely among the decisive elements. Implicit knowledge and teacher beliefs about assessment are generally highly personal, context-specific, experience-based, and difficult to formalize, record, and articulate; they house in teachers' brain, In this chapter, we described the importance of teacher's assessment knowledge, and explain its educational application.

Educational assessment not only evaluates students learning performance, but also plays a vital role in teaching and learning. It enables teachers to diagnose pupil's difficulties, enhance pupil motivation, evaluate their teaching and plan the next teaching and learning steps to be taken (Maclellan, 2004). Effective assessment is vital in educational activities. Educational assessment is an essential aspect of teaching. Researchers have observed that teachers in schools spend more than 35% of their time on assessment and more than 10% of their time on assessment-driven instruction (Conca, Schechter & Castle, 2004). Maclellan (2004) supposed that assessment was taken to mean knowledge of principles and methods. Assessment principle includes:

- Clear purpose (such as diagnosing or aiding learning, evaluating teaching, motivating learners or ranking, selecting and grading learners).
- The basis for comparison (usually taken to mean normative or criteria, but can also include positive).
- Modes (emphasis and timing) of assessment (which are represented as bipolar dimensions such as informal/formal, process/product, formative/ summative).
- Fairness (now perhaps better understood as "just" or "equitable" assessment, but in any event relying on the precepts of validity and reliability).
- Source of assessment (self, peer or teacher/other).

The past decade has been a number of new assessment forms, such as performance assessment, authentic assessment and portfolio assessment, each of which promises a panacea for the assessment of competence (Baartman, Bastiaens, Kirschner & Van der Vleuten, 2007). Assessment methods refer to the instruments through which information is gathered and would include (Maclellan, 2004):

- Tests (objective measures designed to yield a "correct answer" and which might be constructed by the teacher or some external body, may/not be standardized, may be national or local).
- Open-ended writing (which may be short, long or extended and in which the respondent has some choice as to how the piece of writing is formulated).
- The creation of some artefact or performance which can be observed by others.
- Oral work (which might be a formal presentation, participation in discussion with teachers and/or learners, proficiency in discussion or some consultation type task).

In real assessment environments, most classroom assessments involve test items that teachers have constructed by themselves. Teachers usually play a critical role and weight in determining assessments, and they strive to find suitable specific weights in accordance with course goals on course assessments. Meng, Ye, Roy & Padilla (2007) argue that certain goals should be taken into account when developing a test within a certain discipline. These goals include the following:

- To identify the scope of the knowledge points and their distribution proportions in a test.
- To identify the distribution of teaching requirements, which can be represented by Bloom's Taxonomy.
- To identify the difficulty distribution (e.g., a test consisting of 10% very difficult test items, 20% difficult items, 40% medium difficult items, 20% easy items; and 10% of very easy items).
- To identify the structure of a test (i.e., the types of test items and the quantity and score of each type).

Carroll & Moody (2006) proposed that the percentage of points per topic/concept of the test should be directly related to the percentage of instructional time spent on that objective. Thorough coverage of the content can be ensured by outlining the main topics and balancing questions from each topic/concept studied. Teachers think like assessors who must judge what students should know, understand, and be able to do as well as understanding what is worthy, what enduring understanding is desired, and how to determine whether students have achieved the desired results and met the standards (Shepard, 2000). Teachers must rely on advice, opinion, experience, and common sense to direct them when constructing classroom tests that produce reliable and valid scores (Frey, et al., 2005). Cizek and colleagues (1995) surveyed 143 elementary and secondary school teachers and found that assessment practices "were highly variable and unpredictable from characteristics such as practice setting, gender, years of experience, grade level or familiarity with assessment policies in their school district"(Cizek, Fitzgerald &

Rachor, 1995). They concluded that "many teachers seemed to have individual assessment policies that reflected their own individual values and beliefs about teaching". Wang (2000) also argued that teacher-made assessments convey teachers' ideas and beliefs. As icebergs hidden below sea level, these beliefs often determine the teachers' instructional and assessment practices. Xu & Liu (2009) assent that teachers' experiences with assessment reveal that their knowledge is not a static end product, but rather a highly complex, dynamic and ongoing process. They also argue that teachers' knowledge of assessment develops along a temporal continuum in the sense that teachers usually use their prior assessment experience to inform their current assessment practices, which, in turn, further informs their future plans. More recently, researchers also suggest that teachers do not use externally prescribed standards alone as a basis for judgment; they also turn to their own implicit knowledge and beliefs, especially when conflicts arise between their personal assessment and standardized criteria (Arkoudis & O'Loughlin, 2004; Davison, 2004).

Therefore, assessments, embedded with teachers' implicit domain knowledge, play an important role in evaluating learners' comprehension of a subject. It follows from what has been said that valuable implicit assessment knowledge and experience are definitely among the decisive elements. Implicit knowledge and teacher beliefs about assessment are generally highly personal, context-specific, experience-based, and difficult to formalize, record, and articulate; they house in teachers' brain, such as expertise, intuition, understanding, or professional insight formed as a result of experience, and is then internalized as tacit knowledge. Conversely, explicit knowledge, including reports, articles, manuals, pictures, images, video, audio and software, refers to codified knowledge that is easily expressible, verbal and simply to codify. It is transmittable in formal, systematic language and is easily transferred by using Information Technology (IT) (Mitri, 2003; Polanyi & Sen, 2009). Zhao (2010) further mentioned that tacit knowledge has yet to become explicit knowledge, which is often acquired through the long-term accumulation of the knowledge of individual teachers. It is usually difficult to express with words, and it cannot be transmitted to others or spread very easily.

In essence, the assessment of these skills requires faculty to use intuition, judgment, and feeling. Much more thought must go into this type of evaluation, which we will term tacit assessment, than is necessary for judging students' knowledge of simple facts or principles (explicit assessment). Tacit assessment is the area in which curriculum assessment efforts often encounter roadblocks (Mitri, 2003). The problem of tacit assessment knowledge capture is a central theme in the field of education and knowledge management, and assessment management can be thought of as a form of knowledge management. Therefore, tacit assessment management can be facilitated through technologies commonly used in knowledge management systems such as databases, internet architectures, artificial intelligence, and decision support techniques (Mitri, 2003). Namely, the tacit knowledge on the importance of both the concepts and their relationships of a subject, which, if captured, made explicit, properly described and explained, freely articulated, and shared around, may greatly help teachers use and acquire it easily, so far as to construct more effective assessments.

CHAPTER 6 Knowledge and Knowledge Management

In this chapter, we described knowledge and two dimensions of the knowledge which can be classified as: tacit knowledge and explicit knowledge. We also introduced knowledge management, and described how to carry through the construction knowledge management, in particular, we make some introductions about knowledge management in education application.

The Longman Dictionary of Contemporary English defines knowledge as the facts, information, skills and understanding that one has gained, especially through learning or experience (Procter & Ayto, 1978). Knowledge is also defined as a justified belief that increases an entity's capability for effective action, and knowledge refers to meaning and understanding that results from processing information in ways that are actionable (Alavi & Haley, 1999). Davenport & Prusak (2000) defined knowledge as a fluid mix of framed experience, values, contextual information and expert insight. Indeed, knowledge is contextual, relevant, and actionable and can be used to solve problems. This definition implies that knowledge in knowledge management perspectives has been defined in a pragmatic way (Ting & Liang, 2005). In which, knowledge creation and transfer are a spiral process of interactions between explicit and tacit knowledge through socialization, externalization, combination and internalization (Nonaka, 1994).

Alavi and Leidner (2001) considered knowledge from the following five perspectives: a state of mind; an object; a process; a condition of having access to information; and, a capability. Managing knowledge should depend on the viewpoints of knowledge engineers and end-users. In addition, knowledge exists when different transformative processes, such as comparison, consequence, connection and conversation works. They also asserted that knowledge management is much more than technology.

6.1 Tacit Knowledge and Explicit Knowledge

Generally speaking, two dimensions of the knowledge can be classified as: tacit knowledge and explicit knowledge (Nonaka, 1991, 1994, 1995; Sallis & Jones, 2002). This concept is accepted by leading public and private organizations around the world. According to Polanyi's definition (Polanyi, 1967), tacit knowledge is highly personal, context-specific, and therefore hard to express, represent, formalize and communicate, record or articulate (Tiwana, 2000; Wielinga, Bredeweg & Breuker, 1988). Tacit knowledge is knowledge housed in the human brain, such as expertise, understanding, or professional insight formed as a result of experience. Tacit knowledge also refers to personal knowledge embedded in individual experience and shared and exchanged through direct, face-to-face contact (Tiwana, 2000). Conversely, explicit knowledge is indirectly acquired—it is decoded and recoded into a person's mental model, and is then internalized as tacit knowledge. Explicit knowledge can be found in the documents of organizations, including reports, articles, manuals, patents, pictures, images, video, audio and software. Explicit knowledge also refers to codified knowledge that is transmittable in formal, systematic language and is easily transferred by using Information Technology (IT).

Although explicit knowledge is easier to handle, a great amount of knowledge in an organization exists in a form of highly personal and context-dependent one which belongs to tacit knowledge. Tacit knowledge is normally not documented or stored in a system database. Capturing the tacit knowledge and make it in the form of explicit knowledge is important for executing knowledge management to preserve implicit knowledge as corporate property. Moreover, tacit knowledge is a source of sustainable competitive advantage (Teece, 2004) and quite beneficial to a faster decision-making process (Eisenhardt, 1989), effective decision (Agor, 1987), and fewer pertinent factors necessary for a decision (Wagner, 1987). However, if dealt with improperly, tacit knowledge is subject to be wiped away tacit knowledge management. Thence, knowledge management enables tacit knowledge to be reused for another application, and accelerates the improvement of operations in the construction phase (Lin, Wang & Tserng, 2006).

6.2 Knowledge Management

Knowledge is in a sense at the heart of knowledge management. Knowledge management aims at providing the appropriate information for the right person at the correct time (Snowden, 1999), and its objective is to increase the competitive power, elasticity and innovations of the organization through the organization's members. In recent years, the growing awareness and value of specialized knowledge in its various forms has been recognized in an emerging discourse known as knowledge management (Blair, 2002; Gray Southon, Todd & Seneque, 2002). Many organizations focus on knowledge management to provide users with access and retrieval of information. It is widely recognized that good knowledge management leads to higher efficiency and enterprise performance. Knowledge management involves kinds of activities such as discovering, codifying, storing, identifying, disseminating, categorizing, retrieving and sharing information assets throughout the organization (Alavi & Leidner, 1999; Taft, 2000). Noticeably, knowledge management could be used for improving organizations' performance, and becomes a critical issue for academic research and industrial practices (Lai, Wang & Chou, 2009).

Knowledge management is a combinational concept based on a knowledge-based system, artificial intelligence, improvements of software engineering, human resources management and organizational behavior (Liebowitz, 2000). Accordingly, knowledge management is increasingly being recognized by individuals and organizations as an important competitive strategy. People are increasingly becoming engaged in knowledge management processes, such as contributing new knowledge from practice and experience, applying and verifying existing knowledge, and developing intellectual assets for improving individual, group and organizational performance (Wang & Jacobson, 2011).

As we noted, knowledge management is a systematic process for acquiring, organizing and communicating the knowledge of employees so that other employees may make use of it to be more effective and productive in their work (Alavi & Haley, 1999). Knowledge management is a process to identify, select, organize, disseminate and transfer important knowledge and expertise so that it can be shared in a formal manner and reused (Turban, Aronson & Liang, 2005). Besides, knowledge management involves creating, securing, coordinating, combining, retrieving and distributing knowledge (Lin & Hsueh, 2006). In addition, many researchers argued that knowledge is a meaningful resource in an organization to booster the management performance, and knowledge management helps facilitate creating, storing, sharing, and reusing the organization's knowledge by typically using advanced technology (Abecker, Bernardi, Hinkelmann Kühn & Sintek, 1997; Noh, Lee Kim, Lee & Kim, 2000).

Lin & Tserng (2003) identified five phases in the construction of knowledge management life cycle: knowledge acquisition, knowledge extraction, knowledge storage, knowledge sharing and knowledge update. Each phase is briefly outlined as follows:

- Knowledge acquisition: Most information and knowledge are acquired in the knowledge acquisition phase on the job site during the construction phase. Hence, the accumulation of knowledge on a job site plays a significant role in the knowledge acquisition phase. Most knowledge acquisition work is performed in the office because all information and tacit knowledge sent back from the job site can be transferred to explicit knowledge.
- Knowledge extraction: The expert's thoughts and experience are

captured in the knowledge extraction phase. Some knowledge that must be extracted for reuse and storage may only exist in the memories of experts and engineers. Knowledge extraction may also be extended to include capturing knowledge from other sources such as problem-solution descriptions, construction, operation process digital records, virtual communication and collaboration. Moreover, knowledge workers assist experts and engineers and deal with the digital process recording work if they are important or valuable as company assets.

- Knowledge storage: In the knowledge storage phase, all information and knowledge are centralized and stored in the central database to prevent the collection of redundant data. All information and knowledge can be stored in the system by ensuring that all data are in the appropriate electronic file format.
- Knowledge sharing: Knowledge sharing refers to the ultimate objective of knowledge management. After the developing knowledge management, individuals who need to apply knowledge of a particular project can access relevant knowledge for reuse.
- Knowledge update: Available knowledge and experience are continually updated in the knowledge update phase. Reused experience can be evaluated in the context of a new problem to be solved, either in terms of the suitability of the selected experience, or in terms of the accuracy of the retrieved experience. Such evaluation is important to ensure that the process of reusing experience continuously improves. Invalid knowledge must be identified and eliminated or updated.

With the rapid renovation of Information Technology (IT), it has become more important and been applied to several procedures to improve management and store knowledge and data in a more systematic way. As a result, knowledge of how to best manage knowledge by IT is an important issue in academic and industrial domains. Alavi & Haley (1999) identified three perspectives of knowledge management: information-centric, technology-centric and organization-centric perspectives. The information-centric emphasizes the right amount of information. The technology-centric is related to the need for information technology in the knowledge management process and organization-centric perspective suggests that knowledge management should be specific to fit an organization's culture, level and requirement for knowledge. Sound tourism knowledge management systems should possess the right types and amount of information (knowledge), appropriate technology and organizational support. For example, the typical strategy for knowledge management is focused on computer-based approaches for capturing, storing organization's know-how, and disseminating explicit knowledge (Woo, Clayton, Johnson, Flores & Ellis, 2004).

Knowledge management in education field is involved in the process of knowledge acquisition, accumulation, sharing, transformation, application, innovation, integration and diffusion, all of which is impacted by the school leadership, organizational culture, information technologies, performance management and other enablers (Zhao, 2010). School knowledge accumulation is the accumulation of the results of knowledge applications and innovations within the school by school members, equipment entities, and technical documents. Specifically, teacher classroom assessment knowledge sharing is intended to establish assessment knowledge reciprocity and understandings among school members, promoting the sharing of knowledge and experiences and thereby creating a vast collection of knowledge of teacher classroom assessments.

6.3 Reusing Tacit Knowledge

Reusing information and knowledge minimizes the need to refer explicitly to past experience, reduces the time and cost of solving problems, and improves the quality of the solutions. Sharing experience and knowledge means that problems in the similar projects do not need to be repeatedly solved. Reducing problem-solving could reduce costs and the probability of repeating problems. Several enabling activities should be considered to help attain the eventual goal of efficient experience and knowledge reuse; experience and knowledge should be preserved and managed, restated activities should be captured, modeled, stored, retrieved, adapted, evaluated and maintained (Bergmann, 2002).

Polanyi (1997) presented the first theory concerning tacit knowledge in his book, *Tacit Dimension*. Since then, numerous studies have demonstrated the importance of tacit knowledge in real-world performance. In much of the literature, tacit knowledge has been emphasized and regarded as the important strategic resource that assists in accomplishing a task (Baumard, 1999; Sternberg, 2000). Some research done by Sternberg et al. (2000) showed that much of the knowledge needed to succeed in real-world tasks are tacit. Malhotra (2000) also insists that explicit knowledge typically lacks the context required to be truly useful to the knowledge seeker. The first attempt to measure the effectiveness of tacit knowledge was performed by Sternberg (2000) and his colleagues. Their goal was to point out the contribution of tacit knowledge to successful performance and to establish a relationship between the possession of tacit knowledge and job performance. They found that tacit knowledge can be quantified. Their studies also indicate that the amount of tacit knowledge is related to both job performance and school performance. Specifically, they insisted that tacit knowledge can be a source of highly effective performance in the workplace. They also pointed out that the efficacy of tacit knowledge depends on effective acquisition and utilization.

According to the theory of organizational knowledge creation (Nonaka, 1995), the key to knowledge creation lies in the mobilization and conversion of tacit knowledge to explicit knowledge. However, converting tacit knowledge to explicit knowledge often fails because of an unawareness of tacit knowledge and the necessity to make it explicit (Stenmark, 2001). Herschel, Nemati & Steiger (2001) also pointed out that converting tacit knowledge to explicit knowledge is often time consuming and problematic. Sveiby (1997) says that knowledge becomes static when tacit knowledge is made explicit through language. This is why the codification process for the richest tacit knowledge is generally limited to locating experts with the knowledge and encouraging knowledge seekers to communicate (Davenport & Prusak, 2000).

One of the more successful initiatives for sharing tacit knowledge is Communities of Practice. These communities are designed to build a network of knowledgeable experts who work together to learn and solve complex problems when the solutions are needed. In general, they operate informally through meetings, video-conferences, or communications to exchange knowledge and work practices on topics of interest to the members. There are only a few empirical research studies of tacit and explicit knowledge utilization. Experimental research conducted by Herschel et al., (2001) focused on the comparison of tacit and explicit knowledge representation methods. Their results showed that tacit knowledge representation methods excel at sharing knowledge, but that their effectiveness critically depends on whether the recall process is explicitly structured. Somech and Bogler (1999) used survey research to investigate the relationship between tacit knowledge and student learning and achievement. The results revealed that students who scored high in tacit knowledge achieved higher academic grades than students who scored low in tacit knowledge.

In the context, knowledge management involves capturing tacit knowledge and transforming it into explicit knowledge for further sharing. Tacit knowledge management can be facilitated through technologies commonly used in knowledge management systems, such as databases, internet architecture, artificial intelligence, and decision support techniques (Mitri, 2003). Several knowledge acquisition techniques, such as interviewing, protocol analysis, and personal construct theory, are useful for eliciting tacit knowledge from domain experts, and knowledge discovery techniques involve data mining. Combined with induction, these techniques can help to create new knowledge by finding patterns and relationships in data repositories. In this book, we argue that assessment information gleaned from teachers' classroom assessment procedures can be thought of as school knowledge to be managed in the sense that assessment knowledge, experience and know-how reside in the heads of individual teachers. Furthermore, assessment knowledge accumulated during the assessment construction phase from multiple members of the same curricula domain can be more valuable. Tacit knowledge is normally not documented. Therefore, tacit assessment knowledge management can be facilitated through technologies commonly used in knowledge management systems such as databases, internet architectures, artificial intelligence, and decision support techniques. Therefore, methods of capturing and integrating teachers' individual experiences and tacit knowledge, transforming it into explicit knowledge, and spreading it to teacher organizations become an important task for executing school knowledge management and for preserving implicit knowledge as valuable school property.

CHAPTER 7 Knowledge Representation and Visualization

Knowledge representations use some notations or expressions to represent knowledge, such as text, table or graph. Besides, knowledge visualization means that visual imagery is used to construct and convey complex insights for improving understanding and communication. In this chapter, we introduced knowledge representations and knowledge visualization. In addition, different types of knowledge representation and related application are shown in this chapter.

The knowledge conveyed by abstraction is usually schematic and analytical with a format that is typically highly structured and systemic, due to the reduction of conceptual complexity and the articulation of relationships (Ainsworth, 2006). In which, Some research underline the advantages of visualizations (Eppler, 2004): (a) to motivate people, (b) to present new perspectives, (c) to increase remembrance, (d) to support the process of learning, (e) to focus attention and support concentration of the viewer, (f) to structure and coordinate communication. Visual representations of knowledge also can be used for Knowledge management processes, i.e., for the identification, transfer, creation, and application of knowledge.

Knowledge representation and visualization is a new field of research which examines our innate potential to effectively process visual representations in knowledge intense tasks. Many knowledger epresentation methodologies have been devised to date for knowledge-based applications. These techniques provide a bridge between human knowledge and machine knowledge (Kim, Suh & Hwang, 2003). The term graphic knowledge organizer, or knowledge representation tool, is commonly used to describe two-dimensional visual knowledge representations, which show relationships among concepts or processes by means of spatial positions, connecting lines and intersecting figures (Ives & Hoy, 2003). In addition, to deep understanding and high level thinking, knowledge visualization can support meta-cognition by helping users develop an awareness of their mental representations, which may help to foster conceptual change and knowledge transfer (Jacobson, 2004).

Knowledge presentation and visualizations may externalize or reify tacit know-how knowledge into explicit formats such as competency models, workflow charts, business process diagrams, decision-making models, reasoning patterns, and argument processes (Wang & Jacobson, 2011). In these contexts, knowledge visualization offers great potential for the creation of new knowledge from individual or group activities using heuristic sketches or rich graphic metaphors. Innovation or knowledge creation can be fostered by making preliminary ideas or unstable knowledge explicit and debatable (Wang & Jacobson, 2011). Moreover, visualization improves knowledge application and problem solving by providing rich representations to express "know-how" knowledge exercised in the accomplishment of tasks, which is usually tacit and associated with hands-on experience and practice at solving problems (Wang, Ran, Liao & Yang, 2010).

7.1 Knowledge Representation

Knowledge representation involves to represent knowledge that uses some notations or expressions, such as text, table or graph. According to these representations, the graph is more readable and realizable by human than others because it's simpler and more intension to represent (Chartrand & Oellermann, 1993). Knowledge representation can be defined from four perspectives (Markman, 2013). First, the represented world is the domain that the representations are about. Second, the representing world is the domain that contains the representations (Palmer, 1978). Third, a representing rule is "a set of rules that map elements of the represented world to elements in the representing world" (Markman, 2013). Finally, the process that uses the representation should exist. Knowledge representations comprise data of facts, information of summarized data and cases. These representations could be used for procedures, rules, ideas that guide personal and organizational decisions and actions (Liebowitz, 1999). In general, knowledge representations, including rule-bases (O'Leary & Selferidge, 1999), semantic networks (Kuwata & Yatsu, 1997) and frame representations (Gaines & Shaw, 1993), have been utilized in KM systems, and can provide a qualitative representation of knowledge. Besides, there are several methods of knowledge representation that have been devised for AI-type applications. Some of these are also suitable for use and interpretation by humans and can form a bridge between human knowledge and machine knowledge (Gordon, 2000).

7.2 Knowledge Visualization

Knowledge visualization shows how visual imagery is used to construct and convey complex insights for improving understanding and communication. Knowledge visualization examines the use of visual representations to improve the transfer and creation of knowledge (Burkhard, 2005; Schwartz, 2006). It thus designates all graphic means that can be used to construct and convey complex insights. Beyond the mere transport of facts, knowledge visualization aims to transfer insights, experiences, attitudes, values, expectations, perspectives, opinions, and predictions. And this in a way that enables someone else to re-construct, remember and apply this knowledge correctly. Burkhard (2005) argued that an effective transfer of knowledge through visualizations should be considered, which are based on four relevant questions:

- Why should knowledge be visualized? (Aim)
- What type of knowledge needs to be visualized? (Content)

- Who is being addressed? (Recipient)
- What is the best method to visualize this knowledge? (Medium)

In which, the knowledge visualization framework (as seen in Figure 7.1) consists of four perspectives that need to be considered when creating visual representations that aim to transfer and create knowledge: A function type perspective answers why a visualization should be used, a knowledge type perspective clarifies the nature of the content, a recipient type perspective points to the different backgrounds of the recipient/ audience, and finally the visualization type perspective structures the main visualization types according to their individual characteristics (Burkhard & Meier, 2005).

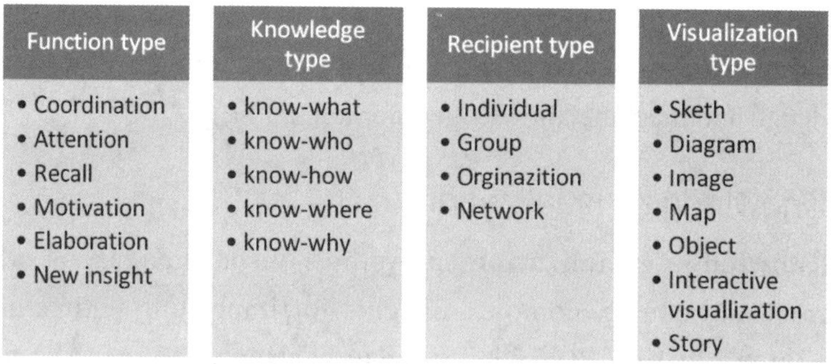

Figure 7.1 The knowledge visualization framework

The visualization type perspective structures the visualization methods are grounded and derived from the seven visualization methods architects use to transfer and create knowledge, and into seven main groups: sketches, diagrams, images, maps, objects, interactive visualizations, and stories (details are as follows). In similar, according to Schwartz's opinion (Schwartz, 2006), six formats can be distinguished in knowledge visualization, there are Heuristic Sketches, Conceptual Diagrams, Visual Metaphors, Knowledge Animations, Knowledge Maps, Domain Structures.

- **Sketches:** represent the main idea, are atmospheric, and help to quickly visualize an idea. Sketches are used to assist the group reflection and communication process by making knowledge explicit and debatable.
- **Diagrams:** abstract, schematic representations used to explore structural relationships among parts. Diagram as a "visual language sign having the primary purpose of denoting function and/or relationship". The type of knowledge that is conveyed by Diagrams is analytic; Diagrams are structured and systematic.
- **Maps:** follow cartographic conventions to reference knowledge. A map generally consists of two elements: A ground layer represents the context (e.g., a network of experts a project, and a city) and individual elements (e.g., experts, project milestones and roads). In the context of knowledge management, maps are called knowledge maps. They illustrate both overview and detail, and interrelationships among these details. Knowledge maps are graphic directories of knowledge-sources, -assets, -structures, or-processes.
- **Images:** are impressive, expressive, or represent reality. Images address emotions and they are inspiring, appealing, motivating, and energizing. Therefore, they are widely used as a key instrument in advertising. Images can be grasped and recalled in less than a second and sometimes be remembered for decades.
- **Objects:** exploit the third dimension and allow experiencing materials. Objects in space are helpful. For example, for information points, knowledge fairs, or exhibitions to complement physical and digital visualizations and to show the content from different points of view.
- **Interactive Visualizations:** allow to access, explore, and make sense of different types of information. This is the domain of interaction design and information visualization applications.
- **Stories:** the last visualization type, are imaginary visualizations that are efficient in transferring and disseminating knowledge across

time and space.

Knowledge visualization is a powerful strategy for integrating high-level human intelligence and knowledge into the knowledge discovery process (Miller & Han, 2009). The human visual system is extremely effective at recognizing patterns, trends, and anomalies. The visual acuity and pattern spotting capabilities of humans can be exploited in many stages of the knowledge discovery process from databases, including OLAP, query formulation, technique selection, and interpretation of results. These capabilities have yet to be surpassed by machine-based approaches. Some researchers described software systems that incorporate visualization techniques for supporting database querying and data mining (Keim & Kriegel, 1994; Lee & Ong, 1996). Keim & Kriegel (1994) use visualization to support simple and complex query specification, OLAP, and querying from multiple independent databases.

Knowledge visualization can also provide a qualitative representation of tacit knowledge (Mitri, 2003). According to the conjoint retention theory (Verdi & Kulhavy, 2002), features and structural information can facilitate both the coding and later recall of the accompanying texts. Visualized features aid in recall when they are visually distinct and drawn in such a way that they activate prior knowledge about the represented place. Structural knowledge establishes a spatial frame that references visual features and verbal knowledge to enable efficient comprehension. Increasing research has produced evidence suggesting that the use of graphic structure to represent knowledge of a focused topic has gained increasing attention in various fields. This knowledge representation framework denotes terms, concepts, or basic knowledge elements through notes in the graph and facts, propositions, or associations by linking two or more nodes to reflect their relationships with each other (Tseng, Chang, Rundgren & Rundgren, 2010). Larkin & Simon (1987) described how diagrams, in comparison of texts, can offer more efficient support for comprehension and problem solving. Maps are a form of knowledge visualization that may lower the cognitive load needed to add new associations to those already linked with previously encountered concepts by allowing a more efficient visual search than text passages.

Knowledge visualization has been widely used in various area, in particular, used for learning environments to augment cognition, facilitate thinking and scientific inquiries, and assist metacognition. By representing cognitive structures or mental models through using various techniques, knowledge visualization has the potential to facilitate the construction of understandings at a deeper level, as well as those understandings with multiple perspectives, such as interpretation and abstraction (Wang & Jacobson, 2011).

CHAPTER 8 Knowledge Map

Knowledge maps are diagrams that represent ideas as node-link assemblies, which involve the display of acquired knowledge and relationships (O'Donnell, et al., 2002). This node-link diagram may enable the users to assimilate new facts and to perceive how detailed information fits in with central concepts, thus facilitating the acquisition and retrieval of the microstructure (Rewey, Dansereau, Skaggs, Hall & Pitre, 1989). In this chapter, we introduced the definition of knowledge map, the types and forms of knowledge map, and many different applications for knowledge map, especially in the education domain. In addition, several knowledge map developments are shown in the last section.

The knowledge map is a two-dimensional graphical display that presents information in the form of node-link-mode assemblies. The nodes contain key ideas, and the links specify the relationships between nodes (McCagg & Dansereau, 1991) and add structure and organization to the map (Rewey, Dansereau, Dees & Skaggs, 1992). Knowledge maps are created by transferring certain aspects of knowledge into a graphical format that is easy to understand knowledge (Abel & Kulhavy, 1986), and facilitated to organize, display and acquisition of information (Amer, 1994). Speel et al. (1999) also define knowledge mapping as the process, methods and tools for analyzing knowledge areas in order to discover features or meanings and to visualize these in a comprehensive, transparent form, such that the complexes or implied-relevant features are clearly highlighted (Speel, et al., 1999; Vail & Andersen, 1999). It can serve as a common framework or context for the purposes of knowledge sharing, decision-making and problem-solving (Rouse, Thomas & Boff, 1998).

Moreover, knowledge maps make the macrostructure of a body of information more salient (O'Donnell, et al., 2002). According to Grey (1999), the knowledge map is an aid in understanding the relationship between explicit information and tacit knowledge, illustrating how knowledge flows throughout the domain. A knowledge map portrays the sources, flows, constraints and terminations of knowledge within the domain. Davenport and Prusak observed that the development of a knowledge map involves locating important knowledge in the organization and then publishing a list or several pictures showing where to find it (Davenport & Prusak, 2000; Prusak & Davenport, 1998). Knowledge maps are diagrams that represent ideas as node-link assemblies, which involve the display of acquired knowledge and relationships (O'Donnell, et al., 2002). The knowledge in a knowledge map may involve various shared contents, such as text, graphics, videos, models and data. The relationships among them are determined by linking concepts or topics discovered from this shared content, sources, flows, constraints, and sinks (losses or stopping points) of knowledge within an organization (Liebowitz, 2005).

Knowledge map techniques serve as a tool for human beings to better understand the structure of important knowledge or competence and their relationships to people, groups or other organizational units that create, hold, seek, distribute or apply the knowledge (Liu, Li & Lv, 2009). Node-link knowledge maps have drawn significant interest among educational researchers (Nesbit & Adesope, 2006). They are often used as media for constructive learning activities and as communication aids in lectures, study materials, and collaborative learning (Cañas, Coffey, Caront, Feltovich, Hoffman, Felotovich & Novak, 2003). More importantly, however, knowledge map can serve as a means of navigating the required knowledge. They have the advantage of simplifying the relational complexity of information and structuralizing information and knowledge (Shaw, 2010). As for the relationships between knowledge map and usefulness, it also can be explained with precision of perceived data, ease for recalling, reducing in the form at invalid, knowledge capture, knowledge reuse, learning, and support collaboration.

Knowledge maps have six key advantages. They can help in the following ways (Thomas, 2009):

- To find key sources, opportunities and constraints to knowledge creation and flows.
- To encourage reuse and prevent reinvention, saving search time and acquisition costs.
- To highlight the islands of expertise and suggest ways to build bridges to increase knowledge sharing and exchange.
- To discover effective and emergent communities of practice where informal learning is happening.
- To reduce the burden on experts in helping staff to find critical solutions & information quickly.
- To improve user response, decision-making and problem-solving by providing access to applicable information, internal and external experts.

There are many types of representation and many different types may need to be integrated in the knowledge map (Markman, 2013). In every format or type produces insights about knowledge structure and all are likely to be the source of future insights (Fisher, Faletti & Quinn, 1990; Novak, 1984). Rather than advocating particular types of representation, using approaches appropriate to each situation is a better strategy assuming the representation method is clear about the specification of the knowledge mapping processes. Maps must deal with details, contexts and relations between knowledge. Depending on the purpose and use of the opportunity, they contain the following different types: knowledge map, cognitive map, knowledge networking chart, list chart, category map, topic map, mind map (Buzan & Buzan, 1993), cognitive map, semantic maps (Carrell, Pharis & Liberto, 1989), scatter chart, contour chart, ontology and concept map (Myers, 1990; Nonaka, 1994; Novak, 1984; Yang, 2007). These maps are similar to each other in knowledge representation but are different in their specific details and application objectives (Tseng, et al., 2010). Some researchers (Cañas et al., 2003) assumed that knowledge maps are synonymous with concept maps, which represent externalizing structures and ideas as node-link assemblies (Novak & Gowin, 1984; Zumbach, 2009). Other scholars argue that knowledge maps can display complex relationships more easily than concept maps (Crampes, Ranwez, Villerd, Neuckovski, Mooney, Emery & Mille, 2006). Ontology, on the other hand, stresses more on the hierarchical relationship of concepts in a domain, but with the non-consanguineous relationship among concepts implicitly specified in the slots. Knowledge maps, however, stress explicitly more on the general relationships among domain concepts. Knowledge maps can be either strategic or tactical, depending upon the need and intent (Thomas, 2009). Knowledge maps display intellectual processes by representing sequences, alternatives, branches, choice points, and pathways that involved in the acquisition and construction of knowledge (Wang, Jia, Sugumaran, Ran & Liao, 2011). The following section provides a detailed description and introductions according to different types of maps currently used for knowledge representation. The advantages and limitations are discussed as follows:

(1) Concept map

A concept map that was proposed by Novak is a visuospatial representation of knowledge with text and graphical elements, such as arrows, lines, ovals, and squares to communicate knowledge structures for sharing and consensus finding (Novak & Cañas, 2006; Novak, 2010). It consists of nodes, containing a concept or item, and links connecting two nodes to each other and describing their relationship, where each node-link relation makes a proposition. Words on the line specify the relationship between the two concepts. In fact, concept maps implement a simple graph theory. Frequent extensions include the implementation of **partitions** or **contexts**, usually in the form of a box drawn around a sub graph. Concept maps are object-oriented, human-centered, and easy to comprehend and use. The way they enable structuring a body of knowledge is much more salient than other forms of knowledge representation such as pure text and logic (Kremer, 1998). They can be used both at an informal level, such as for "brainstorming", as well as at a very formal level, such as representing knowledge in the knowledge base of an intelligent system.

Concept maps are theoretically grounded in cognitive learning theory. In particular, based on Ausubel's theories of assimilation and subsumption (Ausubel, 1968), which state that the most important single factor influencing learning is what the learner already knows, Novak and Musonda (1991) initially developed concept mapping tools to search for better ways to represent the learners' knowledge. Since then, concept maps have been used in various areas such as assessment tools (McClure, Sonak & Suen, 1999), cooperative learning tools (Stoyanova & Kommers, 2002), anxiety reduction tools (Czerniak & Haney, 1998), and tools that increase efficiency of search engines (Carvalho, Hewett & Cañas, 2001). Computer-based environments for concept mapping have been developed, such as the dynamic concept map proposed by Nesbit and Adesope (2005), in which audio presentation is synchronized with a node-link image. Cañas et al. (2005) developed CmapTools, tools that enable concept maps to be combined with multimedia resources. Chu, Lee & Tsai (2011) developed a concept map learning system with ontology technology to help users search the concept map to help reduce the user's cognitive load. (Ruiz-Martínez, Valencia-García, Fernández-Breis, García-Sánchez & Martínez-Béjar, 2011) developed the MCRDR tool for concept acquisition in the biomedical domain.

(2) Knowledge map

Holley & Dansereau (1984) first developed knowledge maps, and Wiegmann, Dansereau, McCagg, Rewey & Pitre(1992) added types of links, which include type, character, part, results in, leads to, and example. Knowledge maps are very similar to concept maps, in terms of structures, goals, benefits and areas of application; however, knowledge maps have specific types of links. A knowledge map is also a two-dimensional graphical display that presents information, but the method of relationship designation in knowledge maps distinguishes the technique from other types of maps (Amer, 1994). O'donnell, Dansereau & Hall (2002) summarized findings in the field of knowledge maps over 12 years: students who use knowledge maps recall a greater number of central ideas than do students who use texts (Hall, Dansereau & Skaggs, 1992); students with low verbal ability or low prior knowledge benefit the most from the presentation of information in a knowledge map format with recall (Rewey et al., 1989); students who use knowledge maps as supports when interacting with peers in cooperative learning environments learn more effectively; and information is recalled better when presented in well-structured maps designed according to Gestalt principles than when presented in less well-structured map. Also, knowledge maps were found to help general purpose conceptualization processes (Gómez, Moreno, Pazos & Sierra-Alonso, 2000) and to help users reduce their anxiety and increase motivation (Hall & O'Donnell, 1996).

(3) Topic map

Topic maps are an abstraction similar to concept maps in that they contain basic concepts, such as Topics, Associations, and Occurrences (Pepper, 2000), and also model concepts-**topics**-and their relationships-**topic associations**. If the word "topic" is generalized to "word", topic maps are more or less similar to concept maps, except that topic maps are more focused on standards. Böhm, Heyer, Quasthoff & Wolff (2002) introduced a way to construct an initial set of topic maps or extend/optimize a given map using text mining technology (Dicheva & Dichev, 2006). Topic maps are also clearly related to various kinds of electronic information resources supporting topical findings, such as documents, graphics, images, audio/video clips, databases, and so on (Dichev et al., 2004). The topics and the associations can be manipulated in different ways (add, delete, modify, move, rearrange,etc.) at a meta-layer, regardless of the physical resources. **Occurrences** instantiate topics to one or more resources. Typically, an occurrence is a URI or a document. In addition, Dicheva and Dichev (2006) developed an environment for e-learning, called TM4L, where people use topic maps for learning. The TM4L is an environment for building, maintaining, and using standards-based, ontology-aware e-learning repositories, based on the idea that concept-driven access to learning material implemented as a Topic Map can bridge the gap between a learner and targeted knowledge. The goal was to support an efficient context-based retrieval of learning content tailored to the needs of a learner working on an educational task. Other learning environments include a ubiquitous learning system (Wang & Wu, 2011), English e-learning system (Wang & Liao, 2011) and performance analysis e-learning system (Jia, Wang, Ran, Yang, Liao & Chiu, 2011).

8.1 The Type of Knowledge Map

Knowledge maps are multi-relational semantic maps that display verbal information in a spatial manner. Nodes containing verbal information are interconnected with differently nameable links, which together, add structure and organization to the knowledge map. The results of studies using expert-generated knowledge maps have demonstrated that knowledge maps: (a) facilitates the acquisition of main ideas (Rewey, Dansereau & Peel, 1991); (b) facilitates the acquisition of procedural information (Patterson, Dansereau & Wiegmann, 1993); (c) is useful as overview tools prior to actual study; and (d) are useful as reference tools for answering questions about a domain (O'Donnell & Dansereau, 1992). Fundamentally, the links on a knowledge map represent information about the relationship between concepts (Novak, 1984), they either consisted of single unembellished lines or they contained the additional information described above (i.e. arrow heads, labels, and shape). Takes into account the structure of the knowledge map, some researches mentioned that maps are based on knowledge prototypes (see in Figure 8.1) and are designed based on gestalt principles (Lambiotte, Dansereau, Cross & Reynolds, 1989; O'Donnell, et al., 2002). Eppler (2001) presented his views that classify knowledge maps into five types, such as knowledge source map, knowledge asset map, knowledge structure map, knowledge application map, and knowledge development map. McCagg & Dansereau (1991) also point out three main categories of links that can be used in knowledge maps: dynamic links that denote a changing relationship between the linked ideas (e.g., a cause and effect relationship); static links that describe structural relationships between ideas, and elaborative links that extend information. With such richness of link categories, knowledge maps can be used in diverse applications, showing the various nodes and links on the screens in accordance with the purpose of the applications, and can be transferred, either directly or by analogy, from one domain to another (McCagg & Dansereau, 1991).

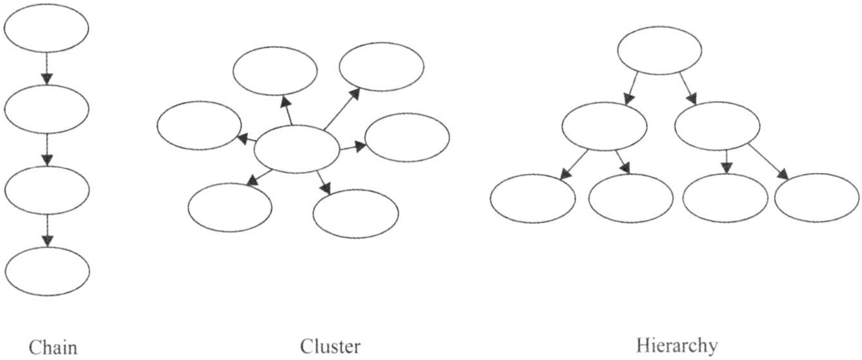

Figure 8.1 Knowledge prototype on knowledge maps

For example, there are several ways in which knowledge maps can be configured spatially and these configurations vary across different systems of mapping (Lambiotte et al., 1989). Maps can be configured in the form of a web. Web configurations consist of a topic node in the center of the map surrounded by supporting nodes. The result is a map that looks like a spider's web (see Figure 8.2).

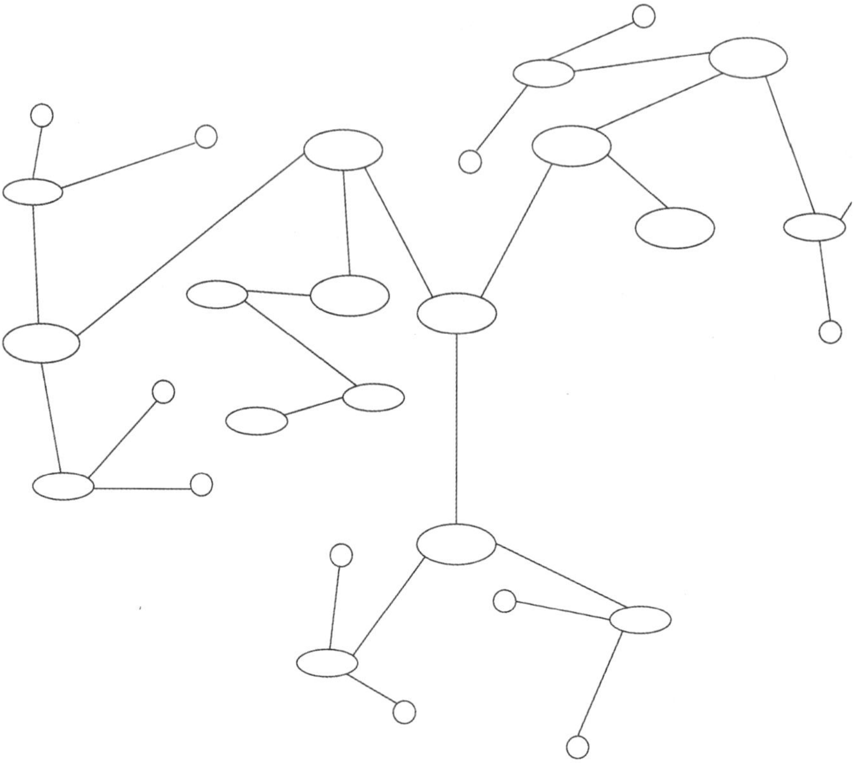

Figure 8.2 A schematic representation of the web-like configuration (Lambiotte, Dansereau, Cross & Reynolds, 1989)

Knowledge maps also can be formatted as a single large map (i.e. whole map; see Figure 8.3) or as a smaller set of interlocked cross-referenced maps (Lambiotte et al., 1989). Whole maps may have advantages in that they provide an overall view of the domain and multiple processing routes through the information. However, whole maps may have problems as associated with size and complexity that potentially reduce their usefulness for instructional purpose (Lambiotte et al., 1989).

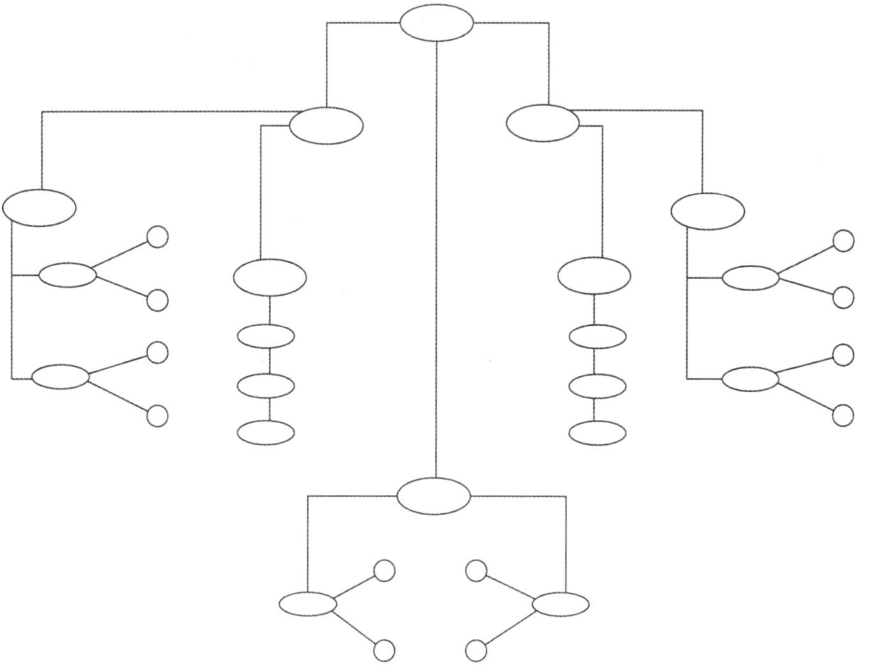

Figure 8.3 A schematic representation of a gestalt map presented in a whole-map format (Lambiotte et al., 1989)

Other techniques include hierarchical configurations. For example, placing the topic node at the top center of the map and then placing subordinate concepts beneath it. This sequence continues down the page with the bottom nodes being the most subordinate concepts in the domain as seen in Figure 8.4 (Wiegmann et al., 1992).

Several additional information can be added to the links by (a) using arrow heads to specify the directionality of the relationships, (b) using words or an abbreviation to label the relationships and (c) using differently shaped lines to classify the types of relationships (Lambiotte et al., 1989).

In addition, the network typed knowledge map is also called causal map which is defined as a technique "for linking strategic thinking and acting, helping make sense of complex problems, and communicating to oneself and others what might be done about them" (Buzan & Buzan, 1993). This approach is normally served for systematizing knowledge about cause and effects. Knowledge source map is a kind of organizational charts that does not describe the functions, responsibility and hierarchy, but expertise (Eppler, 2001). It helps to detect experts in a specific knowledge domain. The last one, knowledge flow map represents the order in which knowledge resources should be used rather than a map of knowledge (Eppler, 2001).

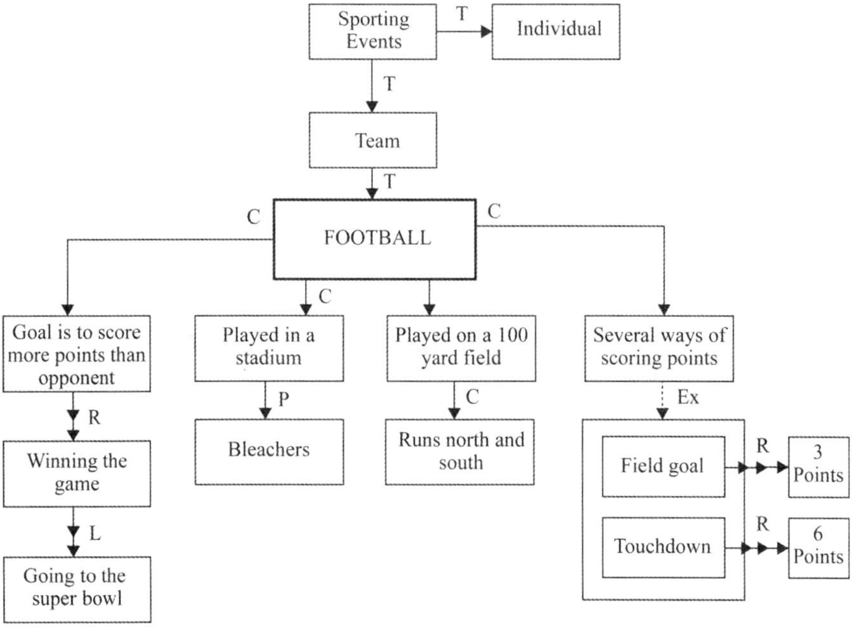

Figure 8.4 Example of a typical knowledge map and link types (Wiegmann et al., 1992)

Recently, an innovative knowledge mapping tool that automatically generated a knowledge map from a set of documents was being developed (Lee & Segev, 2012) (as shown in the Figure 8.5). The map has 18 keywords and 30 relations. Links have different thicknesses. Each link has a different score and thickness, when a higher score yields a thicker link. K-map Tools serves as a K-map learning environment. K-map has a hyperlink for each relation. If the user clicks a relation, all the sentences that have two keywords at both ends of the relation will be visible. For example, if a relation between "Kennedy" and "president" is chosen. In Figure 8.5, all sentences that have the words "Kennedy" and "president" are displayed. The user can read some of the sentences and acquire domain knowledge from them. If the user chooses any sentence, the sentence can be directly accessed in the original document. With K-map Tools, as the user handles the K-map two tasks are accomplished: searching and learning. In current search engines, two steps occur in the searching and learning process. The first step is the user typing in the words the user wants to know about; those words can be considered the topic. Then the search engine shows the user a list of the documents related to the query. The user goes over the list and at some point chooses a document and starts reading it. The same process is repeated until enough has been learned about the topic. With current search engines, there may be inefficiencies—the user may not understand important concepts, may miss key concepts, or may waste time trying to find a right document (Lee & Segev, 2012).

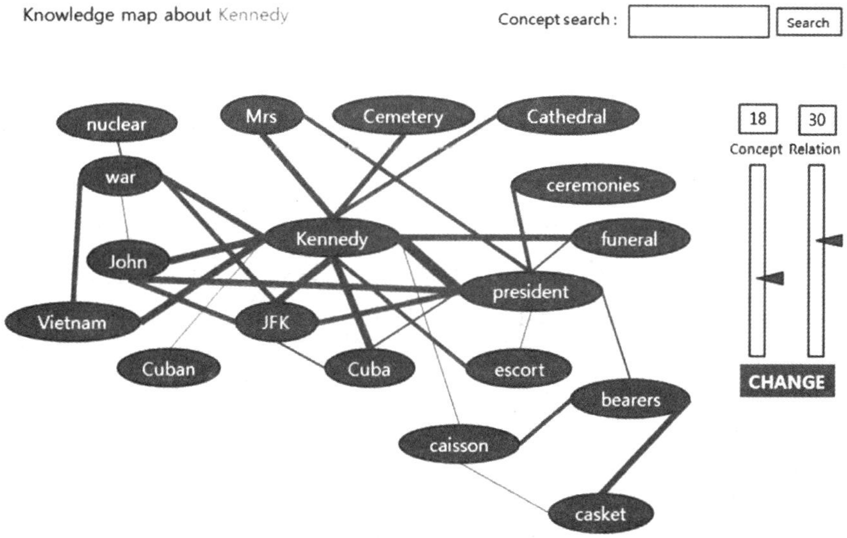

Figure 8.5 Screen shot of K-map tools—knowledge map of John F. Kennedy (Lee & Segev, 2012)

8.2 Various Applications of Knowledge Maps

The knowledge map is defined as a diagrammatic and graphical representation of knowledge, illustrating how knowledge and knowledge attributes are related. A knowledge map is a consciously designed communication medium using a graphical presentation of text, models, numbers or symbols between makers and users (Wexler, 2001). A knowledge map is a structure of concepts with well-defined terms and relationships associating these concepts. The intended meaning so specific concepts are understood well only through these explicit term definitions and associations. Therefore, any specific terms used in the knowledge map have to be explicitly and formally described to avoid misinterpretation during their use within or across disciplines (Yang, Song, Lu & Zhang, 2007). Through exploring a knowledge domain, using the knowledge map can help the user see the holistic picture. We collected various perspectives from using knowledge maps in literatures emphasizing decision-making, information retrieval, or knowledge management, and in particular in educational application (Browne, Curley & Benson, 1997; Chou & Lin, 1998; Hall et al., 1992; Paolucci, 1998).

(1) The knowledge map for decision-making and community communication

Knowledge map functions as a representation tool to visualize knowledge representations and relationships between them (Kang, Park & Kim, 2003). Knowledge representations comprised data of facts, information of summarized data and cases. These representations could be used for procedures, rules, ideas that guide personal and organizational decisions and actions (Wang, 2002). It's not only to elicit the knowledge that a decision maker faces, but also to combine probabilities associated with various factors in order to obtain a final probability (Browne et al., 1997). All these representations can be linked into a network as a knowledge map. It really provides a useful path for the user to reach specific knowledge in the context of knowledge management system.

The map also concerns the relation of casual or influent relationship of decision-making (Eppler, 2001). For example, Chung, Chen & Nunamaker (2003) propose a knowledge map framework for exploring business intelligence to mitigate information overload on the Web. Yang et al., (2007) suggest that knowledge mapping methods are commonly recognized as an effective visual approach for knowledge locating, connecting, and sharing. Moreover, well-structured knowledge objects reveal their relationships between knowledge, and reduce information overloading on knowledge sharing and creation (Paolucci, 1998). Currently, knowledge map could even be applied in other areas such as process design to product development and virtual communities. In the design process of new product development, knowledge maps are often employed to describe what knowledge is needed in which process, who have tacit knowledge, where it resides, or how it flows along a design process. It can assist in the acquisition, utilization,and sharing of both explicit and tacit process knowledge in an unambiguous way (Yang et al., 2007).

On the other hand, within cooperative situations, knowledge maps appear to have some advantages over traditional text when used as communication aids (Reynolds, Patterson, Skaggs & Dansereau, 1991). Knowledge maps are consciously designed communication mediums between map makers and map users (Wexler, 2001), in virtual communities of practice, knowledge map is defined as a concept hierarchy characterizing the taxonomy of documents contributed by members of a community practice. A knowledge map management system facilitates knowledge navigation, knowledge seeking, and advisory learning (Lin & Hsueh, 2006).

(2) The knowledge map for information retrieval

Davenport and Prusak (2000) defined a knowledge map as a knowledge yellow pages or a cleverly constructed database. A knowledge map, which can be used to point to knowledge, does not contain knowledge. Knowledge maps are created by transferring certain aspects of knowledge into a graphic form that is easily understandable by end-users (Speel, Shadbolt, Vries, Dam & O'Hara, 1999). Moreover, a knowledge map is a knowledge representation that reveals the underlying relationships of the knowledge sources, using a map metaphor for spatial display. For example, a knowledge map for news articles could highlight the current major news topics and their relationships by using blocks to represent key concepts and possibly using lines to represent relationships (Ong, Chen, Sung & Zhu, 2005). Based on earlier literature reviews, knowledge maps typically point for people as well as to documents and databases to facilitate the users to find an appropriate knowledge source. For information retrieval, a knowledge map represents the document category with concept hierarchy (Sebastiani, 2002). Some researches and practices have been done through this concept. For example, Lin and Hsueh (2006) applied information retrieve algorithm to create and maintain a knowledge map system for virtual communities of practice. Chung et al. (2003) proposed a knowledge map framework for exploring business intelligence to mitigate information overload on the Web.

(3) The knowledge map for knowledge management

Davenport & Prusak (2000) have observed that developing a knowledge map involves locating important knowledge in the organization and then publishing a list or picture showing where to find it. The knowledge map plays significant roles in implementing knowledge management and facilitating more effective KMS (Herl, O'Neil Jr Chung & Schacter, 1999). All captured knowledge can be summarized and abstracted via the knowledge map (Kim, Suh & Hwang, 2003). Knowledge maps gather explicit and collected knowledge which can be shared, and facilitate the emergence of tacit knowledge of new relationships. Effective knowledge mapping brings map users several returns including economic, structural, organizational culture and knowledge returns (Wexler, 2001). Moreover, partial knowledge returns accelerate learning curves by helping users locate an effective route, plan, and scenario or sequence of actions, and assist participants in communicating with others regarding the new relationships and ideas using a shared vocabulary. Partial knowledge returns also help users identify new areas in the emerging search for actionable information.

Therefore, the benefit of knowledge returns is achievable when a knowledge map for construction scheduling techniques is constructed.

Specifically, knowledge map assists to find key sources conveniently and helps define the constraints of knowledge creation and flows. Since the map increases convenience in knowledge finding, knowledge reuse is encouraged. As a result, costs for knowledge reinvention, search time and acquisition are reduced. Important expertise is most visible in the map and knowledge sharing is induced and increased. From the map, users can discover effective and emergent communities of practices where learning is happening and find opportunities for learning and leverage of knowledge. Knowledge maps can be used as a baseline to measure progress in knowledge management projects, to provide an inventory and evaluation of intellectual and intangible assets and to design a knowledge depository (Pyo, 2005). In addition, Lin & Hsueh (2006) propose a knowledge map management system to facilitate knowledge management in virtual communities of practice. Develop knowledge map creation and maintenance functions by utilizing information retrieval and data mining techniques. The knowledge maps created respectively from the documents of the teachers' professional community, SCTNet, are evaluated by experts of these two domains. Knowledge maps generated by the system are accepted by domain experts from the evaluation since the degree of their modification of the automatically created knowledge maps is proportionally small. The knowledge structure representing the categories of community documents maintains its high purity, diversity, specificity, and structure adaptation by using the knowledge map maintenance function with limited computational cost.

(4) The knowledge map for educational application

Knowledge map is widely used in the education field (Kuo, Lien, Chang & Heh, 2004; Lin & Hsueh, 2006; O'Donnell, et al., 2002; Shaw, 2010); meanwhile, a great deal of research has been conducted to examine knowledge maps as multipurpose educational tools (e.g., as text supplements and substitutes (Hall et al., 1992); lecture aids (Wiegmann et al., 1992); prewriting tools (Wiegmann et al., 1992); note-taking strategies (Novak, 1984); and props during cooperative interactions (Rewey et al., 1989). In the teaching-learning process, a teacher teaches learners what knowledge is and how knowledge relates one to another; in practice, Lwathrum et al. had employed knowledge maps to design an intelligent question system for learning (Paolucci, 1998).

The individual Knowledge Map briefing sheets are meant to serve as quick snapshots of *info*rmation in key areas related to the use of ICTs in education (Trucano, 2005). For example, the variety of the knowledge map linking learning systems, which specify the properties of the relationship among concepts, allows for the use of knowledge map in a variety of learning content areas such as statistics, human physiology, science, math and psychology (Lambiotte, Dansereau, Cross & Reynolds, 1989; McCagg & Dansereau, 1991). Besides, research in cognitive and educational psychology supports the use of knowledge maps as a "spatial learning strategy" to form spatial representations of information. Spatial representations seem to be valuable in learning difficult, unfamiliar expository material (Anderson & Armbruster, 1985; Holley & Dansereau, 1984). Support for the use of such spatial representations also comes from research on the differences between experts and novices in knowledge representation. Research has suggested that experts organize their knowledge in terms of abstract relational schemata that novices do not have or cannot access easily (Amer, 1994; Guri-Rozenblit, 1989).

8.3 Knowledge Map Development and Construction

Traditional knowledge map construction usually adopts mathematical and statistical methods to generate maps on the basis of papers, textbooks, and reports (Pritchard, 1969). However, the range of data for mapping has been extended to citations, authors, titles, indices, and so on. Several researchers considered that knowledge mapping tasks should be an ongoing process and must be updated and maintained in order to be useful. Extensive research and communication for various stakeholders should be performed in relation to issues, processes, organization culture, knowledge base and knowledge transferring and sharing procedures. They also believed that the actual knowledge does not have a static structure but is dynamically constructed by identifying and indexing pieces of information or knowledge components depending on the contexts (Kim, Fillies, Smith & Wikarski, 2002).

At present, several approaches exist for knowledge map development and construction as seen in Figure 8.6. Rouse, Thomas & Boff (1998) proposed a procedure for constructing a knowledge map for R&D/ technology management. Their procedure consists of the following six steps: extraction of knowledge; compilation of knowledge; derivation of assertions; sorting and labelling; representation of relationships; interpretation; and, iteration. Moreover, Kim et al. (2003) proposed a procedure for building a knowledge map that is useful for developing a knowledge management system for an organization. However, available approaches for knowledge map development are not targeted to public knowledge sources. Yang (2007) proposes a novel procedure that is suitable for extracting knowledge from public knowledge sources when developing a knowledge map. The proposed procedure has the following six steps: defining organizational knowledge; process map analysis; knowledge extraction; knowledge profiling; knowledge linking; and, knowledge map validation.

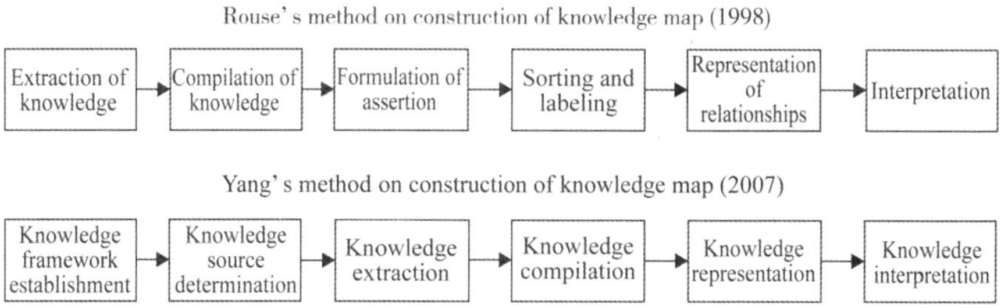

Figure 8.6 Rouse's and Yang's approaches for knowledge map development and construction

In order to create such knowledge structures from diverse information and knowledge sources, Gartner Group has suggested a bottom-up approach that includes data extraction, linguistic analysis, dictionary/thesaurus creation, semantic networks, clustering/categorization, and concept yellow pages (Ong et al., 2005). Among these, mapping textual knowledge sources are more difficult than mapping numerical knowledge sources because the text has limited spatial meaning but strong abstract or conceptual relationships. One example of mapping textual knowledge is Cartia's News Map (Dodge, 2000), which applies sophisticated and proprietary lexical algorithms to analyze and, in some senses "understand" the content of text documents and the relations between them to distill the key topics and form the knowledge map. Another common approach is to use neural networks, which are a class of machine learning algorithms consistent with human mental models (Lippmann, 1987). Woo proposed dynamic knowledge map, it can assist in the reuse of experts' tacit knowledge (Woo et al., 2004). Utilizing knowledge mapping has two advantages. First, the knowledge map is represented in a simple, clear visual presentation in the knowledge management system. Second, the mapping methodology helps users to identify the most critical and easily available knowledge areas of the project.

The most recent trend in knowledge mapping is the application of text mining, which allows automatic tagging and various types of mapping. Thus, co-word maps, citation maps, and co-authorship maps have been developed to enhance the usefulness of knowledge maps. The concept of knowledge map has been suggested to provide the "big picture" of science; this emphasizes the importance of computers for constructing multi-dimensional maps (Doyle, 1961). For example, a typology for demonstrating the intellectual structure of science has been devised to describe patterns of scientific papers (Yu & Van de Sompel, 1965) and track fast-changing research areas that are the focus of special funding efforts by using scientometric journal mapping (Leydesdorff, Cozzens & Van den Besselaar, 1994). In particular, a science map that covers all subject areas of science has been generated on the basis of citation information (Griffith, Small, Stonehill & Dey, 1974) and at the level of the

Institute for Scientific Information (ISI) categories using the aggregated journal-journal citation matrix (Leydesdorff & Rafols, 2009).

8.4 Automated Construction of Knowledge Map

Some researchers have been devoted to the study of automatic construction of knowledge maps in the last few years. For example, Tseng, Sue, Su, Weng & Tsai (2007) proposed a Two-Phase Concept Map Construction (TP-CMC) approach to automatically construct a concept map for a course from the learner's past test data. The first phase uses Fuzzy Set Theory to transform the numeric data into symbolic ones. The second phase uses multiple rule types, to analyze the mined association rules and also uses a heuristic algorithm to remove redundancy and circularity when building concept maps. Relations in the concept map indicate learning paths. Chen & Xia (2009) reviewed research about the automatic construction of knowledge maps. They first presented a traditional knowledge or concept map construction method achieved by hand, which includes the following steps: concept selection, concept classification, appointing the central concept, and connecting concepts and cross-concepts, and then described auto-construction concept map methods based on document information retrieval and concept extraction. Chen, Wei & Chen (2008) proposed a way to construct concept maps automatically from academic papers. They used author keywords as keywords after pre-processing and defined relations. In Lee and Segev's study, an attempt was made to automatically build a domain knowledge map for e-learning by using text mining techniques. From a set of documents about a specific topic, keywords are extracted using the TF/IDF algorithm. A domain knowledge map is based on ranking pairs of keywords according to the number of appearances in a sentence and the number of words in a sentence. The experiments analyzed the number of relations required to identify the important ideas in the text. In addition, the experiments compared K-map learning to document learning and found that K-map identifies the more important ideas (Lee & Segev, 2012); Hou, Ong, Nee, Zhang and Liu (2011) proposed GRAONTO, generating graphs of documents and using the random walk term weighting to estimate the relevance of the information of a term to the corpus from both local and global perspectives. The Markov Clustering algorithm was used to disambiguate terms with different meanings and group similar terms to produce concepts. Urfat and Korhan introduced a way to extract key concepts and relations among learning concepts (Gunel & Nuriyev, 2009). To extract key concepts, n-gram, a sequence of characters that stands for a word, was used with a dictionary of technical terms. To extract relations (relevance) from sentences, three features were considered: word co-occurrences, logarithmic concept weights, and augmented normalized candidate learning concept frequency. Some descriptions about extract key concepts and relations among knowledge maps are shown in the below section.

(1) Keyword extraction

Generally, keywords are extracted from a set of documents in the first phase. The documents can be manually chosen or chosen from the user's query. Each term will receive a weight using the term weighting algorithm. Keywords will be selected from the top-ranked terms set by a limit given by the knowledge map user (Lee & Segev, 2012). Before running the term weighting algorithm, stop words, such as "and" and "the", are deleted from original sentences of a document. Next, a stemming process is conducted with those sentences that don't have stop words. The stemming process cuts the original word down to the root. For example, after the stemming process, the words "run", "running", and "runs" become the same word, which is "run", because all the words have the same meaning. To stem words, porter's algorithm was used in the K-map system (Porter, 1980). Once these pre-processes are finished, we can use a term weighting algorithm to weight terms. The weighting algorithm is based on the Term Frequency/Inverse Document Frequency (TF/IDF) method (Salton & Buckley, 1988). The formula below is the weighting method using TF/IDF. Once words are ordered by weights, keywords are selected from top-ranked words according to the limit that the user set (Lee & Segev, 2012).

(2) Relation extraction

Once the keywords of the knowledge map are decided, relations are also defined. Chen et al., (2008) identified assumptions for defining relations. In the present study, two factors are considered based on these assumptions. One factor is how frequently two keywords appear in a sentence together, and the other is how big a role the two keywords play in a sentence. As the number of the words in a sentence increase, the weight decreases. In other words, the score of a relation in a shorter sentence is higher than the score of a relation in longer sentences. Each relation has its own score, and it is used to rank the relations. The characteristics of important sentences are generally that they contain more important words and have shorter sentence length and a lower number of sub-sentences (Li & Choi, 1997). Clark & Wasow (1998) investigated the origins of repeated words in spontaneous speech. They compared content words and function words. Content words refer to entities, events, states, relations, and properties in the world. They are characteristically nouns, verbs, adjectives, or adverbs.

In summary, Knowledge maps serve as scaffolds or supports to cognitive processing because they can reduce cognitive load, enhance representation of relationships among complex constructs, provide multiple retrieval paths for accessing knowledge and serve as important props for communicating shared knowledge. Knowledge maps are not only effective knowledge management tools for knowledge navigation and searching, but they also specify captured knowledge and its relationships and display them in ordered and friendly forms (Mertins, Heisig & Vorbeck, 2003). O'Donnell, Dansereau & Hall (2002) report that knowledge maps can be used as primary sources for knowledge acquisition, aids for text processing, communication tools for organizing ideas, or retrieval cues. Knowledge maps play important roles in implementing knowledge management by transferring certain aspects of knowledge into a graphic form that is easily understood by end-users. All captured knowledge can be summarized and abstracted through a knowledge map. Knowledge maps gather explicit and collected knowledge, which can be shared and can facilitate the emergence of tacit knowledge of new relationships (Yang, 2007).

Knowledge maps can help to facilitate information research in a specific domain. Moreover, using knowledge maps can help present concept-item relationships of the assessment scope in a more structured manner so that teachers can easily construct their assessments (Su & Wang, 2010). Because of these features, a knowledge map can assist teachers by serving as a tool allowing them to see key concepts quickly, identify important processes and gain insight into associated behaviors. It is important to realize that teachers working on assessment projects act just like knowledge workers who facilitate the collection and management of knowledge from past, current, and even future assessment projects. To enhance knowledge usage, teachers must innovatively utilize the knowledge created and accumulated through historic assessment projects. They must also share this knowledge across future assessment projects, a task which presents the challenge of how to reuse past knowledge and experiences to shorten assessment projects and reduce overhead costs for both the present and the future. Our aim of this study is to utilize knowledge management and knowledge maps to solve the problems mentioned above and to enhance assessment performance.

CHAPTER 9 Test Item Categorization

Item categorization assigns one of the predefined categories to a new item according to the item's topic or contents. In recent years, automatic document categorization and machine learning technology could help us to proceed Item categorization. In this chapter, we introduced some innovative text categorization methods and encourage to be used to analyze assessment and assessment items.

With the rapid advancement of information and the internet technologies, the use of computerized assessments is growing popular in a quick pace. Teachers can now create assessments or exercises using electronic form test items, collected from many sources such as peer teachers, students, schools, textbooks or educational publishing companies. Collected test items are usually put into different item resources without being categorized by topics, or by concepts. When the volume of resources becomes very large, the number of test item combinations increases exponentially, and the item selection process for teachers becomes more time consuming and tedious (El-Alfy & Abdel-Aal, 2008). Moreover, when test items are periodically collected, at each exam or from year to year, test items become grouped by the time rather than by their context (Nuntiyagul, Naruedomkul, Cercone, Wongsawang., 2008). However, teachers always want to retrieve test items according to the categories, not to time, to be in accordance with the curriculum or assessment range. Test items have to be organized and categorized, so that they can be retrieved by subject content, before they can be used effectively (Nuntiyagul, et al., 2008).

Item categorization assigns one of the predefined categories to a new item according to the item's topic or content (Song, Wenyin, Gu, Quan & Hao, 2010). However, manually selecting a suitable category from a long list of categories is time-consuming and inconvenient for a user when asking a new question. Hence, an automatic method for question categorization is necessary to save users' time and efforts, in which some candidate categories ranked by their relevancy can be recommended to the user automatically (Song, et al., 2010). If the user finds a suitable one, he or she only needs to click a button to confirm it. Otherwise, they can still choose the suitable one from the entire category list. Hence, it can save much effort if the assessment system can recommend the categories accurately.

With the recent successes in e-learning and advances in the machine learning techniques, such as information extraction (IE), text categorization and natural language processing, efficient automatic test item categorization has become available (Song, et al., 2010). Some text mining and information categorization techniques are better at managing test items systematically and automatically, allowing items to be efficiently reused and retrieved (Li & Roth, 2002; Zhang & Lee, 2003).

In which, text categorization techniques are regarded as a novel and exceptional technique for enhancing the applicability of educational assessment. Currently, these techniques focus on the document-level texts, which usually consist of at least hundreds of words. They are widely used to predict the predefined class label for semi-structured or non-structured document data. In most of these techniques, including Naive Bayesian (NB) classifier, k-nearest Neighbors and support vector machine (SVM), focus on machine learning to construct a classifier and use it to categorize new documents. A more intelligent application of text mining involves identifying the subjects of documents and summarizing their content (Clifton, Cooley & Rennie, 2004). The scope of subjects in text mining is very broad. First, documents are automatically classified in a predefined class. For this, k-nearest neighbor (k-NN) techniques apply to text classification (Yang & Lee, 2004) and machine learning are utilized for the automatic classification of documents (Sebastiani, 2002). Furthermore, a corpus-based method applies text mining techniques on a corpus of web pages to automatically create web directories and organize them into hierarchies (Yang & Lee, 2004). Second, documents are grouped into several clusters on the basis of the similarity of content. K-means and hierarchical clustering algorithms are adopted for such clustering (Dhillon & Modha, 2001). While such text clustering algorithms utilize the vector space model, recent methods are proposed to apply the sequences of frequent words or meaning (Li, Chung & Holt, 2008). In particular, SOMs are adopted to improve the performance of the process (Kohonen, 2001) and a graph-based approach to document classification allows for a much more expressive document encoding than the more standard bag-of-words approach (Jiang, Coenen, Sanderson & Zito, 2010). Finally, the structuring of documents in an unstructured format is a recent research trend that employs mathematical models of machine learning (Hsu & Chang, 1999). Automatic tools for assisting engineers or decision makers are suggested to facilitate text segmentation, summary extraction, feature selection, cluster generation, and topic identification (Tseng, Lin & Lin, 2007)

Moreover, as Huang proposes, text categorization involves looking for patterns in natural language text and may be defined as the process of analyzing text to extract information (Huang, et al., 2008). Natural language processing technique can be used effectively in the language-based domains, such as dialogue systems, speech recognition, information retrieval and knowledge representation (Alshawi, 1992). The natural language processing is a way of computer processing of human language, and the computer returns a correct response that people expect (Huang, et al., 2008).

Due to documents in a textual format have no structured data fields, it is very difficult to efficiently analyze such textual information. Thus, the first step of text mining is to define key features of documents in order to transform unstructured textual information into structured information. In short, text mining puts a set of labels on each document; further, discovery operations are performed using the labels. The technique is particularly notable because it can cluster similar documents (Dhillon & Modha, 2001) or classify newly generated documents into a category (Sebastiani, 2002).

Before proceeding the text classification work, word segmentation is the first task. Prior research of word segmentation is summarized into three categories: dictionary, linguistic and statistical approaches. The dictionary approach is known to utilize the dictionary to match the lexicons of sentences in each article. The major advantages of this approach are its execution efficiency and ease to implement. Some systems are still using this approach, especially when lexicons in the target articles do not consist of new words (Chien, 1997; Li & Xing, 1998). Word segmentation is used for eliciting words from the text. In English text, words are separated by spaces or terminators, such as comma, quotation mark, period, etc. However, the information retrieval development of western languages has gradually matured, the research on information retrieval from Chinese documents still has many difficulties in morphological, syntactic, and semantic levels (Wong & Li, 1998). To generate accurate word segments is considered the major barrier to text retrieval for Asian languages (Wu & Tseng, 1993). But in Chinese text, a word can be composed of more than one Chinese character, and there are no specific terminators to enclose characters as a word (Lin & Hsueh, 2006). Therefore, to transform unstructured Chinese document to structured data for eliciting key terms, techniques such as word segmentation, text indexing, and term weighting have been adopted (Lin & Hsueh, 2006).

The linguistic approach uses semantic knowledge bases, heuristics, or rules extract lexicons (Wu & Tseng, 1995). The Chinese knowledge information processing (CKIP) project in "Academia Sinica" proposes the Chinese parser to facilitate word segmentation and provides not only the functionality of word segmentation but also the morphological information of each word (http://ckip.iis.sinica.edu.tw/CKIP/). Moreover, in the word segmentation and text indexing phases, the next step is to assign weights to word segments (terms) to represent their importance to represent the main concepts of documents. This weight assignment process is known as feature selection in machine learning, or the term-weighting system in an information retrieval system. Some studies have cited keyword extraction as a way to classify text; keywords are usually used for representing key topics included in a research article and are useful for researchers to locate documents of interest (Barki, Rivard & Talbot, 1993). Luhn (1999) suggests that the occurrence frequency of a word is a useful measurement of word significance. An early classification method often adopts statistics calculations on extracted keywords, then follows up with some of the text categorization techniques that focus on machine learning to construct a classifier and use it to categorize new documents, such as Term Frequency-Inverse Document Frequency (TF-IDF), vector space model (VSM). These techniques are to explore the importance of keywords in documents. For example, the design of the TF-IDF weight means the importance increases proportionally to the number of times a word appears in the document, but is offset by the frequency of the word in the corpus (Salton & McGill, 1983). The term-weighting system calculates the term occurrence in a document as a measure to assess the importance of the term to represent the document. In the information retrieval research, the fully weighted system obtains the best results among the term-weighting systems, where "tf" denotes term frequency, "N" is the total number of documents in the corpus, and "n" is the number of documents to which a term is assigned (Salton & Buckley, 1988; Salton, Wong & Yang, 1975). The vector space model is that various information retrieval objects are modeled as elements of a vector space. Specifically, terms, documents, queries, concepts, and so on are all vectors in the vector space. The VSM is used to handle multiclass categorization by calculating and comparing the distances between terms. The VSM can also be used to acquire similarities through applications, such as training or making lexical share characteristics with tasks such as information extraction, knowledge extraction from texts and text mining (Basili & Pazienza, 1997; Knight, 1999). In addition, the Rocchio algorithm (Hull, 1994) is thc classical mcthod using information retrieval techniques to route and filter documents.

Assessment item topic categorization, which is a bit different from normal text categorization, can be considered as a particular type of (short) text categorization problem (Song, Wenyin, Gu, Quan & Hao, 2011). If we just use a high dimensional space to represent items, the vectors will be very sparse, which may lead to poor performance. This is mainly due to the special properties of questions compared with normal text. First, items contain much less statistic information than long documents. If we use the traditional statistic method, the item vector may be very sparse. Second, items have some additional information such as question type and question focus which may play a more important role than other information on the question (Ittycheriah Franz, & Roukos, 2002; Moldovan, Harabagiu, Pasca, Mihalcea, Girju, Goodrum & Rus, 2000). Moreover, in an item, different words may contribute differently (Song, et al., 2010). These words should be given a higher weight for categorization task. On the other hand, some research works (Li & Roth, 2006; Zhang & Lee, 2003) on item type categorization, which categorize items into some semantic classes that impose constraints on potential answers, which like "person", "location", "definition", and so on. Such constraints can be utilized to find the right answers. In question type classification, the interrogatives like "who", "when" and so on, are very important because they directly indicate the question types. For example, if a question starts with "who", we know the question is about a person; if a question starts with "when", the question is about time. Thus, some heuristic rules can be constructed to assist the categorization. Hence, due to the rapid growth of electronic testing items which are mainly text-based shapes, this study makes use of a text categorization technique, which is able to handle specific characteristics of textual data, to help teachers categorize test items automatically and more efficiently.

CHAPTER 10 Clustering Technology and Clustering in Education Application

In this chapter, we introduced clustering technology, the clustering is the process of grouping the data into classes, so that physical or abstract objects within a cluster have high similarity in comparison to one another, but are very dissimilar to objects in other cluster (Han & Kamber, 2006; Wang, 2006). A cluster is a collection of data objects that are similar to one another within the same cluster and are dissimilar to the objects in other clusters. In addition, two commonly cluster approach, k -means, k-medoids are described. We also introduced the relevant educational application, especially for Item Recommendation on the education assessment environment in the last section.

10.1 Clustering Technology

Data mining technology is a knowledge discovery process to extract information from a dataset and to transform it into an understandable structure for further use (Klosgen & Zytkow, 2002). The objective of the data mining process is to discover new, interesting and useful knowledge of the actions and attributes of users, and could be used to help recommender systems to make recommendations. These mining techniques according to data classification purposes are divided into classification, prediction, clustering, association, detection and so on. Among these, clustering analysis is used to discover interesting data distributions and patterns, and group physical or abstract objects into classes of similar objects, it helps construct meaningful partitioning of a large set of objects based on a "divide and conquer" methodology that decomposes a large-scale system into smaller components to simplify design and implementation (Chen, Han & Yu, 1996).

In general, there are two purposes for using cluster analysis: understanding and utility. Clustering for understanding is to employ cluster analysis for automatically finding conceptually meaningful groups of objects that share common characteristics. It plays an important role in helping people to analyze, describe and utilize the valuable information hidden in the groups. Clustering for utility attempts to abstract the prototypes or the representative objects from individual objects in the same clusters. These objects, then serve as the basis of a number of data processing techniques such as summarization, compression, and nearest-neighbor finding.

Indeed, cluster analysis is valuable for the exploration of unknown data emerging from real-life applications. That is the fundamental reason why cluster analysis is invariably so important. At present, clustering has been used in a wide variety of application domains, including market research, pattern recognition and classification, data analysis, and image processing, business intelligence, psychology and social science, information retrieval, and Bioinformatics. In business, clustering can help marketers discover distinct groups in their customer bases and characterize customer groups based on purchasing patterns. In biology, it can be used to derive plant and animal taxonomies, categorize genes with similar functionality, and gain insight into structures inherent in populations (Han, Lee & Kamber, 2009). Some other interesting examples areas follows:

- Market research: Cluster analysis has become the "killer application" in one of the core business tasks. It has been widely used for large-scale customer segmentation and profiling, which help to locate targeted customers, design the 4P(product, price, place, promotion) strategies, and implement the effective customer relationship management.
- Web browsing: As the world we live has entered the Web 2.0 era,

information overload has become a top challenge that prevents people from acquiring useful information in a fast and accurate way. Cluster analysis can help to automatically categorize web documents into a concept hierarchy, and therefore provide a better browsing experience to web users.

- Image indexing: In the online environment, images pose problems of access and retrieval more complicated than those of text documents. As a promising method, cluster analysis can help to group images featured by the bag-of-features model, and therefore becomes a choice for large-scale image indexing.
- Recommender systems: Recent year have witnessed an increasing interest in developing recommender systems for online product recommendation or location based services. As one of the most successful approaches building recommender systems, collaborative filtering (CF) technique uses the known preferences of a group of users to make recommendations or predictions of the unknown preferences for other users. One of the fundamental tools of CF, is right the clustering technique.
- Community detection: Detecting clusters or communities in real-world graphs such as large social networks, web graphs, and biological networks, is a problem of considerable interests that has received a great deal of attention. A range of detection methods has been proposed in the literature, most of which are borrowed from the broader cluster analysis field.

Clustering is also called **data segmentation** in some applications because clustering partitions large data sets into groups according to their **similarity**. As a data mining function, cluster analysis can be used as a stand-alone tool to gain insight into the distribution of data, to observe the characteristics of each cluster, and to focus on a particular set of clusters for further analysis. Alternatively, it may serve as a preprocessing step for other algorithms, such as characterization, attribute subset selection, and classification, which would then operate on the detected clusters and the selected attributes or features (Han et al., 2009). Clustering techniques conventionally can be categorized into three types: partitioning, hierarchical, and hybrid approaches (Kaufman & Rousseeuw, 2009). On the partitioning approach, objects are viewed as points distributing in a hyperspace, and given the number of clusters, the seed (centroid) points for their corresponding clusters are initially selected. Through iteratively shifting centroid points, we can obtain the final clusters. Several algorithms such as k-means, PAM, CLARA, and FANNY are developed in this manner (Kaufman & Rousseeuw, 1990). In the agglomeration approach, the clustering process starts with forming each data point as its own cluster, and gradually merges clusters until all points have been grouped together as a big cluster. The entire grouping history is preserved, so that the user can choose the level of clustering that works best for the application. The common methods include AGNES, DIANA, CURE, and CHAMELEON (Kaufman & Rousseeuw, 1990). Two-stage clustering is a hybrid approach combining the partitioning and hierarchical clustering (Punj & Stewart, 1983). If the initial parameters of the partitioning clustering are not generated randomly, it will perform better than hierarchical clustering. Besides, they also conclude that the k-means clustering technique has better noise tolerance and the performance is independent from the abnormal instances and the difference of the distance measurement. These related clustering approaches are described in detail in the next section.

10.2 K-means and K-medoids

The most well-known and commonly used clustering methods are k-means, k-medoids, and their variations (Han, et al., 2011). In the k-means algorithm, cluster similarity measures in regard to the mean value of the objects in a cluster, which can be viewed as the cluster's center of gravity. The k-means method, however, can be applied only when the mean of a cluster is defined, which may not be the case in certain applications, such as when data with categorical attributes are involved. Furthermore, this method is sensitive to outliers because an object with an extremely large value may substantially distort the distribution of data. Conversely, instead of taking the mean value of the objects in a cluster as a reference point, the k-medoids method uses the medoid, which is the most centrally located object in a cluster. However, it is necessary to use both methods to specify , which is the number of clusters (Wang, 2006). Both the k-means and k-medoids algorithms are partitioned (dividing the dataset into groups) and both attempt to minimize squared error, the distance between points labelled to be in a cluster and a point designated as the center of that cluster. The detail description of k-means and k-medoids are introduced as follows:

(1) K-means

K-means classification-based clustering algorithm is the most commonly used algorithms in analysis application (Zhangang, 2009). Under the following description in the k-means algorithm, this **algorithm** takes the input parameter, *k*, and partitions a set of *n* objects into *k* clusters so that the resulting intra-cluster similarity is high, but the inter-cluster similarity is low. Cluster similarity is measured with respect to the *mean* value of the objects in a cluster, which can be viewed as the cluster **centroid** or **center of gravity** (Han et al., 2009). For example, given a set of observations (x_1, x_2, ..., x_n) where each observation is a d-dimensional real vector, k-means clustering aims to partition the n observations into k sets (k ≤ n) $S = (S_1, S_2, ..., S_k)$ so as to minimize the within-cluster sum of squares :

Where *ui* is the mean of points in *Si*.

Typically, this algorithm uses an iterative refinement technique. Given an initial set of k-means $m_1^{(1)}$, $m_2^{(1)}$..., $m_k^{(1)}$(see below), the algorithm proceeds by alternating between two steps:

Assignment step: Assign each observation to the cluster with the closest mean.

Update step: Calculate the new means to be the centroid of the observations in the cluster.

The process of iteratively reassigning objects to clusters to improve the partitioning is referred to as **iterative relocation**. Eventually, no redistribution of the objects in any cluster occurs and so the process terminates(as shown in Figure 10.1).

- k initial “means” (in this case k=3) are randomly selected from the data set (shown in color).
- k clusters are created by associating every observation with the nearest mean. The partitions here represent the Voronoi diagram generated by the means.
- The centroid of each of the k clusters becomes the new means.
- Steps 2 and 3 are repeated until convergence has been reached.

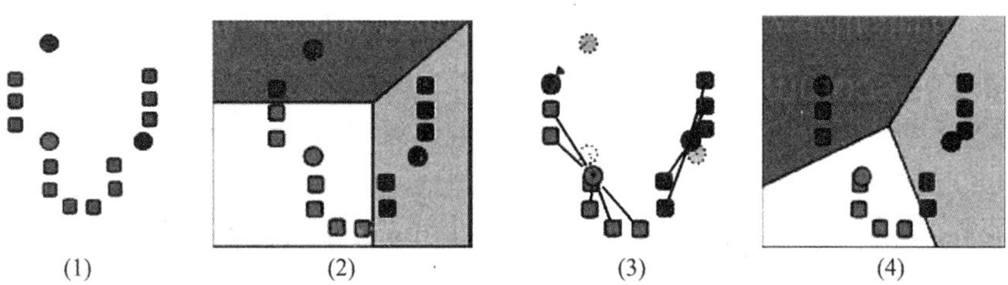

Figure 10.1 The k-means partitioning algorithm (k=3)

The k-means algorithm attempts to determine k partitions that minimize the square-error function. It works well when the clusters are compact clouds that are rather well separated from one another. The method is relatively scalable and efficient in processing large data sets because the computational complexity of the algorithm is $O(nkt)$, where n is the total number of objects, k is the number of clusters, and t is the number of iterations. Normally, $k \ll n$ and $t \ll n$. The method often terminates at a local optimum. In addition, the k-means has some shortcomings. For instance, the k-means method is not suitable for discovering clusters with no convex shapes or clusters of very different size. Moreover, it is sensitive to noise and outlier data points because a small number of such data can substantially influence the mean value (Knorr, Ng & Tucakov, 2000). To deal with this, one research direction is to incorporate some outlier removal techniques before conducting k-means clustering.

(2) K-medoids

In contrast to the k-means algorithm, k-medoids chooses data points as centres. The k-medoid is a classical partitioning technique of clustering that clusters the data set of n objects into k clusters that are known a priori. It is more robust to noise and outliers compared to k-means because it minimizes a sum of pair wise dissimilarities instead of a sum of squared Euclidean distances. A medoid can be defined as the object of a cluster with a minimal average dissimilarity to all of the objects in the cluster is, that is, it is a most centrally located point in the cluster.

- Initialize: randomly select k of the n data points as the medoids.
- Associate each data point to the closest medoid ("closest" here is defined as using any valid distance metric, most commonly Euclidean distance, Manhattan distance or Minkowski distance).
- For each medoidm,
  (a) For each non-medoid data point o
  (b) Swap m and o and compute the total cost of the configuration.
- Select the configuration with the lowest cost.
- Repeat steps 2 to 5 until there is no change in the medoid.

10.3 Clustering in Education Application

Currently, clustering is applied to proceed for statistical data analysis in many fields, including machine learning, pattern recognition, image analysis, information retrieval, and Bioinformatics ("clustering analysis", n.d.). No doubt, the clustering analysis also applies for EDM (Educational Data Mining) when it uses the unique kinds of data that come from an educational setting (Cristóbal Romero, López, Luna, & Ventura, 2013; Romero & Ventura, 2013). Such as: Tang & McCalla (2005) used this technique to find clusters of students with similar learning characteristics and to promote group collaborative learning as well as to provide incremental learner diagnosis; grouping students in order to give them differentiated guiding according to their skills and other characteristics;

Cheng, Lin, Chen & Heh (2005) explores the possibility of using a hierarchical clustering and analytical procedure to diagnosis individual and class learning and misconceptions; Firdausiah Mansur & Yusof (2013) proposed the ontology and the clustering techniques for classifying the behavior of the students which is based on the level of meaningful learning characteristics from their log activities in Moodle e-learning system; Khan, Clear & Sajadi (2012) use the frequency of access and the duration of sessions to establish several categories of learners by cluster analysis, which depict the differences among the cohort in terms of participation; or Cristóbal Romero et al. (2013) used clustering algorithms to compare versus classification for predicting whether students will pass or fail the course on the basis of data about their forum usage.

10.4 Teacher Clusters

At the perspective of knowledge sharing, to reduce unfamiliarity of teaching and assessment for novice teachers, it is important to promote the sharing and exchange of teachers' specialized knowledge associated with teaching and assessments. Teachers occasionally share their valuable teaching experiences, assessment knowledge, and ideas with colleagues in various school situations. Unfortunately, this priceless knowledge is rarely recorded, stored or applied by others. While teachers need this knowledge to enhance their own teaching and assessment techniques, it is not easy to access within the educational environments. This knowledge is especially critical for novice teachers developing content-specific assessments, as they hope to have access to superior testing items written by veteran teachers or follow an experienced teacher's assessment methodology with respect to item selection or concept-item weight allotment policy. However, not all item selecting strategies will conform to an individual teacher's assessment preferences or needs. Therefore, it is important to identify teachers who have similar assessment preferences and recommend appropriate items for those teachers, which can be accomplished via clustering technology and the various recommendation approaches. Accordingly, the first essential work deals with teacher clustering based on grouping teachers together who display similar assessment preferences. As a group, the teachers' assessment experiences and knowledge may be reused effectively and because of the similar assessment preferences, the teachers will have access to test items that match their personal preferences for future assessment development. Therefore, researches associated with clustering and item recommendation are briefly summarized.

The terms "groups" and "clustering" are somewhat interdependent in the context of assessment. Groups are defined as mutually similar data items (Pahl, 2006). Rafaeli distinguishes between "friends group" and "neighbors group". This concept is innovative in suggesting that "neighbors" (a like-minded group) are relevant to low-risk recommendation domains, such as movies, music or jokes, while "friends" are more relevant to higher-risk domains, such as knowledge items used in learning and assessment (Rafaeli, Barak, Dan-Gur & Toch, 2004). In the data mining domain, clustering is a useful technique for discovering interesting data distributions and patterns in the underlying data. It is a process of grouping the data into classes or clusters such that objects within a cluster have high similarity in comparison to one another, but are notably dissimilar to objects in other clusters (Han, Kamber & Pei, 2011). Clustering analysis, therefore, helps to construct meaningful partitioning of a large set of objects based on a "divide and conquer" methodology that decomposes a large-scale system into smaller components to simplify design and implementation (Chen, Han & Yu, 1996). The principle behind clustering is to maximize the similarities inside an object group and minimize the similarities between the object groups (Wang, 2006).

CHAPTER 11 Personalization and Item Recommendation

"Personalization" has been considered to be an important part of the recommendation process to take intelligent decisions. This chapter presents an overview of the field of recommender systems and describes the current generation of recommendation methods (Content-based filtering approach and Collaborative filtering approach) with their limitations and possible applications that can improve the capabilities of the recommendations made suitable for education applications. Finally, this chapter will explain why we use the application of such recommendation techniques in the field of educational assessment.

11.1 Personalization

Personalization, a special form of differentiation, is that a service or product can respond to a different user's unique and particular needs. Mobasher et al. defined that web personalization as an act of response according to the individual user's interestand hobby on Internet usage (Mobasher, Dai, Luo & Nakagawa, 2002). Through personalization, businesses can get to know customers' buying behaviors and accordingly develop more appropriate marketing strategies to attracteach customer of a specific type and efficiently deliver the suitable information and products/ services to him/her.The customer's satisfaction and loyalty can thus been hanced, and the increase in each customer's visiting frequency can further create more transaction opportunities and benefit the Internet businesses

(Lee, Liu & Lu, 2002).

The aim of personalization is to offer users what they want without asking them explicitly and to capture the social component of interpersonal interaction (Mulvenna, Anand & Büchner, 2000). The term "personalization" is often used in the context of recommendation systems that selectively promote products to end-users based on the analysis of earlier interactions (Schafer, Konstan & Riedl, 2001). Actually, Adomavicius and Tuzhilin proposed five stages of personalization: (a) collect user information, (b) profile users, (c) compare similarity, (d) deliver and present personalized information, and (e) measure user responses.In this book, the personalization takes on a broader meaning for the educational purpose of this research project; it involves the item repository and processing of a test paper data bank of educational assessment about each individual classroom teacher with detailed assessment preference and requirements information, and about the assessment system with detailed features and descriptions. This research project's approach to increase the accessibility of assessment systems relies on domain-based personalization of all interactions between the classroom teachers and the assessment system at a fine-grained level. Personalization of interactions with systems can potentially reduce complexities through the automatic filtering and translation of content and the elimination of features not directly related to the task at hand (Chiasson, Hawkey, McAllister & Slonim, 2002). End-user access to computerized systems relies increasingly on personal electronic computing devices such as personal data assistants, organizers, mobile and wearable computers.

11.2 Recommendation Systems

Basically, when encountering many resources and products, we expect to seek appropriate recommendations for sorting and selecting suitable data. According to this argument, personalized recommendation systems were proposed that produce a ranked list of items on which a user might be interested, in the context of choosing a current object

(Crespo, Martinez, Lovelle, Garcia-Bustelo, Gayo & Pablos, 2011). These objects can be any kind of information or articles, such as books, movies, communities, news, articles, electronic commerce, songs, web pages, blogs, and etc. In addition, several recommendation systems have been applied by many Web retailers, such Amazon.com, CDNow.com and eBay in an attempt toretain current customers. Software products for such systems, such as Net Perceptions' Personalization engine, Andromedia's LikeMind and Manna's FrontMind, are available. For another specific example, to help Internet users to search more efficiently, many powerful search tools have been proposed, such as the Google search engine (Google) (Page, Brin, Motwani & Winograd, 1999). Most of these search tools provide personalized recommendation mechanisms to enable users to filter out uninteresting or irrelevant search results. Restated, personalized service has received considerable attention (Herlocker & Konstan, 2001; Mobasher, Cooley & Srivastava, 2000; Rashid, Albert, Cosley, Lam, McNee, Konstan & Riedl., 2002) recently because of information needs differ among users.

The recommendation system is an important application which offers personalized service and maximize user satisfaction, capable of presenting a user a suggestion for an object, obtained on the basis of his previous preferences and the preferences of a community which has likings and opinions similar to his or her. In addition, a personalized recommendation system can provide one-to-one service to users based on users' past behavior and through inference from other users with similar preferences (Mulvenna et al., 2000). Recommendation Systems also can help us reduce the overload of information we suffer nowadays, providing, at the same time, customized access to information for a specific domain (Mirza, 2001). With the increasing applications of recommendation systems in a variety of fields, various approaches to recommendation systems have been developed (Burke, 2002; Cho & Kim, 2004; Liang, Yang, Chen & Ku, 2008). Previously published studies focus on the technique of building personalized recommender systems. In general, recommendation systems for the development of the first recommendation system by Goldberg, Nichols, Oki & Terry (1992), Tapestry is one of the earliest recommendation systems. It is a mail filtering system that allows its members to annotate each document in detail to represent how interesting the reader found the document. This system selects neighbored people to measure their preference similarities. Based on this work, several automated recommendation systems have been developed. (Hill, Stead, Rosenstein & Furnas, 1995) proposed video recommender for movie suggestions. Konstan, Miller, Maltz, Herlock, Gordon, Riedl., (1997) developed a recommendation system for news and movie recommendations. So far, various recommendation systems and related technologies have been reported (Crespo et al., 2011; Schafer, Frankowski, Herlocker & Sen, 2007; Zenebe & Norcio, 2009).

Generally, recommendation systems are decision aids that analyze user's prior online behavior and present information on products to match the user's preferences. Through analyzing the patron's operate history or communicating with them, recommendation systems employ quantitative and qualitative methods to discover the products that best suit the user. Users have come to trust the recommendation system to reduce the burden of navigating large information spaces and product catalogues. The preservation of this trust is important both for the users and site owners, and is dependent upon the perception of the recommender systems as objectives, unbiased and accurate. These recommender systems generally rely on two categories of mechanisms: content-based filtering (CBF) (Zenebe & Norcio, 2009) and collaborative filtering(CF) (Mobasher et al. 2000; Schafer et al., 2007), the former is effective in filtering useful information that fit each user's needs. The latter is expected to provide powerful suggestions for group decision and satisfy users' needs in group activities (Chen, Cheng & Chuang, 2008). In addition, several other data mining techniques, for example, decision tree (Cho, Kim & Kim 2002), association rule (Wang & Shao, 2004), and semantic approach (Liang et al., 2008), are used to proceed with the recommendation. The two main approaches will be presented below:

(1) Content-based filtering approach

Content-based filtering technologies are based on a content analysis of the target items. Target items are described by their attributes (Yu, 1999), such as color, shape and material. The user's profile is constructed by analyzing his/her responses to questionnaires, his/her rating of products has selected in the past, and navigation history. In content-based filtering systems, recommendations are provided for a user based solely on a profile established by analyzing the content of items that the user has rated in the past or the user's personal information and preferences (Balabanović & Shoham, 1997; Lang, 1995). For example, the recommendation systems based on the content filtering are mainly used to recommend documents, web pages, publications, jokes or news. Some examples are: SYSKILL & WEBERT, which recommend web pages (Pazzani, Muramatsu, & Billsus, 1996) or PTV (McCormack & Jones, 1998) that recommends TV programs to the user. The user's profile can be constructed by analyzing responses to a questionnaire, item ratings, or the user's navigation information and, based on those analyses, inferring the user's preferences and interests (Wang & Shao, 2004). However, Cheung et al. argued that a pure CBF system also has its shortcomings. One is that users can only receive recommendations similar to their earlier experiences. The other is that some items, such as music, photographs, and multimedia, are hard to analyze (Cheung, Kwok, Law & Tsui, 2003). Besides, some researchers also criticized two weaknesses for Content-based filtering systems (Shahabi & Chen, 2003):

- **Content limitation:** Content-based filtering methods can only be applied to a few kinds of content, such as text and image, and the extracted features can only capture certain aspects of the content.
- **Over-specialization:** Content-based recommendation system provides recommendations merely based on user profiles. Therefore, users have no chance of exploring new items that are not similar to those items included in their profiles.

In order to solve these problems, a variety of different techniques have been proposed. Some of techniques, such as dimensionality reduction, clustering, and BayesianNetwork, mainly are remedies for the scalability problem. These techniques extract characteristics (patterns) from the original dataset in an offline process and employ only these patterns to generate the recommendation lists in the online process. Although this approach can reduce the online processing cost, it often reduces the accuracy of the recommending results. Moreover, the online computation complexity keeps increasing with the number of patterns (Shahabi & Chen, 2003).

(2) Collaborative filtering approach

In contrast, a collaborative recommendation system is defined as "the system in which recommendations are made based only on the similarity degree between other users" (Balabanović & Shoham, 1997; Shardanand & Maes, 1995). The collaborative filtering (CF) is an information filtering technique that depends on human beings' evaluations of items. It is an attempt to automate the "word of mouth" recommendations that we receive on a daily basis from our family, friends, and colleagues. It identifies users whose tastes are similar to those of a given user and it recommends items those users have liked in the past. Given a target user's record of activity or preferences, collaborative filtering-based techniques, such as the k-Nearest-Neighbor (kNN) approach, compare that record with the historical records of other users in order to find the top k users who have similar tastes or in terests. The mapping of a visitor record to its **neighborhood** could be based on similarity in ratings of items, access to similar content or pages, or purchase of similar items. The identified neighborhood is then used to recommend items not already accessed or purchased by the active user. The advantage of this approach over purely content-based approaches which rely on content similarity in item-to-item comparisons is that it can capture "pragmatic" relationships among items based on how their intended use or based on similar tastes of the users.

Collaborative filtering has become the most widely used technologies for building personalization and recommendation systems. For example, the collaborative filtering is successfully adopted by Amazon.com and Dell.com. It finds a similar user group for the target buyer and recommends products that have been rated by users in the reference group, but not yet viewed by the target buyer (Konstan et al., 1997). In addition, recommender systems using a collaborative filtering approach have also been applied for reducing information overload and finding desired contents (Balabanović & Shoham, 1997; Basilico & Hofmann, 2004; Cho & Kim, 2004; Sarwar, Karypis, Konstan & Riedl, 2001; Schafer et al., 2007).

The collaborative filtering approach was the first attempt at using artificial intelligence for achieving personalization in a more intelligent manner (Mulvenna et al., 2000). It identifies other users who have shown similar preferences to a given user and recommends what they liked (Breese, Heckerman & Kadie, 1998). In general, it observes the behavior of individuals in a like-minded peer group and makes recommendations to individual users based on the behavior pattern of the peer group. Examples of systems using this approach include Ringo (Shardanand & Maes, 1995) and GroupLens (Konstan et al., 1997). Despite their success, their use has been constrained by two major limitations. The first limitation is the sparsity problem (Cheung et al., 2003). Conventional collaborative filtering recommendation systems require users to explicitly input preference ratings about many products. The number of ratings received is relatively small compared to the number of ratings required for prediction. Consequently, predicted ratings accuracy degrades significantly when the received ratings are sparse. One is its difficulty in measuring the similarities between users, the second limitation is the scalability problem (Cho et al., 2002). As the number of customers and products increase, the computation time of algorithms, which perform product comparisons grows, respectively (Ghani & Fano, 2002; Hung, 2005).

Typically, collaborative filtering-based recommendation systems do not use the actual content of the items for recommendation. Moreover, since other user profiles are also considered, user can explore new items. The nearest-neighbor algorithm is the earliest collaborative filtering-based technique used in recommendation systems. With this algorithm, the similarity between users is evaluated based on their ratings of products, and the recommendation is generated considering the items visited by nearest neighbors of the user. In its original form, the nearest-neighbor algorithm uses a two-dimensional user-item matrix to represent the user profiles. Shardanand & Maes (1995) also argued that CF-based recommendation systems suffers from three problems:

- **Scalability:** The time complexity of executing the nearest-neighbor algorithm grows linearly with the number of items and the number of users. Thus, the recommendation system cannot support large-scale applications such as Amazon.com, which provides more than 18 million unique items for over 20 million users.
- **Sparsity:** Due to large number of items and user reluctance to rate the items, usually the profile matrix is sparse. Therefore, the system cannot provide recommendations for some users, and the generated recommendations are not accurate.
- **Synonymy:** Since the contents of the items are completely ignored, the latent association between items is not considered for recommendations. Thus, as long as new items are not rated, they are not recommended; hence, false negatives are introduced.

On the basis of different situation, two filtering approaches are considering to use. Table 11.1 shows a brief comparison between the two filtering approaches (Wang & Shao, 2004).

Table 11.1 Comparison between content-based filtering and collaborative filtering systems

	Advantage	**Limitation**
Content-based filtering	1. A user can receive proper recommendations without help from other users.	1. Some types of items are not easy to analyze.
Collaborative-based filtering	1. It is more feasible to tackle the problems of multiple user interests and interest transference by monitoring the change and evolving of user profiles 2. Facilitate the sharing of knowledge and/or experiences among users having similar interests.	1. It is hard to provide recommendations for users who have unusual preferences. 2. It is hard to cluster and classify users with changing and /or evolving preferences.

11.3 Item Recommendation

With respect to the application of recommendation with other related field, recommendation technology is seldom applied in the education field, but considering the significance and seriousness of education, the help of recommendation system can improve efficiency and increase the veracity of learners in the actual educational situation. Restated, personalized service has received considerable attention recently because of information needs differ among users. Nowadays, most recommendation systems consider learner/user preferences, interests, or browsing behaviors when analyzing learner behaviors for personalized services (Mobasher et al., 2000). The recommendation system is regarded as an intelligent agent that suggests different alternatives for students, having as starting point previous actions from other students with approximately the same characteristics, such as academic performance and other personal information. It is known that before taking a course, the student has to enroll in the course; the most notorious of this process is not enrolment itself, but the previous decision that has to be taken, mainly related to how many and which course or learning path is going to be taken.

Nowadays, many researchers recently have endeavored to provide personalization or recommendation mechanisms for e-learning (Brusilovsky, 1999). Most recommendation systems consider learner/user preferences, interests, and browsing behaviors when analyzing learner/ user behaviors for personalized services (Fu, Budzik & Hammond, 2000; Papanikolaou, Grigoriadou, Magoulas & Kornilakis, 2002; Rashid et al., 2002). These systems should emphasize the importance of learner/user ability for implementing personalized mechanisms. On the other hand, some researchers emphasized that personalized learning should consider different levels of learner/user knowledge, especially in relation to learning (Brusilovsky, 1999; Lin, 2001). That is, the ability of individuals may be based on major fields and subjects. Therefore, considering learner ability can promote personalized learning performance.

In this book, we argued that the recommendation system can not only suggest information or products of greatest interest to users but also facilitate the organization and better managing of their relationships. To put the assertion more concretely, collaborative recommendation is becoming a popular technology. The task in collaborative recommendation is to predict the use of items by a particular user, specifically, the active user, based on the user item ratings database (Gong, 2010). The same observation applies as teachers anticipate finding a useful or suitable test item resource bank that is sorted and selected efficiently and effectively based on their requirements and preferences. As a result, it becomes more important, albeit more difficult, to retrieve the proper information adapted to user preferences. Recommendations rely mainly on human-analyzed sources, such as reviews, rumours, word of mouth, surveys, guides, friends and recommended literature (Resnick & Varian, 1997). With the rapid development of the internet and technology, information filtering techniques and personalized recommendation systems is needed to provide proper recommendations based on user requirements and preferences (Riecken, 2000). There is a strong demand for personalized recommendation technology and improved recommendation services.

Fortunately, recommender systems offer a potential solution to recommendation services. It has become a popular technique to act as "friends of users" so as to recommend the right items that directly meet the users' needs. Recommender systems are computer systems that seek to guide instructors and students in their choice of relevant resources and knowledge items (Resnick & Varian, 1997). The core tasks of a recommender system are recommending interesting and valuable items in a personalized manner and to help the user make good choices from a large number of alternatives without sufficient personal experience or awareness of the alternatives (Oard & Kim, 1998). The collaborative filtering has become a mainstream technique for recommender systems as it is not subject to the above problem. In collaborative filtering, items are recommended to a particular user when other similar users also prefer them. Collaborative filtering utilizes ratings of other users to predict the opinion of a target user, acting as "friends of customers". The target user is matched against the database of other user histories to discover other users, known as neighbors, who have historically similar tastes. Items the neighbors like are subsequently recommended to the target user. The definition of "similarity" between users depends on applications.

Therefore, considering the teacher-to-teacher correlation towards educational assessment affairs, the item recommender systems recommend appropriate assessment items to a teacher based on the correlation between that teacher and other teachers who have similar assessment experience when they compile or arrange their assessment by using the e-assessment system or e-assessment tools. This technology is known as "collaborative filtering", because it originated as an information filtering technique that used group opinions to recommend information items to individuals. This approach is relatively simple and effective. Many variations of this algorithm exist, but the principles are the same. User profiles are built based on past experience. The set of all user profiles constitutes the collective. When a user in need of suggestions or a software agent is about to generate recommendations to a given user, the profile of the user is compared to the collective to find similar profiles. A selection of these similar profiles is used to produce recommendations. Let us illustrate this approach with an example. Table 11.2 shows the profiles for four teachers with regard to seven testing items. The matrix contains the ratings from the teachers for all items they selected. These ratings measure from 5 to 1. Empty cells mean an absence of opinion. We need to recommend an item to teacher A using the correlation measure. We find that teacher A's ratings are highly correlated with teacher D's. Because teacher D selected two items that teacher A did not, and item 7 was highly appreciated by teacher D, item7 is selected to be recommended for teacher A.

Table 11.2 An example of collaborative filtering

Rating of items	1	2	3	4	5	6	7	8
Teacher A	5	3	3	4	2	1		
Teacher B	3	5	4	3	4	5	1	3
Teacher C	4	3	3	2	4	2	4	1
Teacher D	4	2	2	3	4	1	5	2

Focusing on related research, collaborative filtering can be used in an e-learning context (Wang, 2006; Zaliane, 2006). For example, a software agent acting as an academic advisor recommending courses could rely on collective filtering if the opinions of learners are collected after a course is taken. Constraints, such as course prerequisites and requested curriculum paths in a program taken by a learner, could be taken into account in the selection of courses to recommend (Hsieh, Wang, Su & Lee, 2011). Another type of recommendation in the case of e-learning systems is the recommendation of research papers or citations of papers (Tang & McCalla, 2006). Recommender systems are computer systems that seek to guide instructors and students in their choice of relevant resources (Rafaeli, et al., 2004). Similarity is the most mentioned approach in recommender systems. The recommendation of resources should be motivated either by preference or similarity (Herlocker, Konstan, & Riedl, 2000). Participants in the recommendation group, known as neighbors, share similar preferences. In our study, we determined that "similarity" may be defined as teachers who have similar assessment preferences or teachers who have similar item selection behavior. An assessment system should collect and analyze all assessment information after teachers' completed assessment activities on the website and subsequently calculated the similarities among the teachers using collaborative filtering technology. For teachers who have similar assessment preferences or similar item selection behaviors, their assessment portfolios will be categorized into the same teacher group. When a teacher logins into the system again, the system will first analyze his/her assessment preferences and subsequently compute the most similar group using methods such as the k-nearest neighbor to the teacher and, finally, recommend candidate items for the teacher.

CHAPTER 12 Knowledge Map Assisting Assessment System

In this chapter, we propose a new methodology and builds a Knowledge Map Assisting Assessment System (KMAAS) that uses knowledge maps and text mining for assisting teachers in compiling their assessments. The system extracts learning concepts from textbooks for selected course units by using CKIP (Chinese Knowledge and Information Processing), automatically computes weights of these concepts, and generates a knowledge map with an energy appraisal of the concepts. A test item, before puttingin the bank, will be analyzed to figure out the relationship between the test item and learning concepts. Knowledge maps are displayed while teachers are compiling their assessments, and based on which, teachers can select appropriate test items from test banks. In the 12.1, we introduce the KMAAS's architecture how we implement and their modules, and make deeply descriptions focusing on how to create a knowledge map with energy appraisal of domain concepts under specific course units. A formative evaluation examining the Knowledge Map Assisting Assessment System is conducted in the 12.5, and some limitations for KMAAS are illustrated in the last section.

12.1 The KMAAS Architecture and the Methodology

The well-designed computer assisted programs enable teachers to conduct assessment activities anytime, anywhere, and teachers can flexibly log in to check assessment progress (Chen, 2010). In this chapter, we propose a novel approach, which uses a knowledge map with appraisal of concept weights and other ICTs, and implements an assessment system, named the KMAAS (Knowledge Map Assisted Assessment System), to efficiently help primary school teachers in Taiwan, China, or elsewhere, create educational assessments properly. Besides knowledge maps, KMAAS combines natural language processing and machine learning technologies for concept knowledge extraction and test item classification. This chapter details the system's architecture and its implementation.

The architecture of KMAAS is depicted in Figure 12.1, which has six major functional modules, including the item and course material preprocessing, the concept extraction, the concept relation computation, the concept weights computation, the item retrieval processing, and the knowledge map generation modules. The details of each module are described as follows.

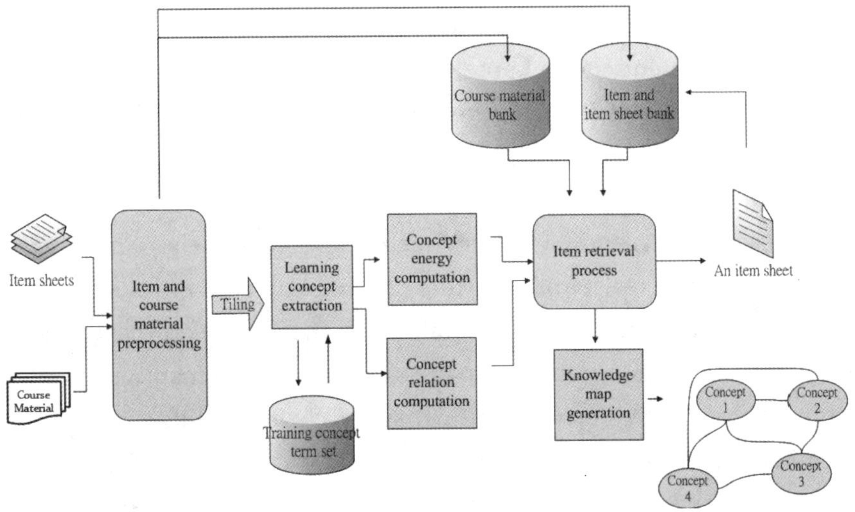

Figure 12.1 The architecture of KMAAS

(1) Item and course material preprocessing module

This module is responsible for performing sentence segmentation and determining morphological features of test items and course materials. In general, specific text preprocessing is required before automated concept extraction and item categorization can be performed. Chinese sentences are characterized by the absence of delimiters to mark word boundaries like those found in English sentences. Chinese sentence segmentation is thus essential for most language processing systems that utilize techniques originally developed for the English language (Wang, Chang & Li, 2008). This study employed the CKIP technology (Chen & Ma, 2002; Ma & Chen, 2003) to perform sentence segmentation and text tagging. This technology automatically locates various Chinese keywords in sentences of test items or course materials and tags them with appropriate morphological feature tags; the module selects among them important concept terms and filters out superfluous keywords so that key concept candidate terms can be identified and sent to the next module.

(2) Learning concept extraction module

This module allows teachers to browse and select course concept vocabularies from the concepts repository produced in the preprocessing stage. Teachers can add or modify concept vocabulary, producing a list of important keywords that are then defined as the vocabularies of the course learning concepts. For example, in the elementary education, textbooks may be used for defining a general set of terms for certain teaching subjects. These important concept terms can be used as the domain knowledge to guide the keyword extraction to represent embedded concepts in documents. Therefore, in this module, learning conceptual vocabularies are like the most important course concept keywords. A hybrid keyword extraction method is employed. The combination of mutual information and a natural language processing method attempts to obtain a more concise extracted keywords. First, we use the auto tag program developed by CKIP projects to identify the morphological information of each word phrase, and prune all words, except noun phrases. Then, the keyword extraction algorithm proposed by Chien (1997) is employed to extract keywords from continuous noun phrases. The module uses one of the training data sets to construct a concept extraction model, which is then employed to extract conceptual vocabularies accurately from test items and course materials.

(3) Concept relation computation module

This module calculates the relationship strength between the concepts extracted from test items and course materials, so that teachers can clearly see the distribution of concepts and the interdependent among these concepts. Formula (1) refers to TF-IDF and calculates the relation between two concepts.

RS (Concept 1, Concept 2) =Frequency/AVG (Distance)··············(1)

Where RS (Concept1, Concept 2) is the degree of correlation between concept 1 and concept 2. The "Frequency" is the number of times that concept 1 and concept 2 appeared in the same sentence in the course materials. The "Distance" between two concepts is measured by the distance between their representing keywords as they appear in the same sentence and "AVG (Distance)" is the average distance between two keywords, i.e. summation of the distances divided by the number of times the two keywords appear in the same sentence (Johnson &Wichern, 2002). The higher the RS value is, the stronger the relationship is. A concept relation database is managed by this module.

(4) Concept weight computation module

This module computes the weight of each concept in the concept repository to represent their relative importance in the course material. An algorithm called RSISF (Relation Strength Inverse Sentence Frequency) is proposed for the concept weight conversion. In short, it converses the summation of the relationship strengths a concept has to other concepts into the weight of the concept. Formula (2) realizes RSISF and works as follows.

$$\text{Concept Weight}=\sum_{i=0}^{n} RS\times\left(\log\frac{N}{n}\right)\cdots\cdots\cdots\cdots\cdots\cdots\cdots\cdots\cdots\cdots\cdots(2)$$

- *RS:* the relationship strength between two concepts stored in the concept relation database, as calculated by Formula (1).

- *N:* the total number of sentences in the course materials.
- *n:* the total number of sentences in which the concept appears together with others in the course materials.

The higher the concept weight is, the more important the learning concept is in the course material. The results of the computations are stored in a concept weight database. In KMAAS, teachers can manually select different versions of course materials on a same topic and combine them for computations to increase the precision of concept weights.

(5) Item retrieval process module

This module helps teachers with the selection of appropriate test items from the item bank and assists them in compiling a test sheet. All collected items follow the concept classification and are stored in the item bank. The weights and relationships of the concepts in the specified course range for assessment are displayed in their strength order for teachers' reference. When a teacher chooses a concept, the associated test items are retrieved and displayed in the order of their importance, which is based on the criteria such as the number of course concepts an item has, concept strength summation the item has, and how many times this test item has been used.

(6) Knowledge map generation module

This module generates graphical knowledge maps that display relationships and concept nodes using Graphviz technology (Low, 2004). Concepts identified by the learning concept extraction module from the course materials of the specified assessment range are used to generate an annotated knowledge map, with concept weights and link strengths both coming from the concept relation database and the concept weight database. The map concretizes and visualizes the importance of these concepts and their relationship's strengths. This module also analyzes the test sheet which is being currently complied by a teacher with test items selected from the item bank or created on the site and displays another similar real-time updated knowledge map to show the balance among course concepts in the test items. This map depicts the overall structure of all the relevant concepts in the test sheet to assist the teacher in developing a comprehensive understanding of the concepts' distribution among test items and in making decisions about item selections and creations.

12.2 KMAAS Implementation and Operations

The operational Knowledge Map Assisted Assessment System, can help teachers select test items that effectively assess teaching objectives of a course and avoid inappropriate distribution of test items and concepts. Cross-referring the real-time generated knowledge maps, teachers can analyze and adjust, according to the course concept weights and relation strengths, the configuration proportion of test items in a test sheet. To make KMAAS more convenient for teachers, it is designed to operate on a personal computer or a notebook, available in most educational settings, and does not require any special CPU configuration.

KMAAS is now being evaluated using the fifth- and sixth-grade "natural science and life technology" curriculum materials in Taiwan, China and the item bank is initially fed with over 830 related test items. When teachers register for accounts and passwords (as shown in Figure 12.2) and then the system provided space for teachers to manage and store their created test items and test sheets. Teachers could perform operations using five major functions, including item input function, course materials input function, data review function, item selection guide function, and relevant records function. Teachers may upload a test sheet with the test items put into the item bank and, in the meantime, receive a concepts distribution analysis knowledge map. Alternatively, teachers could create a new test sheet, using any test items from the item bank, which are in accordance with their testing need and teaching objectives. Either way, a real-time updated knowledge map will always be displayed for their reference. Figure 12.3 shows the item input function. In this function, teachers could add, delete and review electronic test sheets and upload test items in them to the item bank. Teachers hit the "Add a new test sheet" button to add a new text-based test sheet file, fill in the relevant information about the test sheet, and save the file. The system then conducts an analysis on the sheet by, such as CKIP processing, morphological features checking, and automatic concept classifying, on the test item sentences. A knowledge map is displayed afterwards showing the result of the analysis. An example is shown in Figure 12.4.

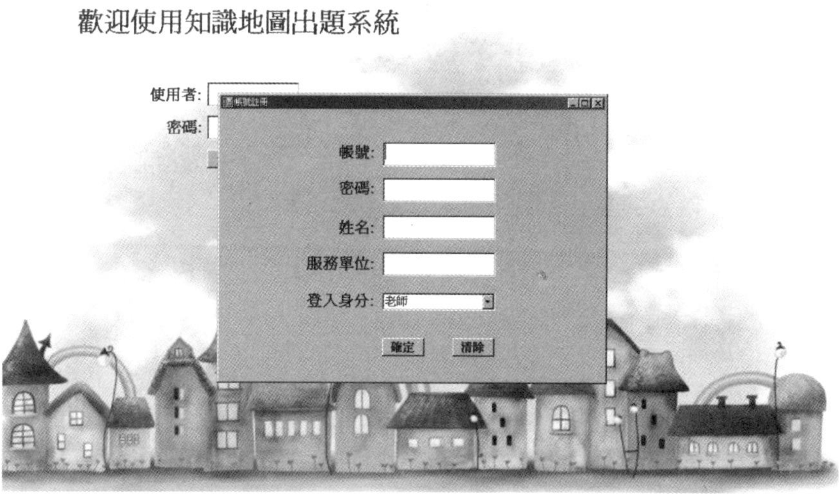

Figure 12.2 The interface of teachers register for accounts and passwords

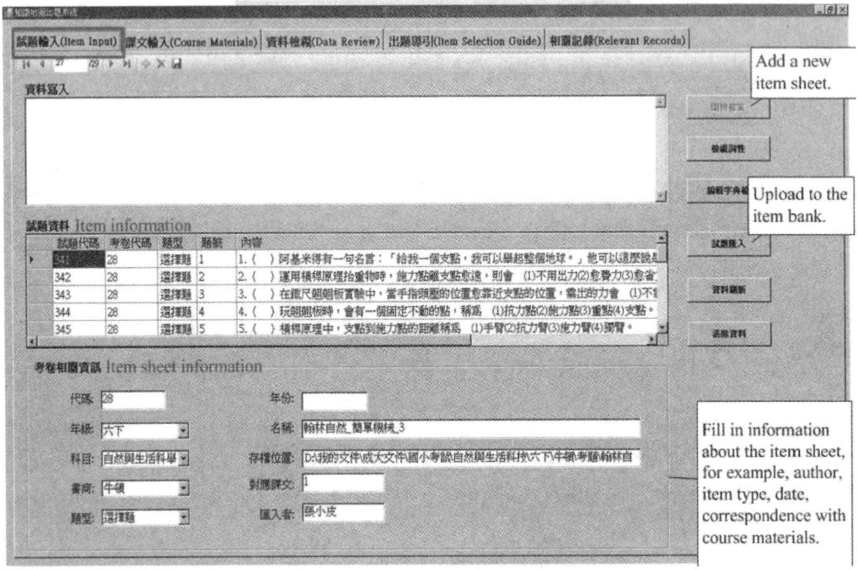

Figure 12.3 The item input function

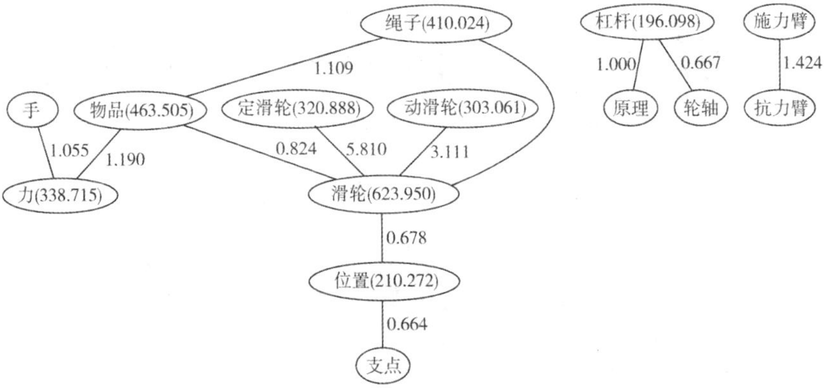

Figure 12.4 A knowledge map from a course material is displayed

Figure 12.5 shows the course materials input function, through which teachers add course curriculum materials into KMAAS to facilitate concept extraction from these course materials. The system uses CKIP technique to mark the morphological features of the course materials, removes redundant contents, and extracts candidate concepts from these materials. The data review function can then be used to help improve the accuracy of automatic concept extractions (as shown in Figure 12.6). Although the system could extract concept vocabularies fully automatically, teachers might want to see how effective the system is in extracting appropriate

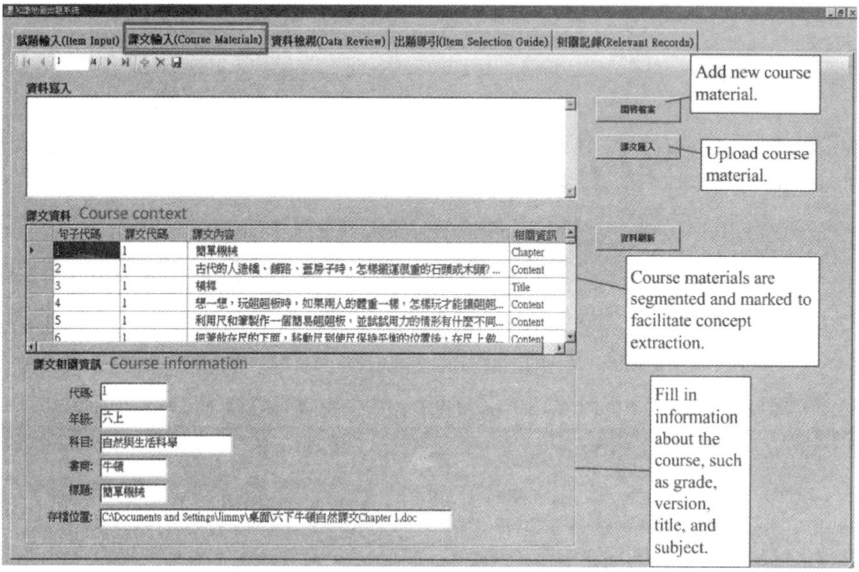

Figure12.5 The course materials input function

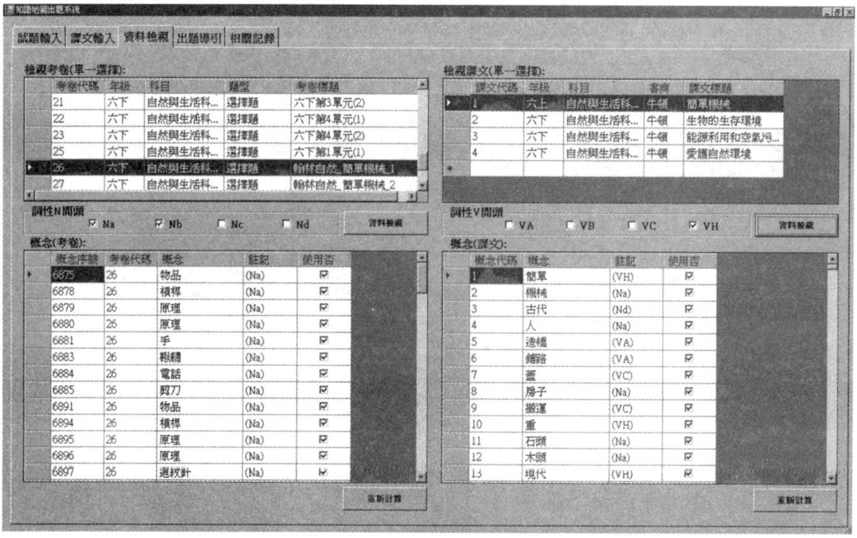

Figure12.6 The interface of data review function

concept vocabularies from textbooks or from any course materials. When inappropriate concept vocabularies do appear, teachers can manually filter out irrelevant or superfluous ones. This practice ensures the extracted concept keywords are more accurate with each use of the system later. The result is then put into the concept extraction training model for further processing.

Figure 12.7 shows the item selection guide function, through which teachers choose one or more electronic test sheets for final analysis. Teachers could choose the students' grade level and then select desired electronic test items with their assessment aims in mind (Four steps are as followsas shown in Figure 12.8 to Figure 12.11). They can use this function to see the overview of concept weights and concept relationships for an archived or just compiled test sheet by generating a corresponding knowledge map. The ranking of concept weights and their relationships corresponds to their importance in the course material.

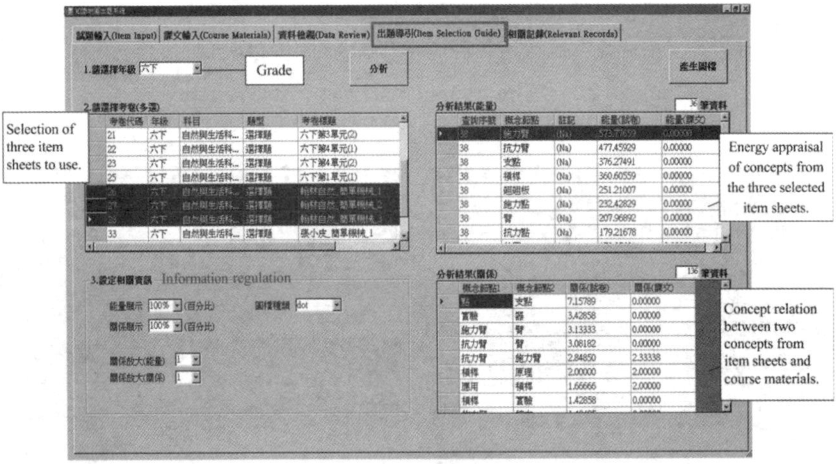

Figure 12.7 The item guide function

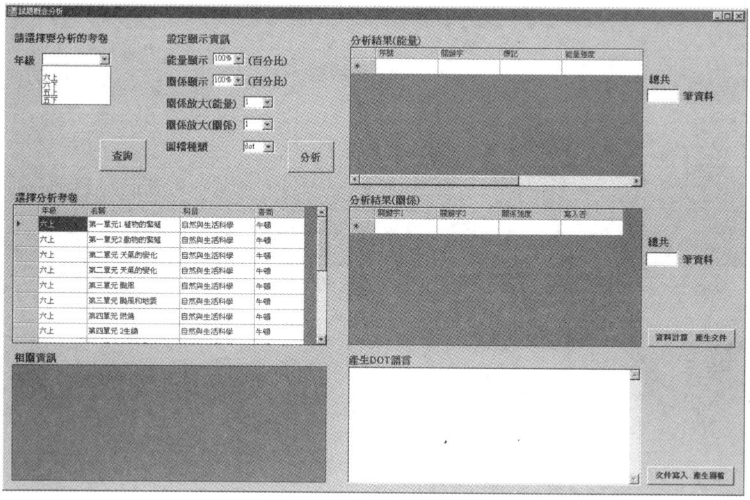

Figure 12.8 Choosing the grade level when teachers want to analyze

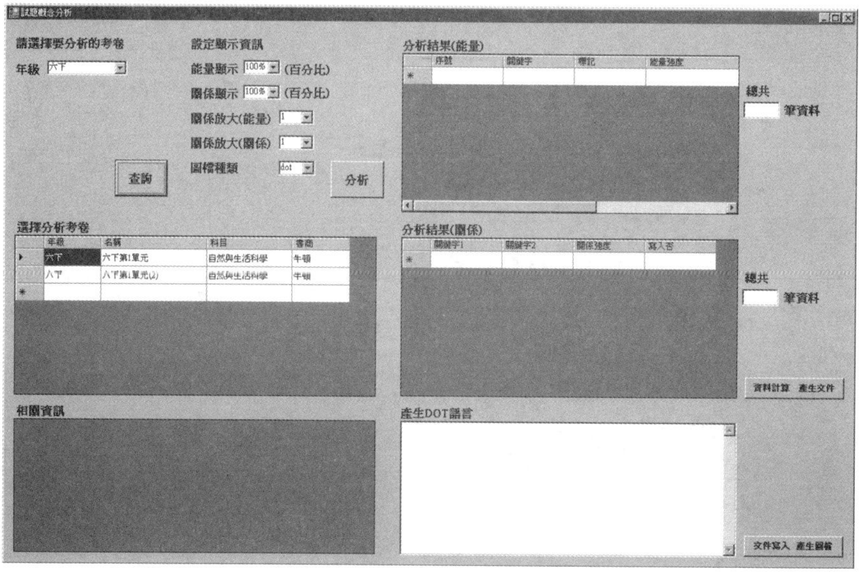

Figure 12.9 Choosing the course range when a teacher wants to analyze

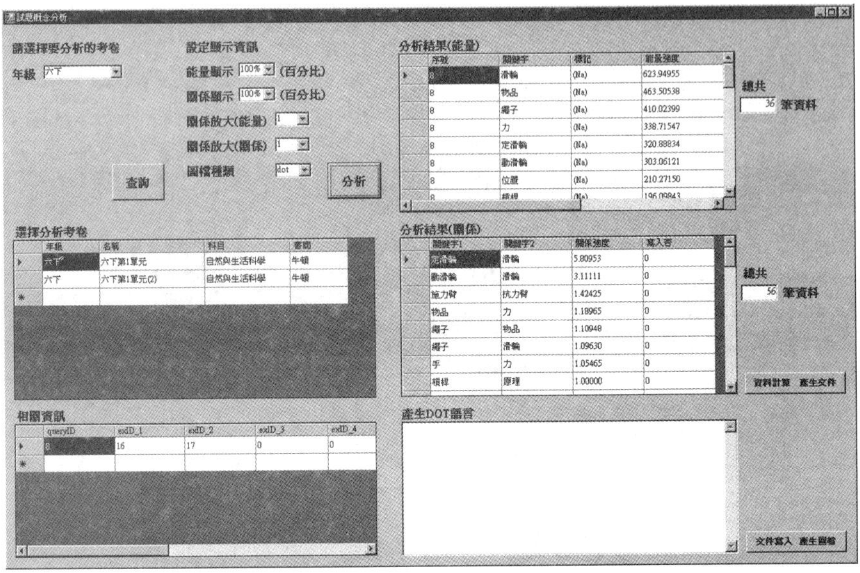

Figure 12.10 Viewing the sorts of course concept when a teacher wants to analyze

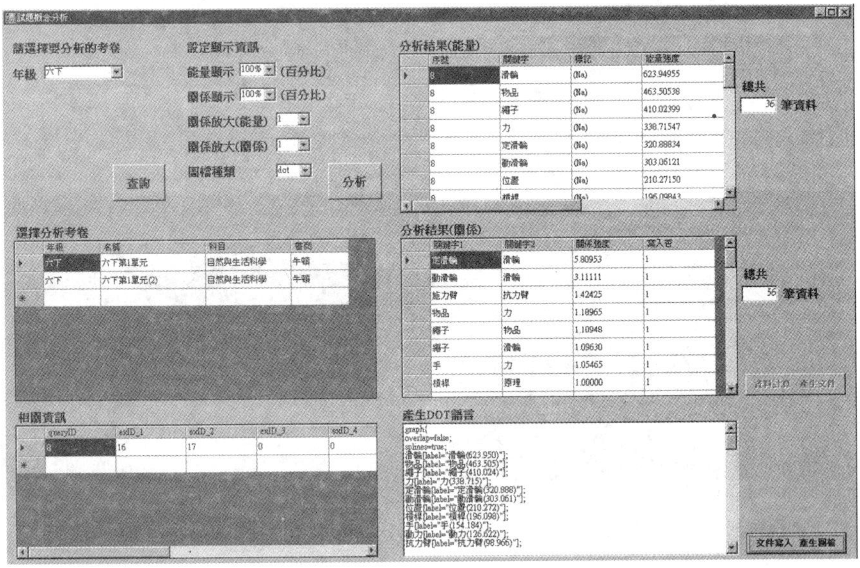

Figure 12.11 Producing the knowledge map when a teacher wants to analyze

Figure 12.12 shows the appraisal of concept weights and their relationships of a knowledge map example on a primary school course on levers. It is created from the combination of three related test sheets after the systematic analysis and shows the whole picture of the core concepts distributions, with regard to the concept trends in terms of distributive test items about the specific subject domain “levers”.

When teachers click on a concept in the concept list column of the item selection guide function, all the test items related to this concept would be displayed in the order of their importance, which is based on the criteria such as the number of course concepts an test item has, the concept strength summation the test item has, and how many times this test item has been used before, as shown in an example in Figure 12.13. Teachers could select test items from this list in accordance with their assessment objectives. After test items selection is done, teachers could export these items into a test sheet text file, which consists of the selected items and the proportion of each concept, as shown in Figure 12.14. They could also transfer the file into an assessment portfolio and save it in the test sheet bank for sharing with other teachers. Finally, the relevant record function could help teachers to query these concept terms, if they used in the knowledge map presentation, or store these commonly concept terms and filter redundancy terms (as shown in figure12.15).

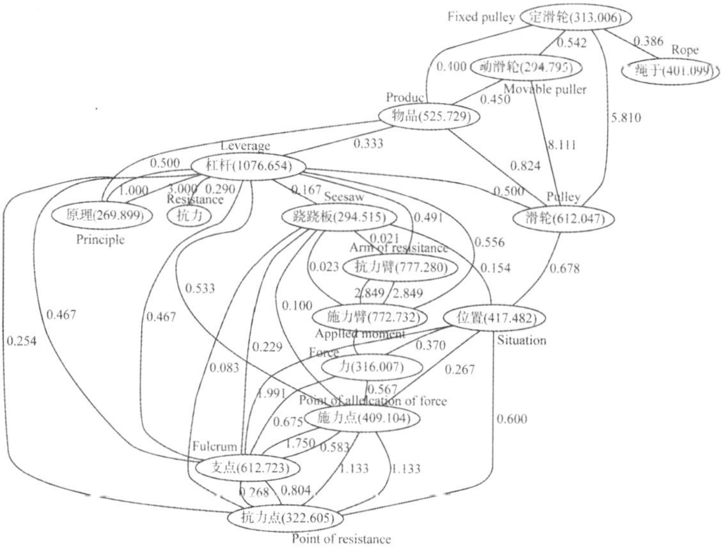

Figure 12.12 The knowledge map presents the result of the integration of three electronic item sheets related to course content on the topic of leverage

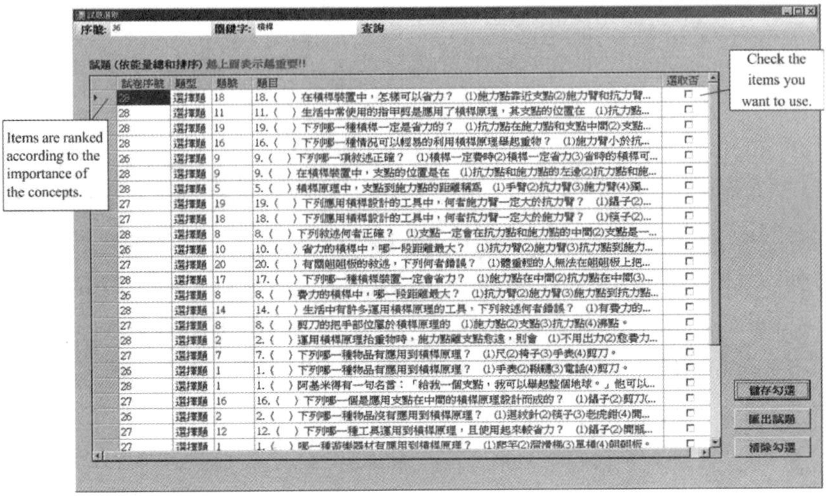

Figure 12.13 The item selection functions

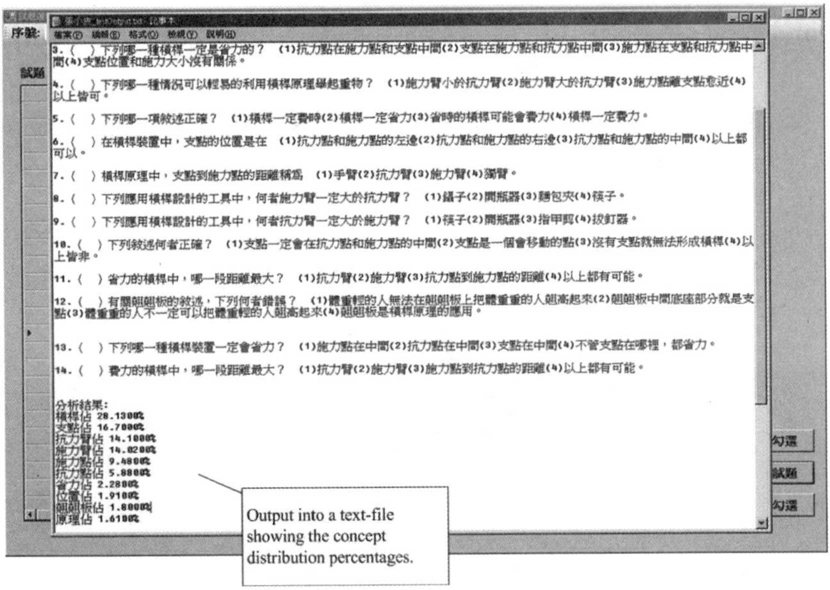

Figure 12.14 The text file presents the exported items and the proportion of concepts

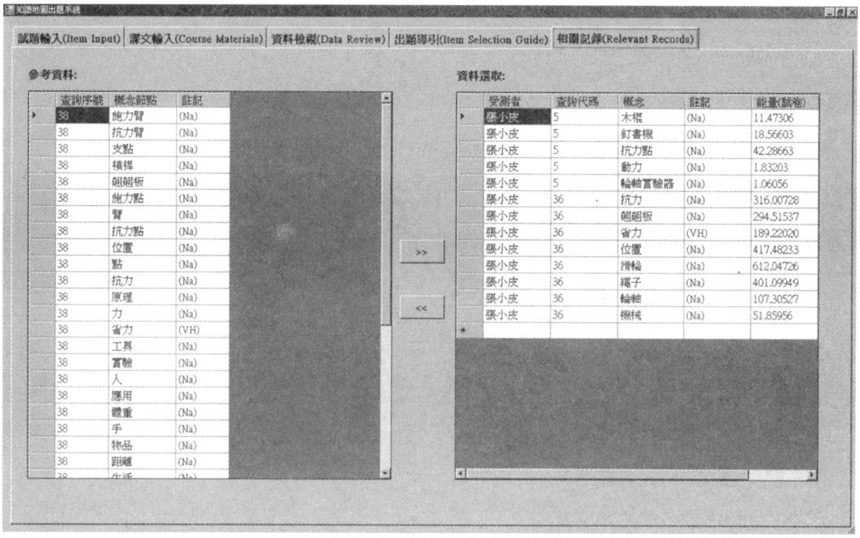

Figure 12.15 Help teachers to query these concept terms, if they used in the knowledge map presentation

12.4 Experiment Design

In this section, we conducted an experiment to evaluate the effectiveness of the method proposed and the usability of the assessment system prototype. The KMAAS contains the fifth- and sixth-grade "natural science and life technology" curriculum materials, and the item bank is initially fed with over 830 related test items. Six elementary school teachers who teach a physics course on "levers and forces" in southern Taiwan,China were invited to use and evaluate KMAAS. The experiment aimed to investigate whether the visual overview of the distribution of the concepts covered by the test items and provided by KMAAS via knowledge maps could help teachers select test items that effectively assessed the teaching objectives of a course and avoid the inappropriate distribution of test items and concepts. The entire experimental process design, displayed in Figure 12.16, can be divided into several parts, as follows:

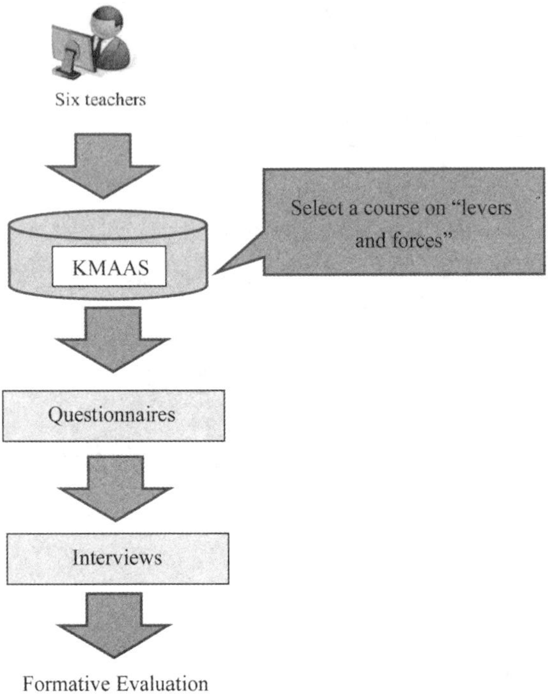

Figure 12.16 The first stage of the experimental process design

12.5 Evaluation and Discussion of KMAAS

The evaluations conducted are to investigate, in addition to its usability and appealing, how to improve KMAAS in order to make assessment compilations more effective and more efficient. The method of formative evaluation is successful in that it has resulted in an improved quality of the system. The method, typically involving a small group of users or participants in the project, has been extremely useful in producing modules which are suitable for their target audience, are easy to use, and are instructive. It is also relatively easy for developers to modify the modules according to the recommendations of the evaluators (Phelps & Reynolds, 1999). Using such a method, six elementary school teachers who actually teach a physics course on "levers and forces" in Taiwan, China were invited to use and evaluate KMAAS. System performance was evaluated in terms of user satisfaction and extraction accuracy. The teachers reported on the usefulness and usability of the system in a Technology Acceptance Model (TAM) questionnaire by providing written feedbacks about their satisfaction in using the system. These evaluations are discussed in the follows. For the extraction accuracy evaluation, as we know that precision and recall are widely used as relevancy measures for information retrieval (Salton & Buckley, 1988). Precision measures the percentage of relevant documents in relation to the number of documents retrieved. Recall measures the percentage of the total relevant documents retrieved by the query. In this study, standard performance measures, precision and recall, were examined by comparing the concepts and their rankings as extracted and obtained by the system to those obtained by participating teachers, with special focus on whether the concept importance ranking provided by the system are similar to that of by the teachers. The precision and recall measures are defined as that shown in Formula (3).

$$\text{Precision (p)} = B / (B + C); \quad \text{Recall (r)} = B / (\text{A} + B); \qquad \cdots\cdots (3)$$

Where A is the concept selected by teachers, C is the concept selected by KMAAS, B is the intersection of A and B.

Fifteen most important concepts of the "levers and forces" course automatically extracted by the system were compared to the 15-20 concepts considered important by teachers. Eleven concepts were common to both lists, and each concept in the list generated by KMAAS was picked an average of 4.27 times from a total of 6 teacher lists. The average precision is 0.733, with the highest being 0.865 and the lowest being 0.61. This result demonstrates that the comparison between automatic system extraction and teachers' selection reaches up to 73% consistency.

Numerous researches have shown that ICT technology can enhance and transform teaching and learning in educational environments. Recently, increasing attention has also been paid to understanding what drives teachers' usage of technology. In addition, the pivotal role that teachers play in ensuring effective integration of technology in education has been acknowledged (Teo, Lee, Chai & Wong, 2009). For this reason, first of the evaluations of this study is set to examine teachers' satisfaction with the KMAAS. The Technology Acceptance Model (TAM) is a robust and widely-used framework for assessing users' satisfaction with some technology (King & He, 2006; Venkatesh & Davis, 2000). The questionnaire used in this study is based on the TAM model and responses are collected using five-point Likert scales. Six teachers were invited to complete a questionnaire eliciting information concerning attitudes and responses; the results are shown in Table 12.4. The findings show that the mean score for most of the items is greater than 4, except for 10th and 15th items. Four of the teachers mentioned the disfluency of the interfaces, but suggested that their problems could be overcome by reading the manual or using the system more frequently. The results are overall very positive. After completing the questionnaire, teachers were interviewed for about 30 minutes on their views on using the system. Some examples of the feedbacks are as follows:

- This system is very novel, I can use it to analyze my post-test sheets and get some important information to help me to comprehend or regulate my ideas on the assessment work (teacher B).
- This system assists me in compositing a proper test sheet, in addition to helping me select test items, I could see the concept distribution percentage by the knowledge maps helping (teacher F).

Furthermore, several comments in the interviews regarding the presentation of the user interface and knowledge map are as follows:

- Although the interfaces seem to be a little bit rough, they did not affect my operations, in contrast, I was looking forward to it helping my assessment works in the future (teacher A).
- I thought that this system is very meaningful for teachers' assessment works, especially the knowledge map. I suggest that the concept node might attach color labels in next version as well (teacher C).

In the evaluations, in general, all teachers felt that the system, which provided them with knowledge maps and weight appraisal of concepts, was very novel; they reported favorably on the value of the system for assisting with their assessment works. The knowledge maps, by aggregating the concepts and presenting the whole assessment structure, enable teachers to make inferences and to reflect on test items and allowing them to make good decisions on item selection.

Table 12.4 A questionnaire eliciting information concerning attitudes and responses

Items	Mean	Standard deviation
Perceived usefulness		
1. Using the KMAAS improves my educational assessment work performance.	4.333	0.51640
2. Using the KMAAS increases my making educational assessment productivity.	4.333	0.51640
3. Using the KMAAS enhances my effectiveness in my assessment work.	4.333	0.51640
4. I find the KMAAS to be useful in my assessment work.	4.333	0.51640
5. Using the KMAAS would make my assessment work easier.	4.0000	0.00000
6. Using the KMAAS would enable me to make assessment quickly.	4.0000	0.63246
Perceived ease of use		
7. It would be easy for me to become skillful at using the KMAAS.	4.1667	0.75277
8. My interaction with the KMAAS is clear and understandable.	4.0000	0.89443
9. I believe that it is easy to get the KMAAS to do what I want it to do.	4.1667	0.40825
10. Interacting with the KMAAS does not require a lot of my mental effort.	3.8333	0.40825
11. Overall, I find the KMAAS to be easy to use.	4.3333	0.51640
Attitude		
12. I like using the KMAAS.	4.1667	0.40825
13. The KMAAS is fun to use.	4.1667	0.40825

(continued)

Table 12.4 (*continued*)

14. The KMAAS provides an attractive working environment.	4.0000	0.63246
Technological complexity		
15. Learning to use the KMAAS takes up too much of my time.	3.8333	0.40825
16. Using the KMAAS involves too much time.	4.0000	0.63246
17. It takes too long to learn how to use the KMAAS.	4.0000	0.63246
Concentration		
18. I was absorbed intensely in the educational assessment activity.	4.3333	0.81650
19. My attention was focused on the educational assessment activity.	4.1667	0.75277
20. I was deeply engrossed in the educational assessment activity.	4.1667	0.40825
Usage Intentions		
21. Assuming I have access to the KMAAS, I intend to use it.	4.5000	0.54772
22. Given that I have access to the KMAAS, I plan to use it.	4.5000	0.54772
23. I intend to increase my use of the KMAAS in the future.	4.5000	0.54772
24. It is worth to use the KMAAS.	4.5000	0.54772
25. I will frequently use the KMAAS in the future.	4.3333	0.51640

Note. n=6

12.6 Limitations of the Evaluation of KMAAS

The evaluation objective set for this study is to let participants use KMAAS for their actual assessment works when teaching 5th and 6th grades primary school "natural science and life technology" courses in order to get more precise feedbacks. Owing to the short overlap period between the semester and the evaluation, the first limitation of this paper so far concerns the amount of time that the teachers spent on using the system. Teachers have busy work days, and could not spend too much of their time for evaluations; they were pleaded to use the system as much as possible within the period of the evaluation. The second limitation is the number of participants because the evaluation wanted to invite teachers with actual experience in teaching targeted courses, which in this case is the "levers and forces" courses, and it was not easy to fulfill the criterion. So a small number of teachers who participated in this study does not meet this basic condition for statistical analysis, which may possibly affect the results of the questionnaire analysis. The final limitation concerns the interface design which was then preliminary and rough. However, the result of this research has the undeniable merit of offering valuable insights into this fast growing ICT-based educational assessment domain, and some of the limits may be offset by the use of TAM based questionnaire for evaluation surveys.

CHAPTER 13 Internet-based Knowledge Map Assisting Assessment System

This chapter describes the knowledge accumulation and knowledge extraction methodology, and introduces the architecture of the Internet-based Knowledge Map Assisted Assessment System (IKMAAS), which uses knowledge maps to display teachers' accumulated assessment knowledge. IKMAAS draws tacit assessment knowledge from teachers' historical assessments and refines, converts, and employs this knowledge to assist teachers in assessment compilation and test item arrangement. The IKMAAS's operation is described in the 13.3. Several experiments in the 13.4 were conducted in the third grade natural science courses of elementary school in Taiwan, China by teachers who were actually teaching the courses. The usability evaluation examining the Internet-based Knowledge Map Assisting Assessment System is conducted in the 13.5.

13.1 Knowledge Accumulation and Visualization Methodology

In order to provide more support for the teachers, we update KMAAS into the Internet-based KMAAS.One of the most important functions of IKMAAS is to automatically accumulate and extract teachers' assessment experience and knowledge of specific courses. After being compiled and saved in an assessment bank, a test sheet has a configuration of the proportions of test items to each concept. The configuration keeps exactly the item-selecting records of its creator in a specific range of a course and the proportions are exactly reflective of how the creator sees the importance of each concept (i.e., her/his assessment experience and knowledge) in the course range. Thus, each of the test sheets in the assessment bank becomes a source of assessment knowledge. Such proportions of test items to each concept in every test sheet of a course range are accumulated and calculated as weight appraisal that reflect the common consensus of all of the teachers on the importance of each concept in the course range. Each of the concepts keeps a weight to reflect its degree of importance. KMAAS have established the cold-start weight of each concept automatically (Su & Wang, 2010). The weight of a concept may change when a completed test sheet is put into the assessment bank. It all begins when a teacher selects a course range and the number of test items for an assessment. All the concepts within the range are shown in the first knowledge map, with their weight percentiles given to show their relative importance. Formula (4) normalizes a concept weight to its percentage, in which there are *n* concepts found in the selected range, *CWPa* is the weighted percentile of concept *a*, and *CWa* is the original concept weight of *a*.

$$CWP_a = \frac{CW_a}{\sum_{i=1}^{n} CW_i} \times 100\% \quad \cdots\cdots (4)$$

According to the weight percentile of all the concepts and the number of test items given by the teacher, IKMAAS calculates and recommends for each concept a proper number of test items to test in the assessment. After a test sheet is compiled, the number of test items given by the teacher to test for a concept might be different from what IKMAAS recommends. To adjust the weights of all the corresponding concepts in the accumulated assessment knowledge base, into which the assessment knowledge of the test sheet is fused, the proportion of test items to each concept on the test sheet must be examined and a dynamic weighting adjustment for each concept be computed. Formula (5) computes the dynamic weighting adjustment for each concept, in which x is the number of test items that IKMAAS suggests for concept a, which is at least 1; y is the number of test items given by a teacher for concept a; and m is the number of test items for the assessment given by the teacher.

$$DWA_a = \frac{y-x}{m \times 100} \sum_{i=1}^{n} CW_i \cdots\cdots(5)$$

Negative DWA_a indicates that a teacher sees a concept less important and gives fewer test items than what IKMAAS suggests, in which case the weight of the concept will be decreased, and vice versa. The new weight of the concept a is then its original weight plus DWA_a as in Formula (6).

$$CW_a(new) = CW_a + DWA_a \cdots\cdots(6)$$

CW_a is the original weight of concept a and CW_a (new) is the new weight of concept a. The total summation of all the concept weights in the selected range will remain the same and will only be redistributed to the concepts. An example of computations by Formula (4), (5) and (6) is shown in Figure 13.1 and Table 13.1. When teacher X selects a course range for assessment and decides to use 20 test items to test the students, the IKMAAS refers to the original weighted percentile of the, in this case, 5 concepts ($CWP_{1\text{-}5}$) in the range and gives the item number suggestions, i.e. C_1=3, C_2=5, C_3=1, C_4=9, C_5=2. Teacher X refers to the suggestions but finally gives the items for C_1=4, C_2=4, C_3=4, C_4=5, C_5=3. The variation in item numbers triggers Formula (4) and (5) to update the concept weights of the five concepts accordingly.

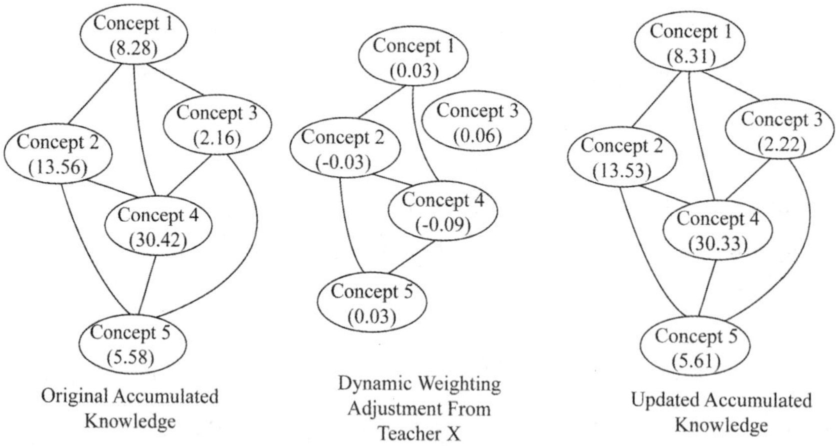

Figure 13.1 An example of knowledge accumulation

Table 13.1 Anexample of knowledge accumulation

Concepts	*CW*	*CWP*	Number of items suggested by IKMASS	Number of items given by a teacher	Dynamci weighting adjustment	$CE_{(new)}$	$CWP_{(new)}$
C1	8.28	13.80%	3	4	0.03	8.31	13.85%
C2	13.56	22.60	5	4	-0.03	13.53	22.55%
C3	2.16	3.60%	1	4	0.06	2.22	3.70%
C4	30.42	50.70%	9	5	-0.09	30.33	50.55%
C5	5.58	9.30%	2	3	0.03	5.61	9.35%
Total	60.00	100%	20	20	0.00	60.00	100%

Another statistic is used to examine all of the test items in the assessment bank and calculate the relationship closeness between each concept pair by recording the probability of their simultaneous appearance in test items. Such information in a selected range of a course will be presented to teachers when they select the range for an assessment. This kind of knowledge reflects the common consensus of all of the teachers on how close two concepts are related and the tendency these two concepts are tested together in a test item. At here, the association rule serves as a useful approach for discovering correlations among concepts in same large course range. It explores the probability that when certain items are present, which other items are also present in the same affairs. Two important threshold values used in the association rules: **support** and **conference**. **Support** indicates the frequencies of the occurring patterns in the rule. Confidence denotes the strength of the implication of the association rule.

Therefore, the Apriori Algorithm is simplified in this study for calculating the probability of simultaneous appearance of each pair of concepts and its parameters, the minimum support and the item sets, are set to 1 and 2 respectively. Figure 13.2 demonstrates an example with three test items which test concepts (A, B, C), (A, B, D) and (B, C) respectively in a same assessment; it shows the first two steps that find the supports of each pair of concepts. The first step is to find the support for each concept, which turns out to be 2, 3, 2, 1 for concept A, B, C, D, and finds out the concepts with support 0, which, in this case, does not happen. Because the supports of the four concepts are all larger than the minimum support 1, they all are entered into the second step that pairs all the concepts, finds their supports, and filters out the pair with support 0 as well, which, in this case, does not happen either.

Minimum support count =1

Sample Database	
TID	Item ID
Paper 1	{A,B,C}
Paper 2	{A,B,D}
Paper 3	{A,B}

C_1	
Item set	Supp
A	2
B	3
C	2
D	1

L_1	
Item set	Supp
A	2
B	3
C	2
D	1

C_2	
Item set	Supp
{A,B}	2
{A,C}	1
{A,D}	1
{B,C}	2
{B,D}	1
{C,D}	0

L_2	
Item set	Supp
{A,B}	2
{A,C}	1
{A,D}	1
{B,C}	2
{B,D}	1

Figure 13.2 An example of support calculation

The next step is to calculate for a concept the value of confidence on the other, and vice versa, in a pair by Formula (7).

$$Confidence(A \rightarrow B) = P(B \mid A) = \frac{(Support\_Count(A \cap B))}{(Support\_Count(A))} \cdots\cdots\cdots\cdots \quad (7)$$

Where *Confidence (A→B)* is the confidence that concept *A* has on concept *B*.

Both *Confidence (A→B)* and *Confidence (B→A)* are calculated, but to keep the knowledge map used to show the relationship strengths between concepts simpler and clearer only the minimum between them is used with the assumption that one of them is supposed to be the major concept to be tested in the test item. As seen in Figure 13.2, concept A has supported 2 whereas B has 3, so Equation 4 yields *Confidence (A→B)* to 1 and *Confidence (B→A)* to 0.67, which is minimum and is then chosen as the relationship strength between concepts *A* and *B*. All the concept pairs left in Figure 13.2 go through the same calculations too.

IKMAAS manages these accumulated assessment knowledge for all the concepts in a course and renews it when there is a new test sheet goes into the bank. It uses two knowledge maps to graphically reveal the two accumulated assessment knowledge in a specific range to help teachers making decisions when they are creating assessments for that range.

13.2 IKMAAS Architecture

The architecture of the IKMAAS, as shown in Figure 13.3, comprises four main modules: the Assessment Editor, the Online Testing Module, the Assessment Result Analysis Module, and the User and Authority Administration Module. Two Internet-based user interfaces, one for teachers and one for students, allow users to interact with various modules of the system to access all of the designated functions of the IKMAAS.

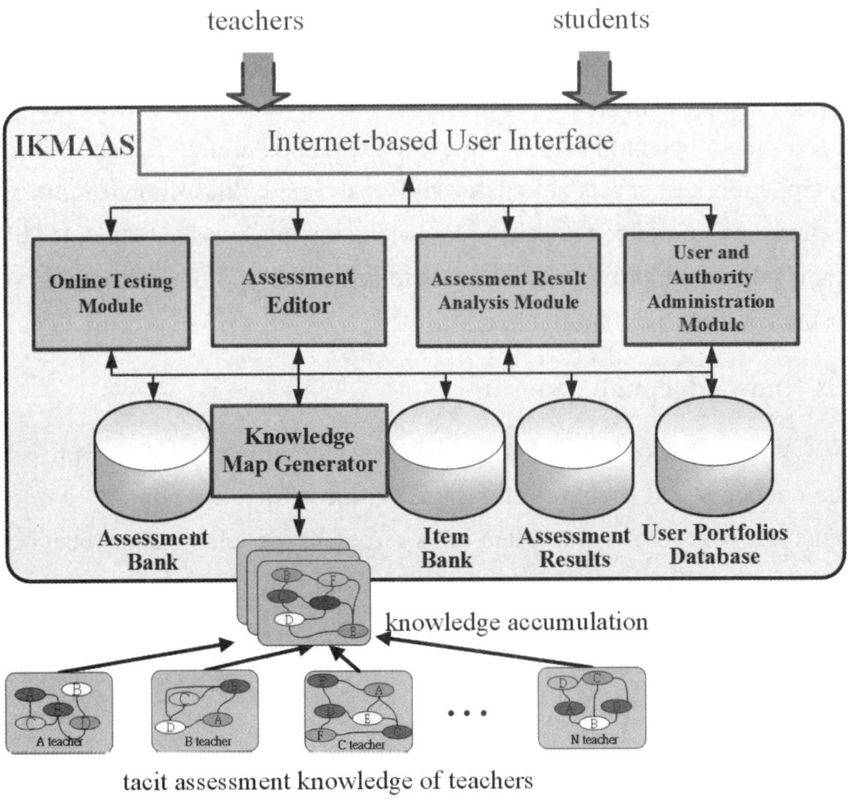

Figure 13.3 The architecture of the IKMAAS

(1) Assessment editor

The assessment editor is the core of the system, which uses two knowledge maps generated by the Knowledge Map Generator to offer appropriate information for teachers to use in guiding their assessment compilations. The first knowledge map explicates teachers' accumulated assessment knowledge by showing the importance weights of all of the relevant concepts and their interrelationships. The weight of a concept represents the importance of the concept according to all teachers who are using the IKMAAS; this importance is reflected in the average number of test items selected for the concept by the teachers. The second map shows the current concept distribution of the test items on the test sheet being compiled. These maps can help teachers develop a comprehensive understanding of the relative importance of the concepts and their proportions among the test items. It can also assist them in making decisions regarding test item selection and creation. After a teacher selects a test range, percentiles given to show their relative importance. During compilation, test sheets are analyzed in real-time by the Knowledge Map Generator to produce the second knowledge map (described above). This knowledge map allows the compiler to select the appropriate number of test items from the Item Bank.

(2) Knowledge map generator

A knowledge map is a graphical presentation method that expresses the concepts and their interrelations within a specific context. Nodes represent concepts, and labelled links represent the relationships between the concepts. In this study, the keywords listed in the textbook or teaching materials are used as nodes to represent concepts to construct knowledge maps for an assessment range in a given curriculum. Knowledge maps are generated by Graphviz and indicate the importance of concepts using the color marks shown in Figure 13.4 (concepts marked with colors on the left hand side of the color bar are more important).

(3) Online testing module

This module allows students to use online tests for practice. In addition, it allows teachers not only to schedule official online tests for students, but also to manage the item bank. Only authorized pupils who are registered for a course are given access to official tests. Each test sheet can be taken online with or without time limits. This module offers additional options, such as random question ordering, login restrictions, and tools to prevent students from copying their peers' answers.

(4) Assessment result analysis module

This module analyses and collects assessment results after students complete the tests. It provides essential statistics, including total score, answer outcome and corrections. If the configuration option is set, it will give detailed feedback, including explanations for correct and incorrect answers. It also collects students' assessment results for each test in the assessment portfolio and supports knowledge map analyses to help teachers understand students' mistakes so that they can make corrections on future tests.

(5) User and authority administration module

This module allows administrators or teachers to manage users and their authority in the system, such as users' personal details, domain teacher group membership and authorization. Teacher groups are arranged and managed in accordance with different disciplines to collect peer teachers' assessment knowledge. The module allows teachers to choose whether to share their own test items and assessments at the single-subject level.

13.3 IKMAAS Implementation and Operations

The operational IKMAAS gives teachers all the conveniences to construct their assessments and accumulate, manage and share their assessment knowledge. Teachers can reuse, edit, and create test items,

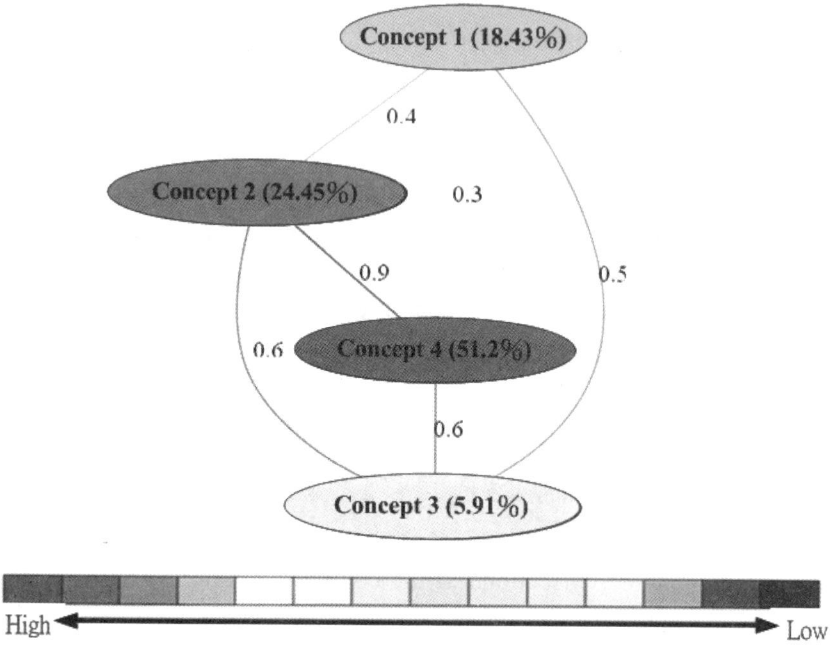

Figure 13.4 Color-marked concepts in the knowledge map

compile assessments, and share assessment knowledge. This IKMAAS is developed by using Microsoft Visual Studio 2005, and using Microsoft. NET as the system operation platform; the back-end database of this system is using Microsoft SQLServer 2000, and the support of maintaining data operation by Stored Procedure. Moreover, knowledge maps were mainly generated by using Graphviz. Graphviz (http://www.graphviz.org/) is an open graphical visualization software that was developed by Bell Labs (AT & T Research Labs). The users can use Dot Language to express the relationship between the property and a node by Graphviz generated graphics(Ellson, Gansner, Koutsofios, North & Woodhull, 2003). The user interface has two parts: one for teachers (see in Figure 13.5) and one for students (see in Figure 13.6).

Figure 13.5 The teachers' interface that teachers could use to log into the IKMAAS

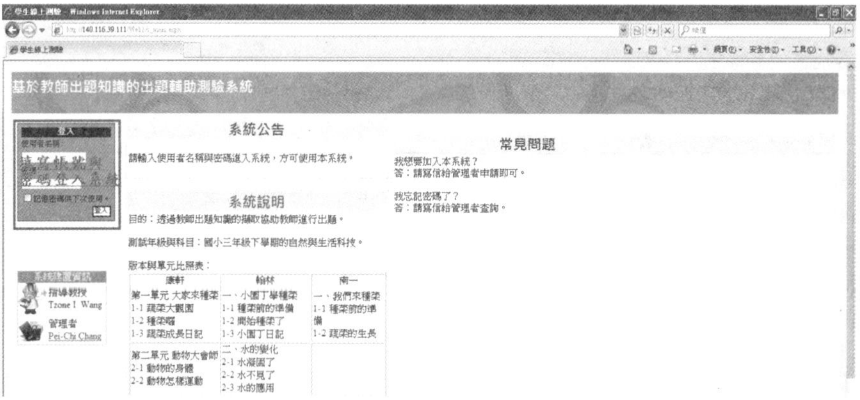

Figure 13.6 The students' interface that students could use to log into the IKMAAS

The web-based IKMAAS is accessible at anytime and from anywhere. In the teacher interface, when teachers register their accounts and pass into the system, they can operate several functions from the left menu, as shown in Figure 13.7, also they can edit their personal information as shown in the Figure 13.8.

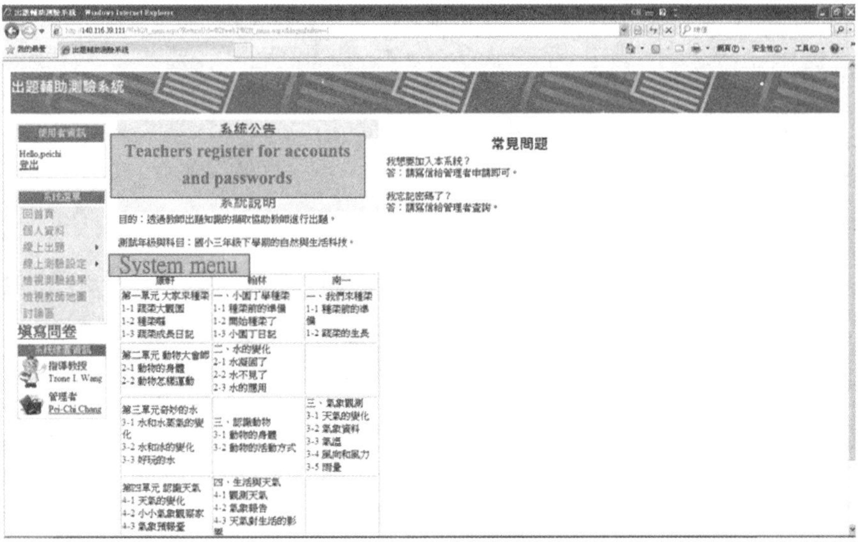

Figure13.7 The teacher logs into the IKMAAS and view several functions from the left menu

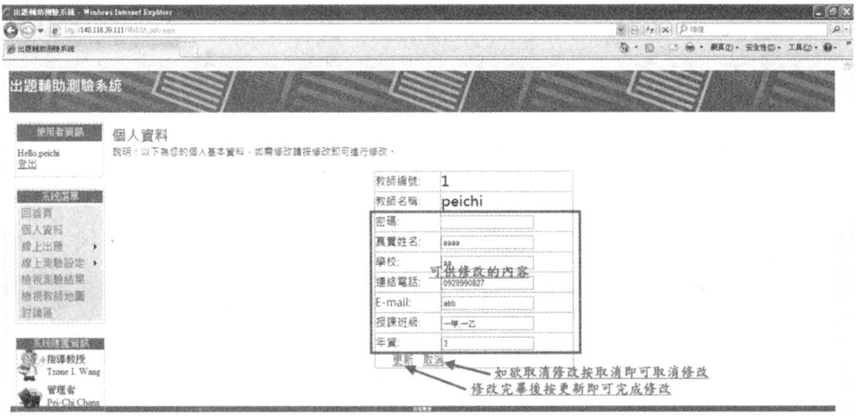

Figure 13.8 Teacher can edit their personal information in the IKMAAS

An example of an assessment compilation regarding the natural science course of the third grade in a Taiwan, China primary school is shown in Figure 13.9 to Figure 13.12. A teacher can arrange an assessment in four steps. Step one selects the scope of a course or the learning material to be tested and determines the maximum number of test items within the assessment scope (as shown in Figure 13.9). Step two involves selecting test items from an item bank. Items related to the testing scope appear in an item table (as shown in the lower part of Figure 13.10), which also contains information about learning goals, subjects, themes, difficulty levels and the skill levels according Bloom's cognitive taxonomy. Some real time statistics about the selected test items, including the number of concepts covered and the numbers of test items in different indexes of Bloom's cognitive taxonomy, difficulty, and discrimination, will appear just below the item table for the teachers' reference.

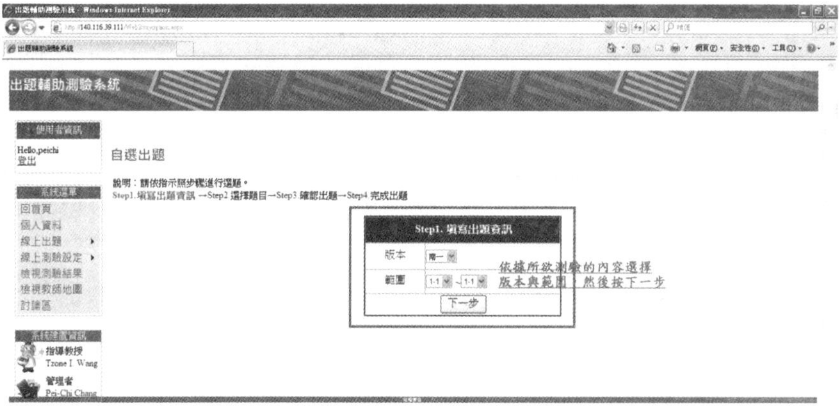

Figure 13.9 Step one—selecting the scope of a course or the learning material to be tested and determines the maximum number of test items

An extra option allows teachers to modify selected test items or to create new ones using an item editor (as shown at the bottom of Figure. 13.10). At the same time, this step uses two knowledge maps displaying the accumulated assessment knowledge that is designed to help teachers compile their test sheets. The example shown in the highest frame of Figure. 13.10 reveals how all teachers who use the IKMAAS rate the relative importance of the relevant concepts in the selected test range. Oval nodes in the figure represent concepts, and the percentile numbers within them are their degrees of relative importance. When this number is higher, it means that teachers more often selected or created test items to test that

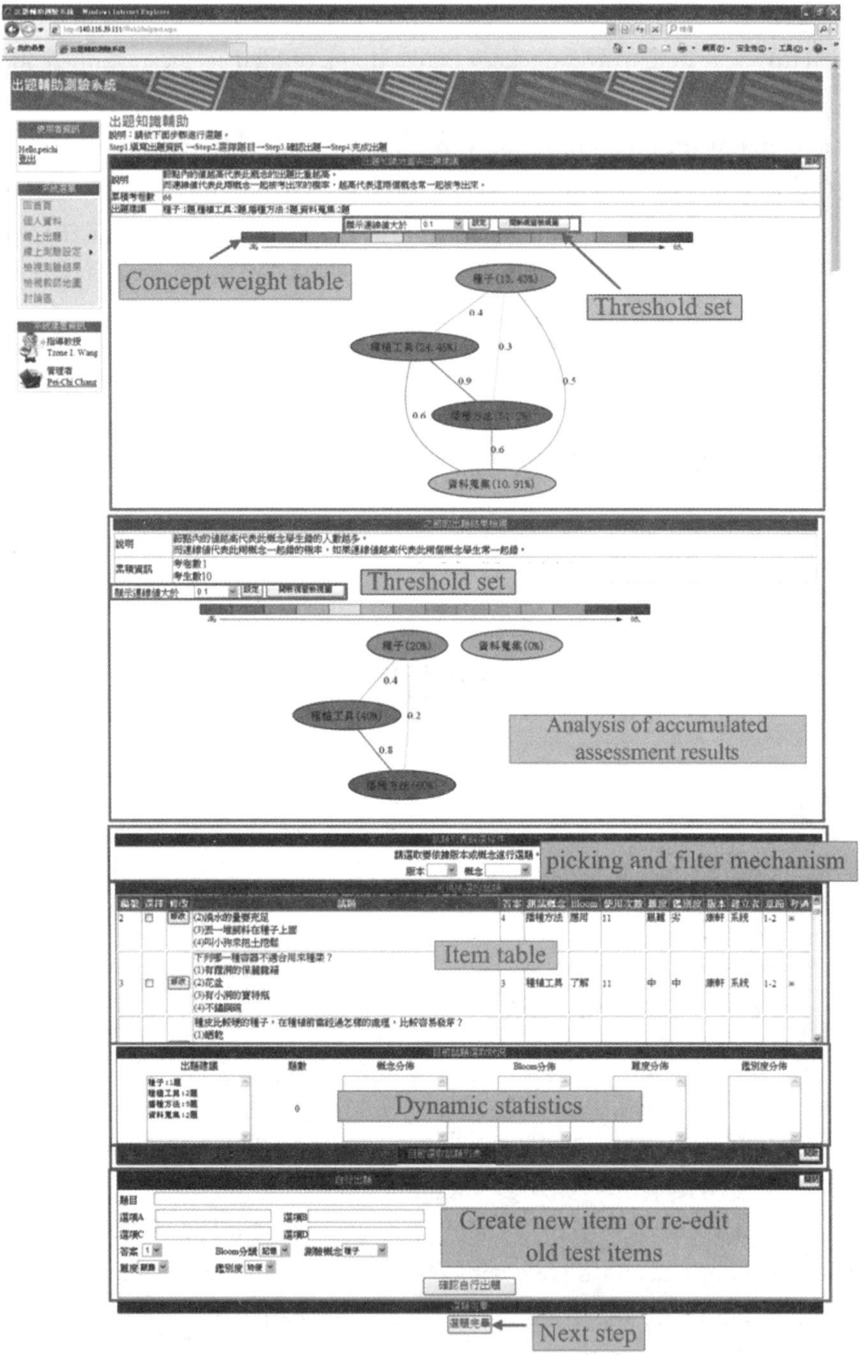

Figure 13.10 Step two—the process teachers follow when using the teacher interface

concept. The number labelled on the link between two concepts represents how often the two concepts are tested together in the same assessment. For each concept, these numbers provide teachers with suggestions on how many test items should be arranged, selected from the item bank or created on-site as well as advice on how the concepts should be organized.

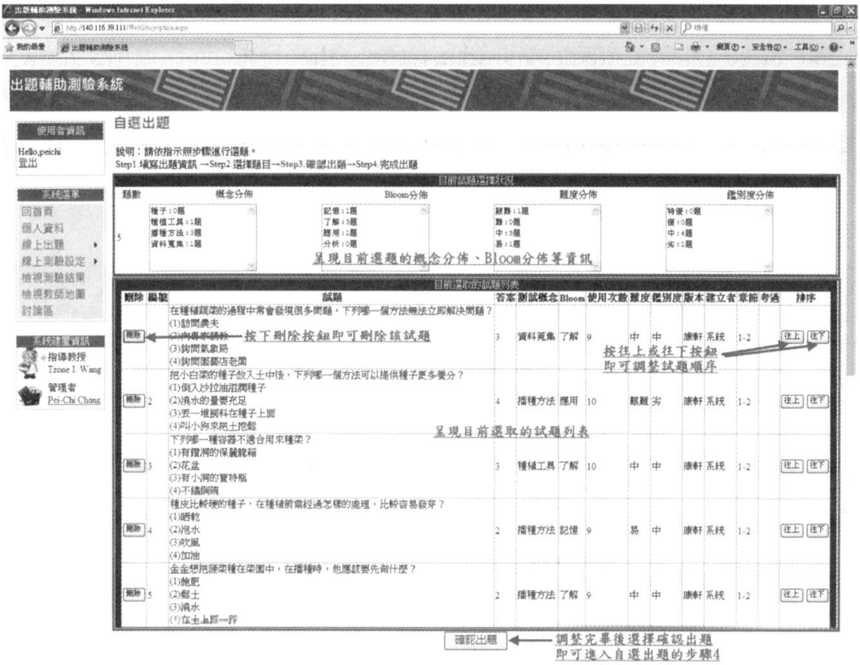

Figure 13.11 Step three—adjust these items or delete these selected items

Another knowledge map, shown in the second frame of Figure. 13.10, provides teachers with an analysis of the accumulated results of assessments within the same selected range. The number in a concept node represents the percentage of students who incorrectly answered test items for this concept; when the number is higher, more students misunderstood the concept. The number labelled on the link between two concepts represents how often the two concepts are misunderstood together in the same assessment. Step three is to generate an assessment for the students after all of the test items are arranged (as shown in Figure 13.11). Step four is checked and save the final assessment arrangement (Figure 13.12). An assignment is transformed into online quizzes or a printable test sheet. It can be saved in the Assessment Bank for sharing with other teachers. Teachers can set assessment time and choose what classes they want to assess (Figure 13.13, Figure 13.14, Figure 13.15).Teachers can then use these documents to create additional assignments by editing test items according to their needs. In addition, teacher can adjust these items or delete these selected items, and transfer into the document file (as shown in Figure 13.16), or view the historic record of assessment arrangement (as shown in Figure 13.17). Of course, teachers are free to make their own choices as to the number of test items for each concept; their decisions, however, will later affect the accumulated assessment knowledge.

Figure 13.12 Step four-check and save the final assessment arrangement

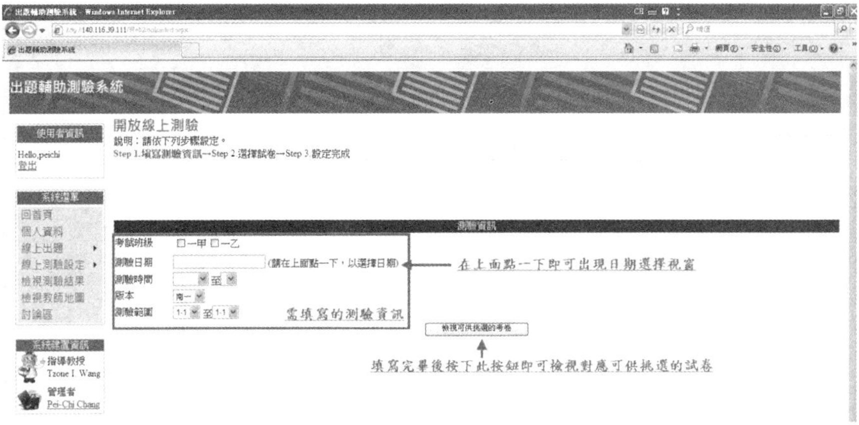

Figure 13.13 Choose classes what they want to assess

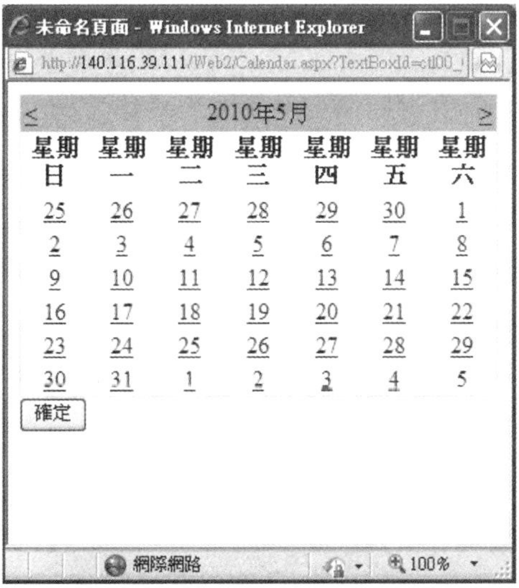

Figure 13.14 Set assessment time

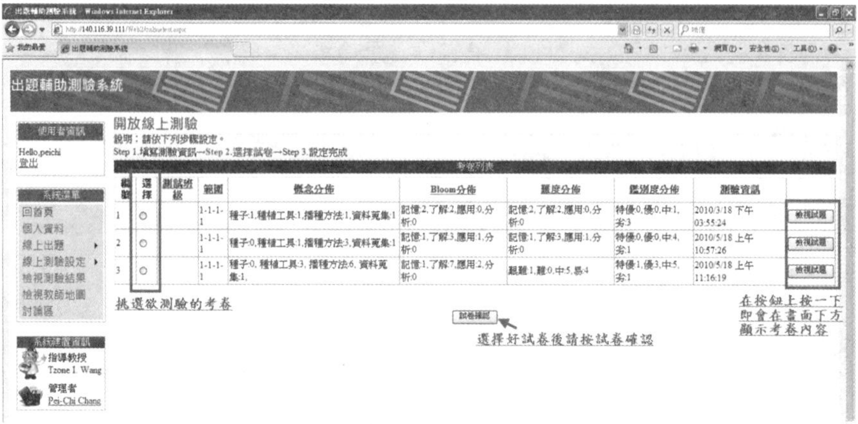

Figure 13.15 Choosing an assessment file

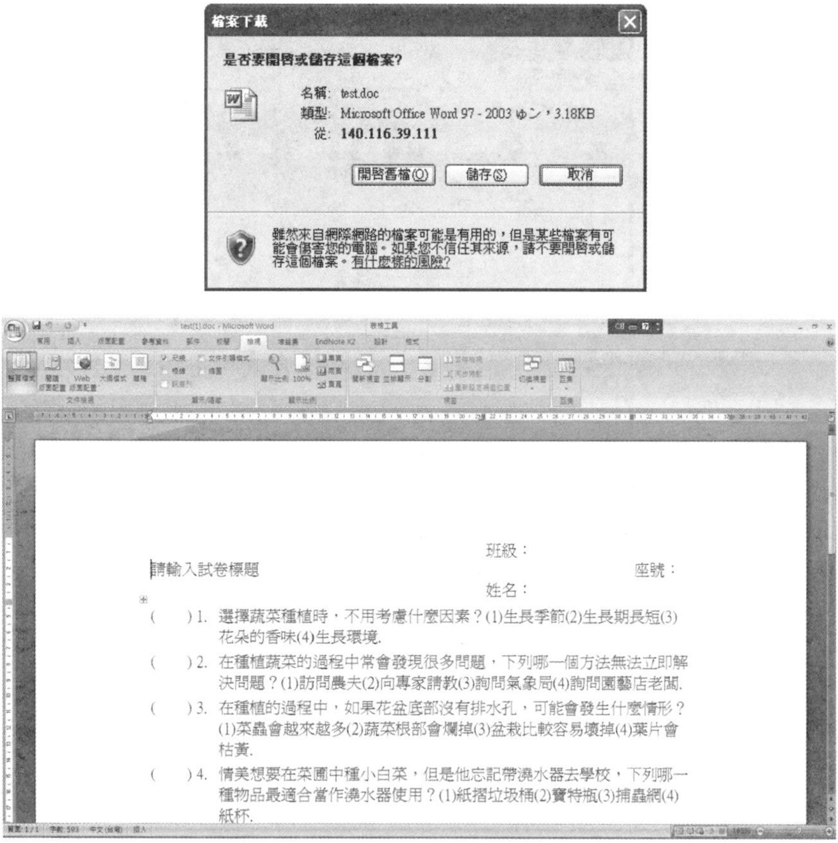

Figure 13.16 Save and transfer into the document file

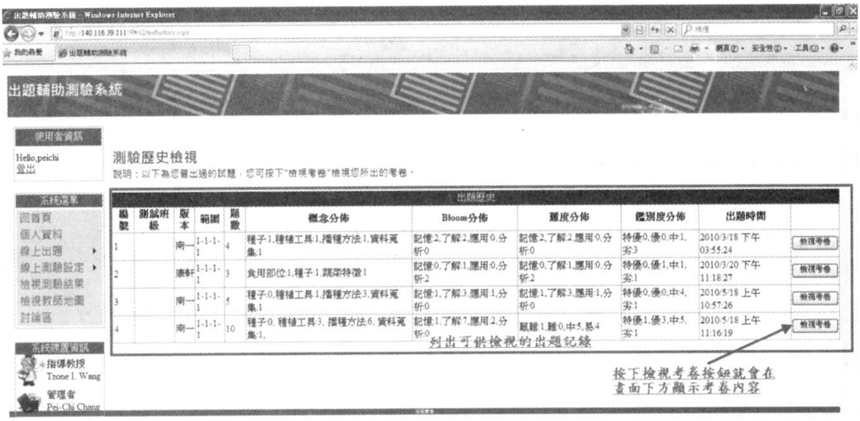

Figure 13.17 Viewing the historic record of assessment arrangement

When students login in the IKMAAS, and completed their online assessment that teacher conducted (Figure 13.18), the Assessment Result Analysis Module of the IKMAAS also provides helpful information for teachers by utilizing a knowledge map that shows the proportion of misunderstood concepts in some specific courses (as shown in Figure 13.19). Such information is produced from the accumulation of assessment results taken from either online quizzes or classroom tests; it provides important statistics that will help teachers assist their students in the future. The students' user interface allows students to receive feedback immediately after finishing an online test. An essential statistical table presents the total score and the proportion of correct to incorrect answers (as shown in Figure 13.20).

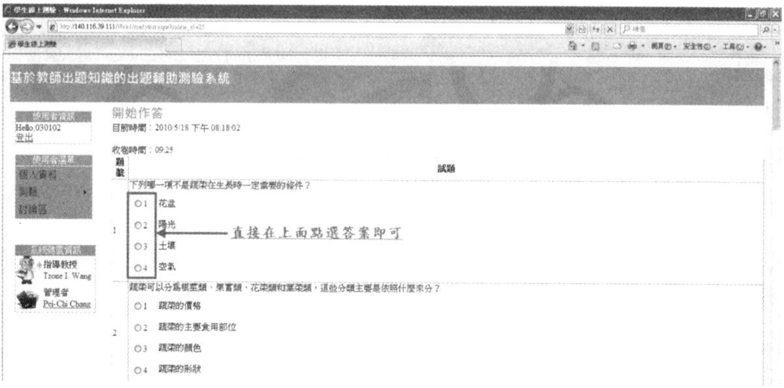

Figure 13.18 Students lagging in the IKMAAS, and completed their online assessment

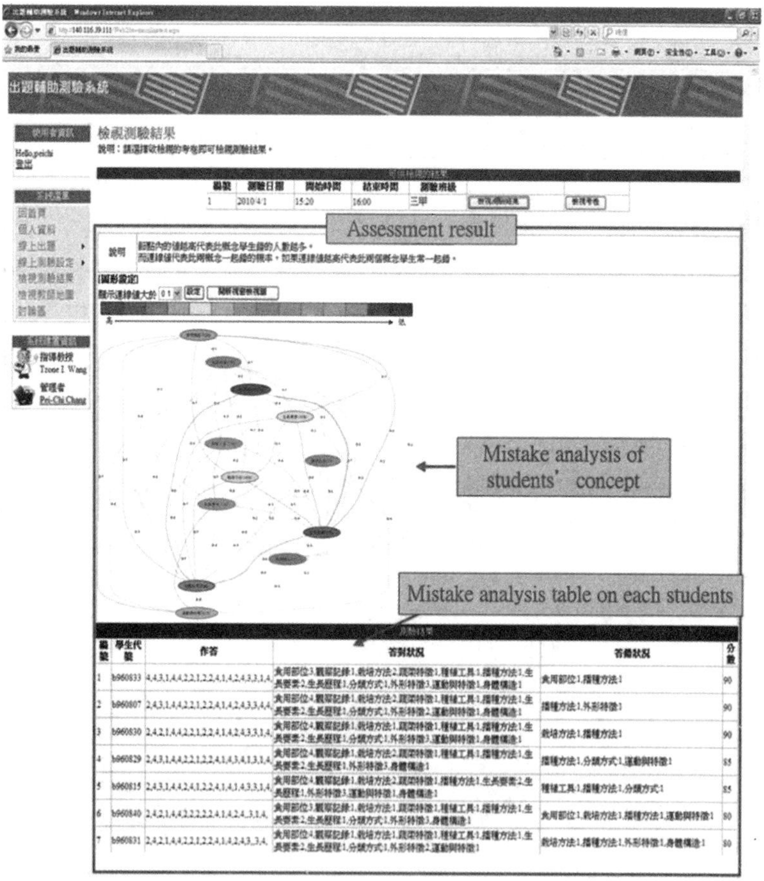

Figure 13.19 A chart of students' mistake analysis

Figure 13.20 A statistical table presents the total score and the proportion of correct to incorrect answers

13.4 Experiment Design

In this section, we conducted an experiment to evaluate the effectiveness of the proposed method on teachers' assessment knowledge accumulation and the usability of IKMAAS. The IKMAAS contains four third-grade "natural science and life technology" curriculum materials, and the item bank is fed with over 1000 related test items. Several experiments scheduled for one semester (over four months) were conducted in the third grade natural science courses at elementary schools in Taiwan, China. Eighteen teachers currently teaching or having taught the courses participated in the experiments, and each of the courses had approximately thirty students enrolled. Two stages were scheduled and were alternately conducted on four different subjects within the courses. In the first stage, teachers used the IKMAAS to compile assessments without using the features of the knowledge map. In the second stage, teachers used the IKMAAS and the various knowledge maps available. The entire experimental process design, as shown in Figure 13.21, can be divided into several parts, as follows:

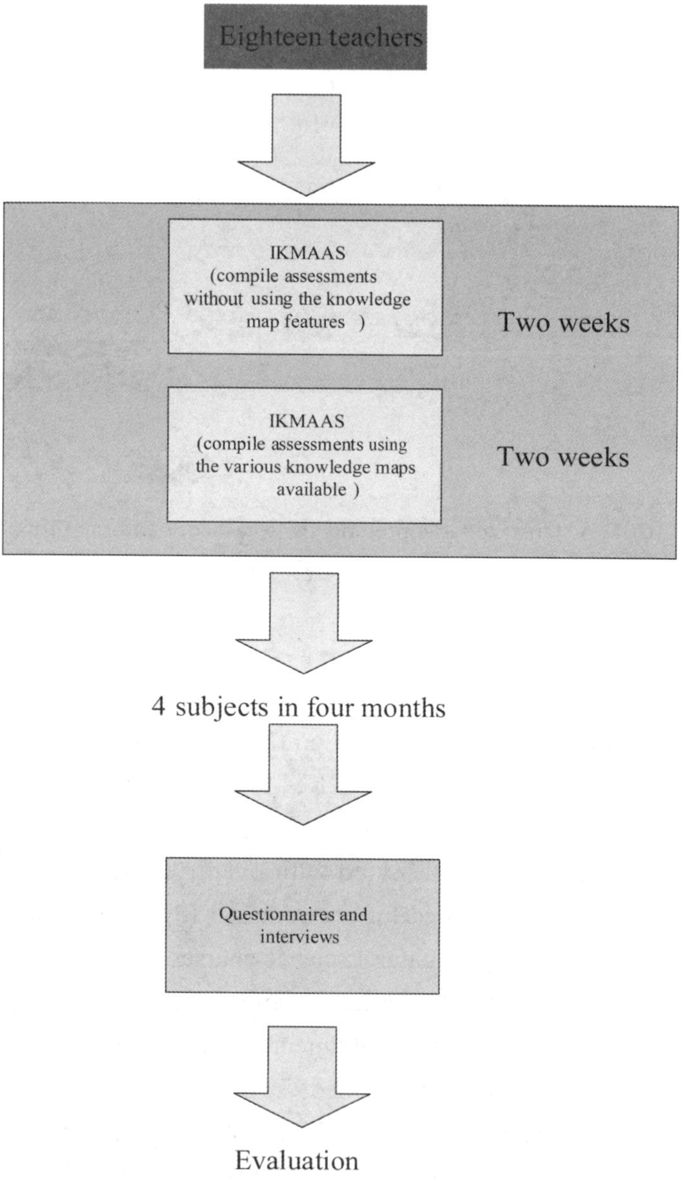

Figure 13.21 The second stage of the experimental process design

13.5 Evaluation and Discussion of IKMAAS

The IKMAAS has been operational for one and a half years, and actually used for compiling many school assessments. While, to precisely evaluate the feasibility of the IKMAAS, several experiments scheduled for one semester (over four months) were conducted in the third grade natural science courses at elementary schools in Taiwan, China. Eighteen teachers currently teaching or having taught the courses participated in the experiments, and each of the courses has about thirty students enrolled. Two stages were scheduled and were alternately conducted on four different subjects within the courses. In the first stage, teachers used the IKMAAS to compile assessments without using the knowledge map features. In the second stage, teachers used the IKMAAS and the various knowledge maps available. Evaluations of the experiments included system usage records, questionnaires and interviews with all of the teachers. These data were collected to examine teachers' experiences with assessment knowledge-sharing, their satisfaction and opinions about the system's functionalities, and more in-depth information on why teachers responded toward the IKMAAS as they did. The results provide evidence that supports the IKMAAS's potential for improving the assessment tasks of teachers in various domains. Analyzed with regard to system usage logs, the dispersion of the standard deviation was calculated to compare the similar dispersion on the item selecting for two different assessment records: items selecting without using knowledge maps, and items selecting using knowledge maps. The formula (8) for calculating the standard deviation is presented below, where N represents the number of samples; x_i represents the value of x, and $\bar{x}$ represents the average value of N. The degree of similarity between the two item selecting (using knowledge maps or without using knowledge maps) is presented in Figure 13.22:

$$\sigma = \sqrt{\frac{1}{N}\sum_{i=1}^{N}\left(x_i - \bar{x}\right)^2} \cdots\cdots (8)$$

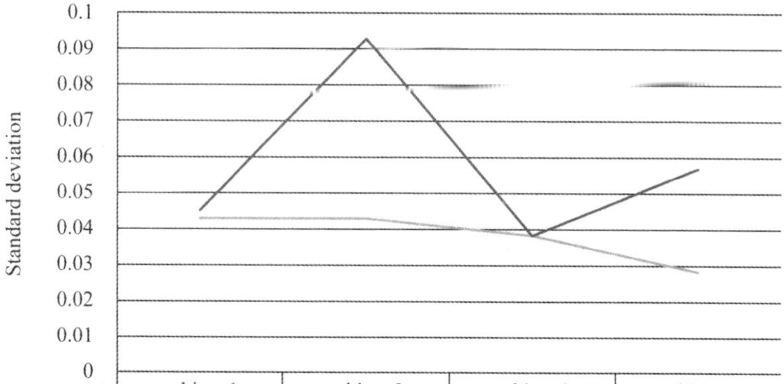

	subject 1	subject 2	subject 3	subject 4
No using K-map (black line)	0.04518997	0.092217011	0.039046886	0.056790415
using K-map (grey line)	0.042798599	0.042798599	0.038104743	0.028786911

Figure 13.22 The degree of similarity between the two item selecting

An important phenomenon was observed by analyzing usage records from the second stage: the more a teacher used the IKMAAS, the more he or she tended to adopt the suggested weights of concept distributions for test items on his or her assessments. Only a few teachers consistently ignored the suggestions from the IKMAAS and used their own concept weight proportions on test items in their assessments. However, the final proportions of concepts among test items on the assessments produced by these teachers were still quite similar to what the system suggested, as shown in Figure 13.23 For the 1-st subject, the average proportion of all the assessments produced saw 83 percent similarity, which rises to 91 percent for the 4-th subject. This means, overall, teachers appeared willing to follow the suggestions pertaining to concept weights that were calculated using the accumulated assessment knowledge. Teachers also agreed that they became more aware of the need to change their assessment practices to avoid inappropriate concept-test item weights on future assessment compilations.

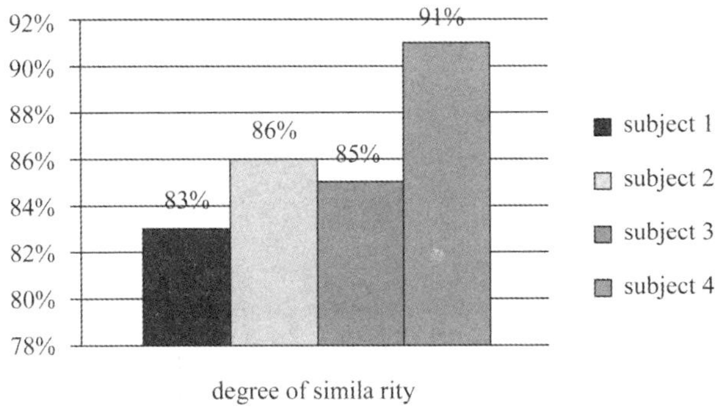

Figure 13.23 The degree of similarity on concept weight proportions between system suggestions and teacher decisions

Thirty two items on the questionnaire, as shown in Table 13.2, covered nine different dimensions among: **usefulness, easiness, attitude, technological complexity, concentration, intentions, satisfaction, system stability and knowledge map presentation.** Responses were defined using a Likert-type scale radar chart, as shown in Figure 13.24. As can be seen, every individual answer to all of the questions were positive, although those related to **technological complexity**, **satisfaction**, and **system stability** were slightly lower than the others. These results suggest that the IKMAAS would benefit from a friendlier user interface. However, the high score on **concentration** also confirms that the IKMAAS can indeed help teachers by providing a supportive overview of the relative importance of concepts and allowing them to concentrate on the distribution of concepts among the test items.

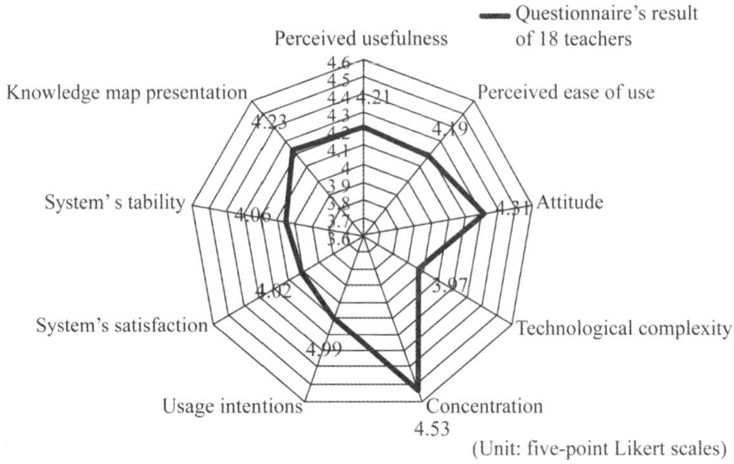

Figure 13.24 Results of questionnaire responses

Some examples of the feedbacks from the interviews are listed as follows:

- This system is amazing; it helps me see the proper concept distribution percentage by knowledge maps when compiling a test sheet. In addition, I can also refer to the maps of other teachers' assessment knowledge to help me determine… (Teacher C).
- I got some important assessment information easily from this system; it helps me to comprehend or regulate my ideas on the assessment work. It also solved some of my problems, for example, the inadequate proportion of concepts in my assessment works… (Teacher H)
- It is convenient for me to review my faults in the previous assessment works and to understand the misconception distributions of students… (Teacher A)

In short, teachers believe that the primary benefits of the IKMAAS are as follows:

- The knowledge map can clearly and visually identify key assessment knowledge (e.g., concept weights and item configuration) that is most strategic and critical to assessments;

- The knowledge map can assist teachers in identifying the necessary knowledge easily and effectively;
- Other teachers' assessment experiences and knowledge accumulated in the IKMAAS were easy to acquire and refer to using the knowledge maps.

One piece of negative feedback is worth noting, and some teachers will give an advice on increasing test items in the future. Most teachers were willing to refer or use questions from others created. However, few teachers were actually willing to share or contribute their questions. Some senior teachers and experts were not willing to share their knowledge and experiences due to security concerns about test items on the IKMAAS. Most teachers did find that the IKMAAS is a helpful platform for editing test items, managing assessment assignments, sharing assessment knowledge, and improving their assessment tasks.

The evaluations confirm that, by integrating knowledge maps and teachers' accumulated assessment knowledge, the IKMAAS is able to provide teachers with novel forms of assistance. All of the teachers' captured assessment knowledge could be summarized and concretized as knowledge maps that were useful to both veteran and novice teachers. Knowledge maps played such a significant role in knowledge management that they were also useful blueprints for implementing teachers' assessment knowledge management systems.

Although IKMAAS was experimented in this study using a science course subject with its related items or assessments, it is not necessarily that IKMAAS is confined to such a limited domain. The methodology and technologies IKMAAS employed are all well developed and all domain independent. To transfer IKMAAS to other subject course material, test items, and test sheets, would require no further labor work than download/upload and creating files.

Table 13.2 Thirty-two items on the questionnaire

Items	Mean	
Usefulness		
1. Using the IKMAAS improves my educational assessment work performance.	4.18	4.21
2. Using the IKMAAS enhances my effectiveness in my assessment work.	4.29	
3. I find the IKMAAS to be useful in my assessment work.	4.24	
4. Using the IKMAAS would make my assessment work easier.	4.12	
Easiness		
5. It would be easy for me to become skillful at using the IKMAAS.	4.35	4.19
6. My interaction with the IKMAAS is clear and understandable.	4.12	
7. I believe that it is easy to get the IKMAAS to do what I want it to do.	4.06	
8. Interacting with the IKMAAS does not require a lot of my mental effort.	4.24	
Attitude		
9. I think that using the IKMAAS is beneficial.	4.35	4.31
10. I think that the IKMAAS is worth to use.	4.35	
11. The attitude of using the IKMAAS is positive.	4.65	
12. I like to use the IKMAAS.	3.88	
Technological complexity		
13. Learning to use the IKMAAS takes up too much of my time.	2.00	3.97
14. Using the IKMAAS involves too much time.	2.06	
Concentration		
15. I was absorbed intensely in the educational assessment activity.	4.59	4.53
16. My attention was focused on the educational assessment activity.	4.47	
Intentions		
17. Assuming I have access to the IKMAAS, I intend to use it.	4.12	4.09
18. I intend to increase my use of the IKMAAS in the future.	4.06	
System satisfaction		

(*continued*)

Table 13.2 (*continued*)

19. The interface of IKMAAS is easy to use.	4.18	4.02
20. The text style and forms are suitable.	4.00	
21. Operating instructions and tips are clear and I can understand easily.	4.06	
22. Making assessment of IKMAAS's interface is very convenient.	4.18	
23. The IKMAAS meets my needs.	3.71	
System stability		
24. The IKMAAS is stable for me.	4.06	4.06
25.The functions of the IKMAAS are faultless.	3.59	
26. The IKMAAS infrequently happened error.	4.18	
Knowledge map presentation		
27. Teachers' assessment knowledge can be shared effectively by the IKMAAS.	4.24	4.23
28. Sharing teachers' assessment knowledge is useful for me.	4.24	
29.Teachers' assessment knowledge can be presented appropriately by knowledge map.	4.18	
30. The color of the node in the knowledge map helps me discriminating the importance of the concept.	4.29	
31. The assessment suggestion proposed by the IKMAAS presented the accumulating and visualizing tacit knowledge of teachers properly.	4.24	
32. The assessment suggestion proposed by the IKMAAS is beneficial to me.	4.18	

CHAPTER 14 Item Recommendation Uses the Teacher Cluster-based Collaborative Filtering Approach

Personalized item recommendation enables the educational assessment systems to make deliberate efforts to perform appropriate assessment strategies that fit the needs, purposes, preferences, and interests of teachers. In chapter 14, we propose an innovative, personalized item-recommendation that automatically adapts to the similar clustered groups of teachers' assessment interests and preferences. When teachers compile their classroom assessments, the best-fit candidate assessment items will be available recommended from clustered the historical assessment knowledge of teachers in the item repository and by displaying item allocation information. How to cluster teachers' assessment knowledge and the item-recommendation method we proposed in the 14.1 and 14.2. The mechanism of personalized item recommendation is implemented and the evaluated results for the effectiveness of the item-recommendation via experiments are respectively presented in the last section.

A recommender system enables to automatically provide personalized recommendations based on the historical record of users' activities (Zhang, Zhou & Zhang, 2010). It is now considered to be the most promising way to efficiently filter out the overload of information or provide favorable information by adopting knowledge discovery techniques to provide personalized recommendations. So far, the recommender systems and related recommender technologies have successfully found applications in e-learning and e-education, to help instructors and students to seek relevant educational resources(Rafaeli, et al., 2004). These resources may be learning materials, contents or learning objects toward particular goals which are being proper recommendations based on different requirements and preferences (Farzan & Brusilovsky, 2006; Krištofič, 2005). It seems to be as "friends of learners and instructors" which recommend the right educational items that directly meet the needs of different learners, or help the individual instructors make better teaching choices from a large number of alternatives without sufficient personal experience or awareness of the alternatives. Likewise, these applications of personalized recommendation could also be used in e-assessment or educational assessment systems, such as, driving personalized recommendation that advises different teachers on the appropriate assessment items selection or efficiently provides suitable item recommendations based on previous assessment activities.

Rafaeli has strongly advocated that the development of educational assessment system should integrate useful recommend technologies for the item selecting and in turn enhancing the effectiveness of educational assessment system at classroom assessment tasks in his previous research. Besides, he also directly raised some essential issues on the development of item recommendation(Rafaeli, Barak, Dan Gur & Toch, 2004). How can item recommendations be performed most effectively? Who are the appropriate recommenders? What needs to be performed in constructing the recommendation algorithm to improve the use and acceptance of recommendations?

As mentioned above, we argue that item recommendation method motivated by referring these historical similar item compiling behaviors could have the potential to help address these issues. The terms "groups" and "neighbors" depending on similarity are somewhat interdependent in the context of recommendation. Groups are defined as mutually similar data items (Pahl, 2006). This concept is innovative because it suggests that "neighbors" (a like-minded group) are relevant to low-risk recommendation domains, such as movies, music or jokes, whereas "friends" are more relevant to higher-risk domains, such as knowledge items used in learning and assessment (Rafaeli, et al., 2004). People may obtain the proper recommendation referred to the individual or neighbor group's preference or experience similar to themselves.

In this chapter, we considered that the item recommended scenarios could be happened among multiple teachers' assessment perspectives when they compiled their educational assessments by assessment systems or tools. Providing appropriate item recommendation based on the "similarity" which finding out teachers who have similar assessment preferences and interests, or teachers who have similar item selecting or assessment compiling behaviors. Therefore, even though the teachers had various assessment preferences and interests based on different levels of expertise and prior knowledge, motivation and criteria in regard to compiling assessment, it could be found out as "peer friends" by data mining technology to find the similarity in overall assessment constructing patterns from these stored historical assessment usage profiles. Moreover, a great amount of assessment usage profiles is preserved in the educational assessment system, which contain useful information in the assessment behavior of teachers. The set of all teachers' assessment profiles constitutes the collective. In particular, among data mining and information extraction techniques in which clustering has become possible to discover similar data distributions and patterns, and group physical or abstract objects into classes of similar objects.

This personalized item recommendation approach initially applied a implemented clustering algorithm is employed to distinguish teacher groups who might have similar assessment selecting behaviors, and then provide item recommendation as an integrated module in a previously developed assessment system to assist teachers to find the proper items and carry out the assessment construction more effectively. An experimental design was adopted to understand the effectiveness of personalized item recommendation in collecting and analyzing teacher assessment knowledge of item preference behaviors to perform an educational assessment compiling and in improving teacher assessment work performance.

As previously mentioned, we can apply a clustering algorithm to group teachers into several clusters according to assessment features of teachers. In the same cluster, every teacher with high assessment preference displays similar item selection behaviors. Moreover, while the IKMAAS, when integrated with the item recommendation mechanism, is responsible for gathering assessment information from the teachers, generating the "friends" group, running the recommendation algorithms and retrieving the recommendations, the IKMAAS was initially designed to reach out across institutions and promote assessment collaboration and assessment knowledge-sharing among instructors. IKMAAS has a smaller granular focus on items and on a process that emphasizes knowledge sharing among instructors. IKMAAS serves as an online platform for teachers to work "together apart" by sharing their assessment knowledge. We propose that IKMAAS provides instructors with important opportunities to share "craft wisdom" in a professional online assessment culture.

14.1 Clustering Teacher's Assessment Knowledge

In order to perform personalized item recommendation based on clustered teacher's assessment knowledge to assist teachers in classroom assessment construction. The first and foremost mission is to proceed cluster work from the IKMAAS's item repository. In general, a measure of similarity is usually defined as a proximity measure in a multi-dimension space spanned by selecting object attributes (Michalski & Stepp, 1983). Most of the previous work on a clustering concern about finding the similarity between nodes through their distance and intensity (Firdausiah Mansur & Yusof, 2013). Some clustering techniques, such as K-means or Fuzzy C mean, which have often been used by many engineering and scientific disciplines for applications such as image segmentation, pattern reorganization and data mining (Chen & Chen, 2009).

At here, we adopted K-means clustering algorithm, because it possess iterative refinement characteristics based on a Euclidean distance metric, and has become a popular, simple, useful and the automatic clustering method (Krishna & NarasimhaMurty, 1999; Sarkar, Yegnanarayana & Khemani, 1997). K-means clustering partitions n items into k clusters is in which each item belongs to the cluster with the nearest mean. This algorithm allows us to specify the number of clusters (k), which given an initial set of k-means, …, the algorithm proceeds by alternating between two steps:

First step: Assign each item to the cluster with the closest mean.

$$S_i^{(t)} = \{x_j : \|x_j - m_i^{(t)}\| \le \|x_i - m_{i*}^{(t)}\| \; for \; all \; i^* = 1, 2, \cdots, k\}$$

Second step: Calculate the new means to be the centroid of the items in the cluster.

$$m_i^{(t+1)} = \frac{1}{|S_i^{(t)}|} \sum_{x_j \in S_i^{(t)}} x_i$$

The algorithm is said to converge when the clustering assignments no longer change. Therefore, in respect of performing teacher's assessment knowledge by using the k-means clustering algorithm, we set four mainly critical assessment information regarding item-concept weight, Bloom's Taxonomy, item difficulty, and item discrimination which as meaningful attributes is used to find similar clusters for classifying the teachers' assessment construction behaviors. These assessment information involved with different teachers' item selecting data has previously stored in the IKMAAS's item repository. Each of the four critical assessment information is basically divided into high and low degree of the parameter, and transformed to interval-scaled variables to facilitate k-means clustering. For example, the definition is as follow Table 14.1. Four variables (1-4), as previously hypothesized, were defined for the following three parameters: item difficulty, item discrimination and Bloom's cognitive taxonomy (as shown in Table 3.1). For instance, teacher A determined that the proportion of item difficulty on one assessment was: very difficult (i_1) 10%; difficult (i_2) 20%; average (i_3) 40% and easy (i_4) 30%. When one teacher's item selecting behavior on each parameter is similar to another teacher's behavior, we indicate that the teachers have similar assessment preferences and assessment determinations; therefore, the IKMAAS can calculate the similarity of each parameter instantly and fulfil the k-mean's clustering analysis to categorize the teacher's item selecting behaviors from the database stored in the IKMAAS. Besides, the k-means clustering need some centroid for the cluster initialization. We initially assume k-value is 4, that means the participating teachers are divided into four groups and ensures that each group included at least two teachers, to resolve the issue of outliers and avoid each cluster that included just a single teacher. Therefore, these similar assessment item selecting preferences will be analyzed by using clustering to provide the next stage of the item recommendations.

Table 14.1 Four variables for each parameter for item difficulty, item discrimination and Bloom's cognitive taxonomy

Element	**Parameters**			
Rating scale	4	3	2	1
Concept weight	≥46(%)	45-31(%)	30-16(%)	15-0(%)
Item difficulty	Very difficult (i_1)	Difficult (i_2)	Average (i_3)	Easy (i_4)
Item discrimination	Superior (i_5)	Good (i_6)	Average (i_7)	Poor (i_8)
Bloom's cognitive taxonomy	Knowledge (i_9)	Comprehension (i_{10})	Application (i_{11})	Analysis (i_{12})

14.2 Item Recommendation Methodology

The personalized item recommendation approach was executed to predict the active teacher's assessment preference for a particular item by comparing and clustering other teachers' similar assessment knowledge, and then give a favorable item recommendation for active teachers. The underlying framework on the item recommendation for the cluster-based filtering method is presented in Figure 14.1. The item recommended scenario assumes a set of n teachers, $U=[u_1, u_2, ..., u_n]$, and a set of m assessment items, $I=[i_1, i_2, ..., i_m]$. Each teacher u_i has a list of items I_{ui} (where $I_{ui}I$, and I_{ui} could be an empty set) for which the teacher has expressed assessment preferences. The preference of a teacher u_i on item i_j might be an explicit numerical scale rating or an implicit measure based on teacher-compiled assessment activities. In this study, the frequency of being selected items represents the degree of preference so that the items selected by the teachers in the group are an implicit measure of teachers' assessment preferences. In addition, items are grouped into distinct clusters based on similarity of assessment preferences, and similarities between item clusters are measured during the clustering process. For each cluster Cr, the average item preference score of a teacher u_i is given as. Based on concept weight, item difficulty, item discrimination and Bloom's cognitive taxonomy for a specific teacher u_a (where u_a U), the recommended decision predicts the preference of that teacher-termed an active teacher- for a particular item that this teacher has not rated. In this recommendation framework, the similarity between the active teacher and another teacher is determined by the similarity of their assessment preferences both within and between item clusters.

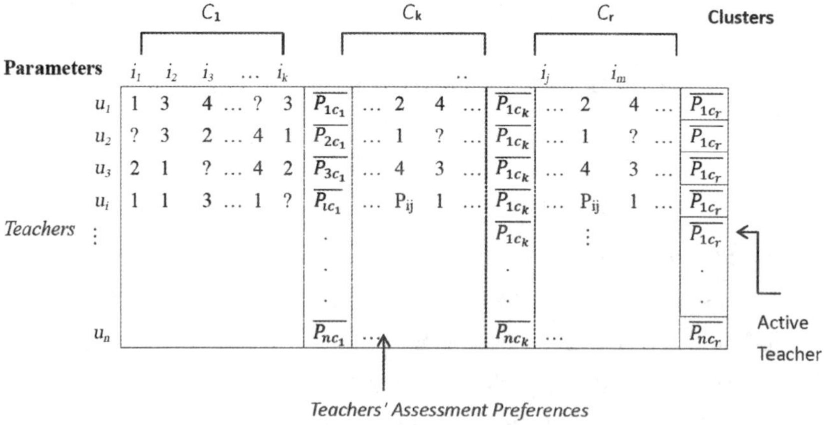

Figure 14.1 The Framework of the Teacher Cluster-based Collaborative Filtering Recommendation Approach

14.3 The Mechanism of Personalized Item Recommendation in IKMAAS

Before executing the item recommendation, the teacher must initially complete the registration to create a personal assessment profile by the IKMAAS (see in Figure 14.2). In case the teachers construct an assessment by the IKMAAS, and the assessment constructed and item selected record portfolios are stored in the IKMAAS. All of these personal assessment portfolios are involved with various of personal assessment information included identification and login information, previous assessment knowledge, discipline, assessment frequency and some detailed assessment operating information regarding assessment conducting and item selecting records.

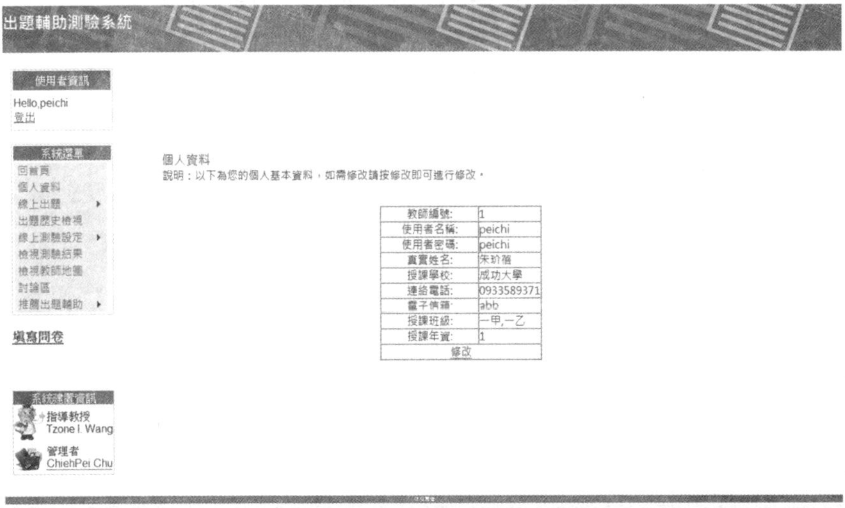

Figure 14.2 The system interface about a personal assessment profile

The mechanism of personalized item recommendation based on clustering the teachers' assessment knowledge profiles consists three modules: teacher assessment data aggregation, clustering pattern analysis and item recommendation (see Figure 14.3). All modules are performed online in the IKMAAS. The module of teacher assessment data aggregation automatically transforms teachers' assessment log files and profiles in the database into the proper format. The module of pattern analysis is used to perform the k-mean cluster analysis of these assessment profiles. And the module of item recommendation is used to provide the specific teachers with proper personalized item choices by the analyzed assessment patterns. Moreover, when teachers want to construct the assessment by the IKMAAS in turn, and then that they can search and select the items, three alternative user interfaces for item selecting were provided: manual item selection, item recommendation employing clustering assessment knowledge and automatic item selection. Also, teachers can manage the assessment created, adding or deleting items.

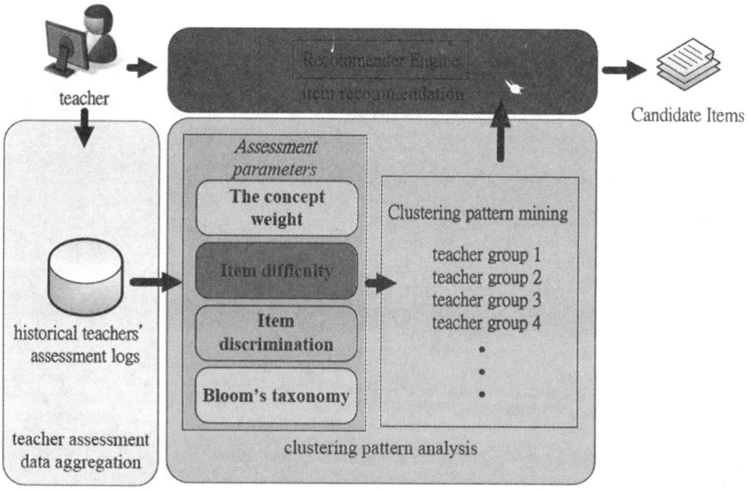

Figure 14.3 System structure for item recommendation

(1) Manual item selection

The interface of manual item selected displays all of the items in the IKMAAS database and the teacher could search or select specific items freely. Four stages about manual item selection is presented as follows: (a) selecting assessment range (Figure14.4); (b) selecting assessment items (Figure14.5); (c) checking the selected items (Figure14.6); iv completed assessment (Figure14.7).

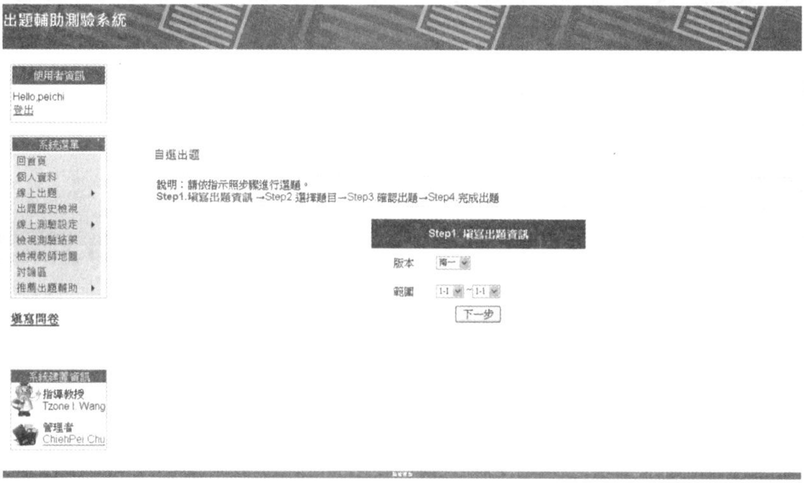

Figure 14.4 Selecting assessment range

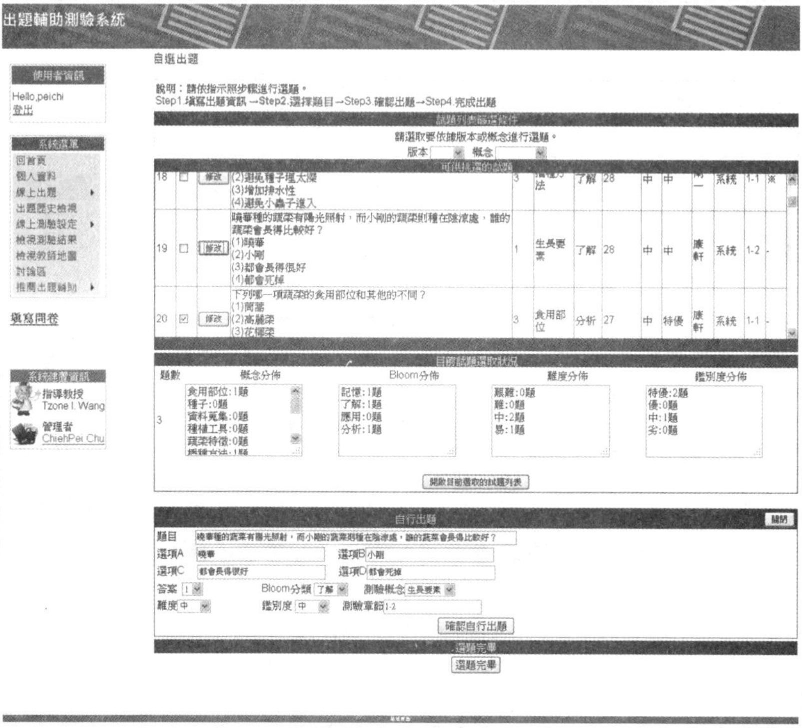

Figure 14.5 Selecting assessment items

Figure 14.6 Checking these selected items or adjusted item sort

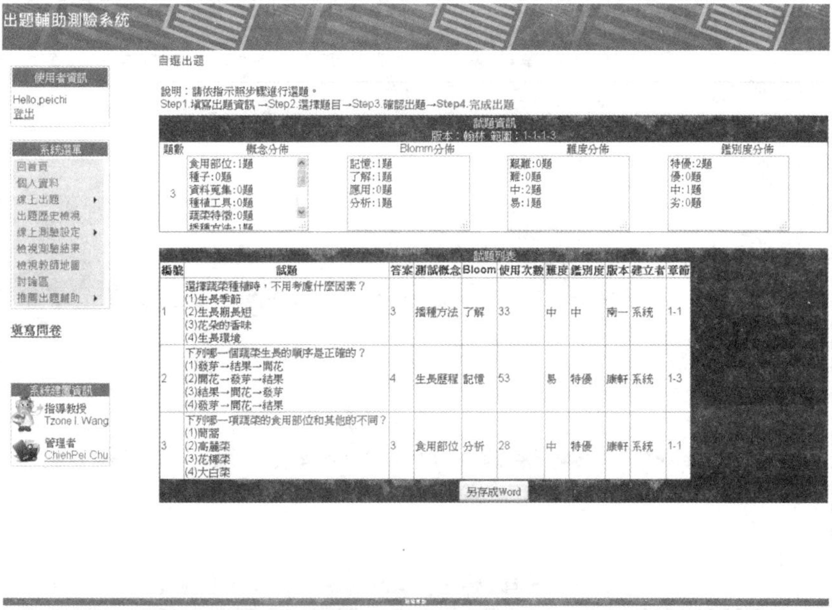

Figure 14.7 Completed assessment arrangement

(2) Tem recommendation based on clustering assessment knowledge

The interface of item recommendation based on clustering assessment knowledge can provide appropriate item recommendations according to predict his or her particular assessment preference and then searching the closed teacher's clusters (Figure 14.8). In this interface, several candidate items involved with the particular teaching concept were shown, and the teacher could add into the assessment lists by accepting or rejecting the recommendations. In addition, the examination of item similarity could help teachers to avoid the two similar items that had selected in this assessment range (see Figure14.9). One limitation is that the new used teacher might obtain a poor item recommendation if his or her current assessment behaviours are not analysed or stored.

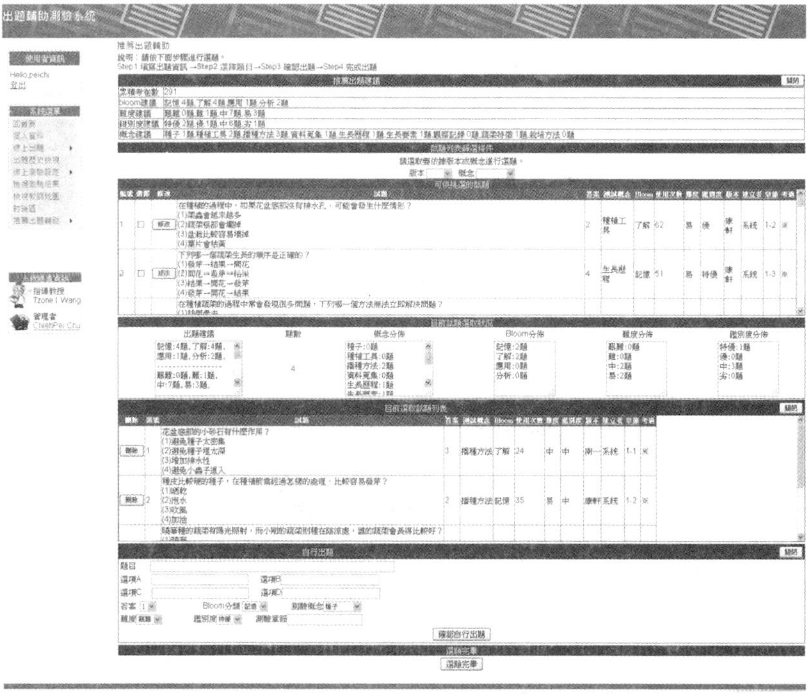

Figure 14.8 Item recommendations according to predict teachers' assessment preference and then searching the closed teacher's clusters

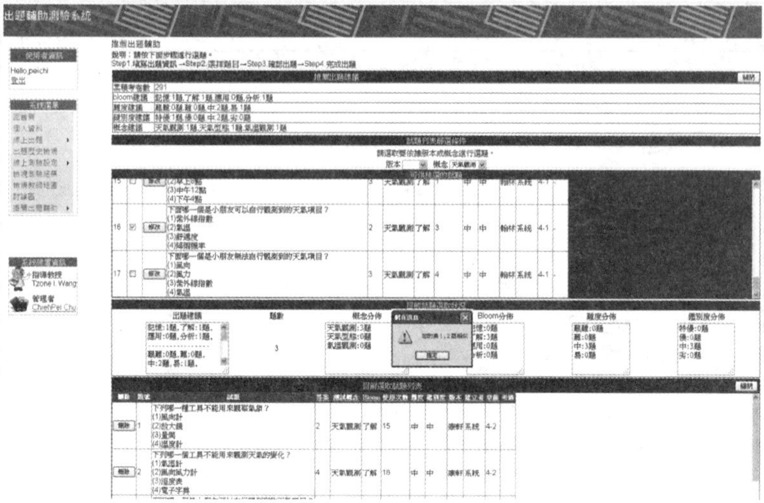

Figure 14.9 The examination of item similarity

(3) Automatic item selection

The interface showed an item list according to the teacher identifies the number of the items desired. These items were selected by personalized item recommendations from clustering similar teacher assessment knowledge. Three stages about automatic item selection is presented as follows: (a)select assessment range and item amount of each course concept (See Figure 14.10); (b)item modification or adjustment, and check the selected items (See Figure14.11); (c) view the completed assessment (See Figure 14.12).

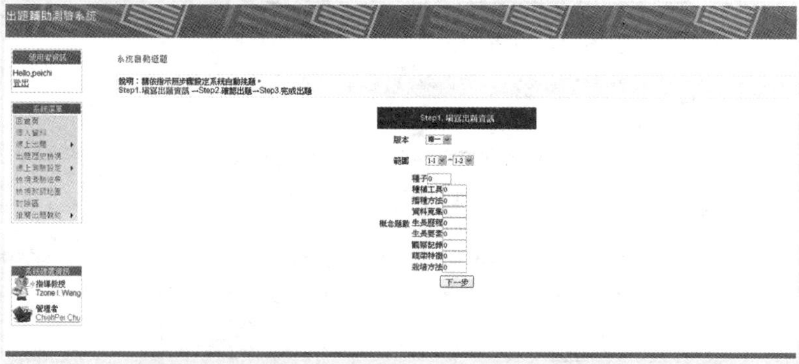

Figure 14.10 Select assessment range and item amount of each course concept

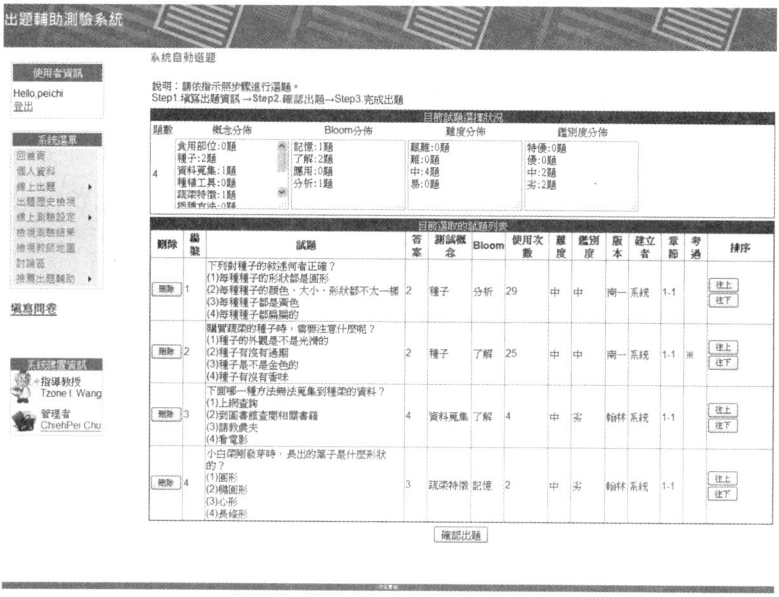

Figure 14.11 Itemmodification, adjustment and finally check the selected items

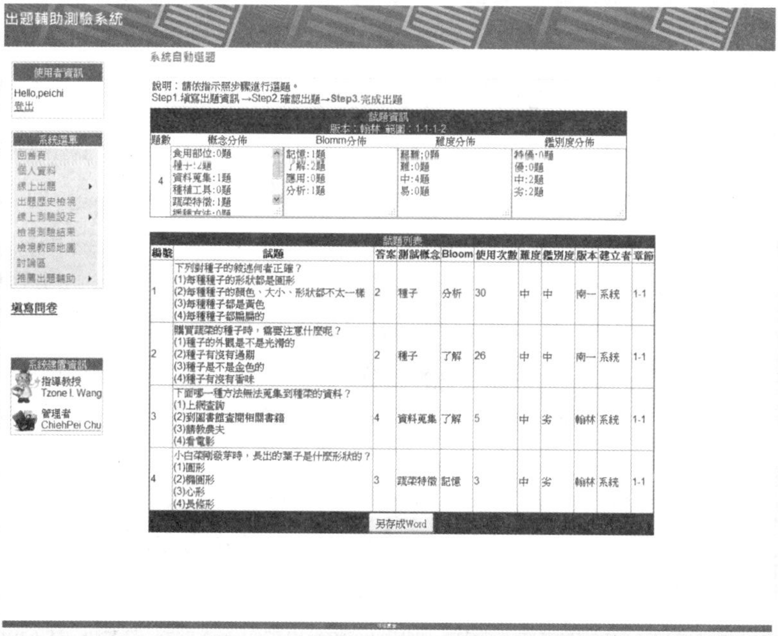

Figure 14.12 Viewing the completed assessment

14.4 Experimental Design

A two round experimental design was used to compare the effects of different ways of providing item recommendation, and to evaluate the feasibility and usability of item recommendation based on clustering of teachers' assessment knowledge. Currently, the IKMAAS contains more than 1000 test items related about three different versions of the third grade "natural science and life technology" curriculum unit. Figure 14.13 presents the overall structure of experimental design, which consists two-round assessment activity performed during a semester; 18 in-serve teachers at elementary schools in Taiwan, China participated in. Four topics of item selecting for different course was scheduled repeatedly and conducted in the two-round assessment activity. During the first item compile round, teachers construct assessments without using the personalized item recommendation. During the second item compile round, teachers using personalized item recommendations to construct assessments by the IKMAAS.

14.5 Results and Discussion

This section presents the experimental results which evaluated the item-recommendation approach based on clustering teacher assessment knowledge. A cluster analysis was performed after participating teachers finished their assessment construction in the first-round assessment activity, and then the system will be executed to calculate these similarities of teachers' assessment constructing behaviors. When the teachers go on to construct assessment by applying item recommendation mechanism from IKMAAS in the second-round assessment activity. The system will immediately identify his/her assessment preferences and recommend appropriate candidate items from searching the closed k-nearest neighbor teacher groups with the highest similarity. Within the current experiment, system usage logs were used to investigate whether there was a difference between the behaviors of assessment construction. And the questionnaire and interview were also used to investigate the usability on item-

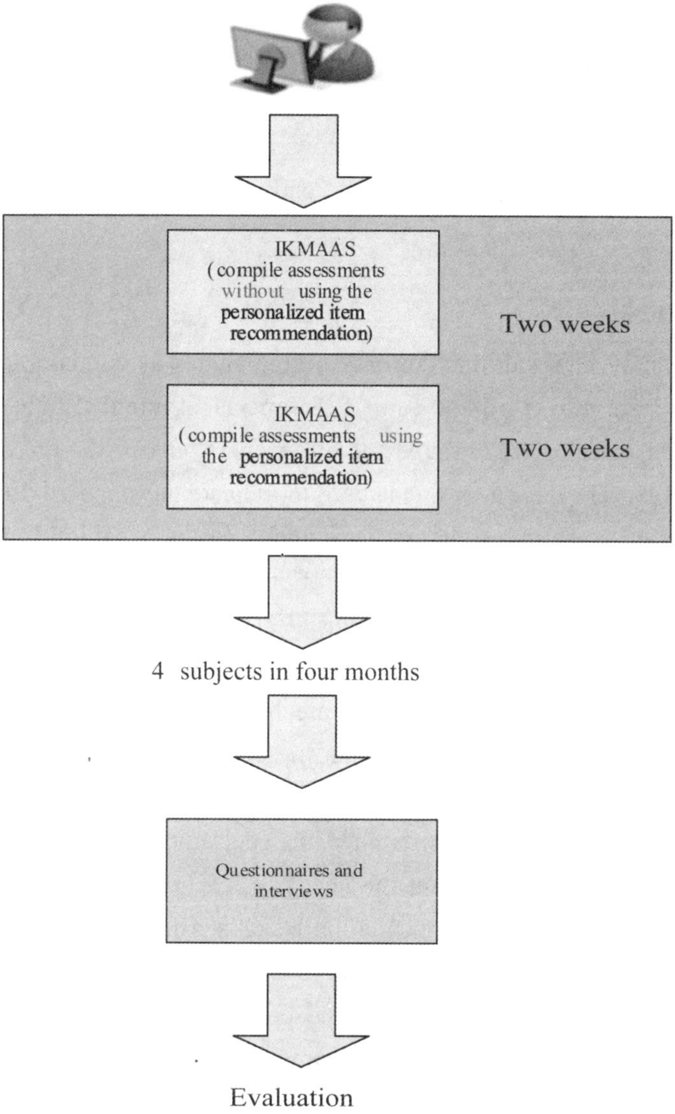

Figure 14.13 Two round experiment design process

recommendation mechanism made constructing assessments more effective and efficient. The results are discussed and interpreted below. Above all, with regard to system usage logs, the dispersion of the standard deviation was calculated to compare the similar dispersion on the item selecting for three different assessment records: items selecting comparable among all teachers selected items, each teacher within the clustering and group clustering groups and item recommendation by clustering teacher assessment knowledge.The formula (9) for calculating the standard deviation is presented below, where N represents the number of samples; x_i represents the value of x, and $\bar{x}$ represents the average value of N.

$$\sigma = \sqrt{\frac{1}{N}\sum_{i=1}^{N}(x_i - \bar{x})^2} \quad \cdots\cdots (9)$$

The analyzed result that compared three values of standard deviation between item selection for four different assessment topics among individuals, the clustered groups and all teachers' group was presented in Figure 14.14. The dark grey line is used to indicate the standard difference between compared with each teacher's item selected behavior. Light grey line is used to indicate the standard difference between compared with each teacher within his or her clustering group and different clustering groups, and grey line is presented to the standardized difference between their adopted item recommendation mechanisms. Here, we notice that grey line is presented the lowest than the other two lines, it meant that if teachers are not grouped, the degree of dispersion for recommended items will have a significant difference, the central value of group for item recommendation will not meet the needs of teachers, but compare with teachers through item recommendation by clustering teacher assessment knowledge have the smallest differences. Moreover, we founded that more than half of teachers directly chosen these items which generated out from the item recommended mechanism. This system usage analyzed result could support the claim that item recommendation is beneficial to assisting teachers' assessment construction. Moreover, an experiment was conducted to evidence the precision and evaluate the efficiency of the item recommendation. Precision implies the reliability and validity of a test. Reliability means the trust worthiness of a test and validity indicates the accuracy of an assessment (Black & Wiliam, 1998). Therefore, evidencing the precision is to ensure that the item selection procedure in the system is feasible.

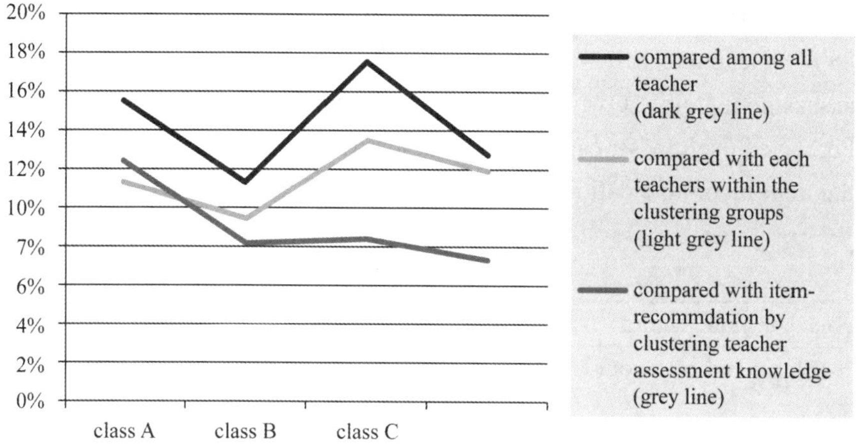

Figure 14.14 Comparison of item similarity of the three items-selecting modules

In addition, one questionnaire was used for gathering the instructors' attitudes toward the usability of the item recommendation. It's mainly intended to measure seven different dimensions involved with teacher background, teacher motivation, assessment judgments, perceived test difficulty, perceived usefulness, perceived ease of use, assessment attitude, intentions, and especially access teachers' perception of using item recommend mechanisms. The questionnaire consists 32 items which be measured by the five point Likert scale. These questionnaire results are being out of statistics and analysis, which showed in the Table 14.2 As we can see from these data, they usually consider the priority of the assessment criterion is student learning conditions (100%) and their teaching schedule (83.33%), when most of participated teachers constructed their new educational assessments,

And teachers still considered these assessment factors in the assessment: Course concepts (100%), Item difficulty (94.44%), Item discrimination(55.56%), and Bloom's Taxonomy (33.33%), when they were constructing assessments. It could be used to prove that the developed item recommendation approach considered these assessment factors matched the teachers' assessment belief. About 94.44% teachers are willing to use these similar assessment items from other teachers as well as share their assessment information with other teachers, as well as 88.89% teachers will revise these previous items when they reuse these assessment items. Overall, participants' responses are positive on the Perceived usefulness, ease of use, attitude, intentions and satisfaction with the item-recommendation.

Table 14.2 Questionnaire

Teacher background					
1. Please indicate your age.	20-30 (11.11%)	31-40 (61.11%)	41-50 (16.67%)	51-60 (11.11%)	Over 61 (0%)
2. Please indicate your gender.	Female (44.44%)			Male (55.56%)	
3. Please identify your educational degree.	Bachelor's degree (11.11%)		Master's degree (83.33%)		Doctorate (5, 56%)
4. Please indicate how many years of teaching experience you have.	0-5 (22.22%)	6-10 (16.67%)		11-15 (33.33%)	Over 16 (27.78%)
Assessment judgment					
5. When constructing an assessment, do you consider:	Testing time for all items (27.78%) Student learning conditions (100%) Teaching schedule (83.33%) School policies (27.78%) Other (5.56)				
6. How much time do you spend constructing a test?	0-1 hour (22.22%) 1-2 hours (22.22%) 2-3 hours (38.89%) Over 3 hours (16.67%)				
7. When constructing an assessment, what factors do you consider:	Course concepts (100%) Item discrimination(55.56%) Item difficulty (94.44%) Bloom's Taxonomy (33.33%) Other (0%)				
8. When constructing an assessment, what factors do you consider in regard to course concepts?	Items assess central course concepts (61.11%) Items assess both central and peripheral course concepts (0%) Items assess course concepts that have relevance beyond the course (38.89%)				

(continued)

Table 14.2 (*continued*)

9. When constructing an assessment, how distinct are items from each other?	Most of the items are very distinct from each other (11.12%) Most of the items are not very distinct from each other (5.56%) Half of the items are very distinct from each other and half are not very distinct from each other (27.27%) Items are randomly chosen with no focus on item distinctness (54.55%)
10. When constructing an assessment, what role does item difficulty play?	Most of the items are very difficult (0%) Most of the items are not difficult (44.44%) Half of the items are very difficult and half of the items are not difficult (44.44%) Items are chosen randomly with no focus on item difficulty (11.12%)
11. When construct an assessment, do you consider Bloom's Taxonomy? (If the response is no, please go directly to item 14.)	Yes (55.56%) No (44.45%)
12. Based on the previous question, please indicate the extent to which test items involve each category of Bloom's Taxonomy (e.g., K 30%, C 30%, Ap 20%, An 10%, S 10%, and E 0%) (where K=Knowledge, C=Comprehension, Ap=Application, An=Analysis, S=Synthesis, and E−Evaluation)	K 15%, C 30%, Ap 25%, An 20%, S 5%, E 5% (5.56%) K 30%, C 20%, Ap 20%, An 20%, S 10%, E 0% (5.56%) K 30%, C 30%, Ap 20%, An 10%, S 10%, E 0% (5.56%) K 30%, C 25%, Ap 25%, An 10%, S 10%, E 0 % (11.12%) K 20%, C 30%, Ap 20%, An 30%, S 0%, E 0% (11.12%) K 30%, C 30%, Ap 25%, An 25%, S 0%, E 0% (5.56%)

(*continued*)

Table 14.2 (*continued*)

13. When constructing an assessment, to what extent do you consider previous exposure to test items?	I reuse previous test items (11.11%) I revise previous items (88.89%) I never reuse previous items (0%)	
14. If assessment items of other teachers are similar to yours, do you use these items?	Yes (94.44%)	No (5.56%)
15. I am willing to share my assessment information with other teachers.	Yes (94.44%)	No (5.56%)

Perceived usefulness	Mean	Standard deviation
16. Item information from IKMAAS improves educational assessments.	4.17	0.60
17. Using the item-recommendation system enhances the effectiveness in my assessments.	4.22	0.63
18. I find the item-recommendation system useful for assessment.	4.29	0.45
19. Using the item-recommendation system makes assessment easier.	4.17	0.60
Ease of use		
20. It is easy for me to learn how to use the item-recommendation system.	4.06	0.52
21. The item-recommendation system is clear and understandable.	4.06	0.52
22. I believe that it is easy to get the item-recommendation system to do what I want it to do.	4.00	0.88
23. Using the item-recommendation system does not require a lot of mental effort.	4.24	0.63
Attitude		
24. I think that using the item-recommendation system is beneficial.	4.06	0.52

(*continued*)

Table 14.2 (*continued*)

25. I think that the item-recommendation system is worth using.	4.17	0.60
26. I have a positive attitude toward using the item-recommendation system.	4.06	0.52
27. I like using the item-recommendation system.	4.06	0.52
Intentions		
28. If I have access to the IKMAAS, I intend to use the item-recommendation system.	4.00	0.67
29. I plan to increase my use of the item-recommendation system in the future.	3.89	0.87
Satisfaction with the item-recommendation system		
30. The operating instructions and tips are clear and easy to understand.	4.22	0.71
31. Constructing assessments using the item-recommendation system is very convenient.	4.18	0.61
32. The item-recommendation system meets my needs.	4.06	0.52

We also explored teachers' opinions by interview for the usefulness and clarity of the item recommendation mechanism. Some teacher comments are as follows.

- Teacher A: I could refer to the item-recommendation based on other teachers' assessment knowledge to identify or filter redundancy items; I could select the items I wanted.
- Teacher H: It is convenient; I can find similar assessment knowledge teachers' assessment items by using the item-recommendation system, which reduces the time spent constructing a test.
- Teacher K: Although this system helps me construct a test, I think the item-recommendation system could be improved by adding the degree to which an item is recommended.

In general, the teachers thought that this approach serves to improve teachers' assessment work, and most teachers approved of the efficiency and the convenience of the item recommendation and the benefits of its implementation mechanism. It enhanced assessment construction and that the item-recommendation mechanism reduced the time spent constructing assessments. Although a few teachers consistently avoided items recommended by the IKMAAS due to concerns regarding the ability to control for previous item exposure.

In this chapter, the assessment systems (IKMAAS) developed using this approach by clustering teacher assessment knowledge should be easier to maintain and provide more applicable item recommendations. However, it should be noted that this approach requires obtaining teachers' assessment knowledge, which is a time-consuming process that is not included in data mining or statistical approaches. Overall, the results of this study confirm these envisioned benefits. The teachers' responses to the survey questions reveal that most teachers held positive attitudes toward the IKMAAS and its item recommendation mechanism. They agreed that this assessment method was efficient, convenient and time-saving, and that the assessment procedures fostered interaction and reflection.

CHAPTER 15 Summary and Future Work

This book concentrates on the Knowledge Map Assisting Assessment System based on accumulating and visualizing tacit knowledge of teachers, and in particular on the construction and analysis of educational assessment using knowledge maps with weight appraisal of the concepts, accumulating and visualizing tacit knowledge of teachers, and providing personalized item recommendation based on clustering assessment knowledge of teachers. In this chapter, we conclude several study results and with the indication of future work, and opportunities for you to take your interest in The Knowledge Map Assisting Assessment System Based on Accumulating and Visualizing Tacit Knowledge of Teachers Forward.

Sharing teachers' assessment knowledge may be useful in convincing them to use assessment methods found to be effective in certain situations. The phrase, "accumulating assessment knowledge of teachers" as used in this study refers to the elicitation and accumulation of teachers' assessment knowledge; it may or may not refer to a generic assessment theory that is prescriptive in nature. However, it is assumed that the sharing is focused on concept - and item weight - related issues only and that the sharing is done using the collected assessment information in the database. Assessment knowledge - management is effectively utilized during the construction stage of an assessment to enable teachers' assessment experience and knowledge to be captured and reused for similar assessment projects.

The techniques used and reviewed in this study are based mainly on knowledge maps and accumulated teacher assessment knowledge on the computer-assisted assessment. This book proposes a novel methodology that harnesses knowledge maps with a weight appraisal of concepts and concept relationships from which an assessment system for assisting primary school teachers in creating assessments is built. The source of content knowledge for the knowledge maps was obtained from domain-specific assessments developed by teachers. This knowledge was subsequently used to calculate the weight of each concept and the relationships between concepts and test items. In Chapter 12, the prototype assessment system (KMAAS) enabled teachers to analyze and reorganize their collection of test sheets and test items, thereby providing a conceptually-organized method for retrieving test items. This approach is accomplished by performing learning concept extractions and automatic classifications on each test item to establish the associations between concepts and test items. When compiling a test sheet, teachers may refer to an automatically constructed knowledge map that presents the level of importance of specific course concepts and the interrelationship among course concepts and test items. This map helps teachers to understand and evaluate test-item distribution according to the appraised weight of each concept. The map also serves as a useful blueprint for assisting teachers as they design various assessment projects. Moreover, teachers can use KMAAS to create and manage their own assessment e-portfolios and to share their portfolios with each other via the network. KMAAS has been evaluated with respect to the accuracy of learning concept extraction and user satisfaction by way of a questionnaire given to those teachers who tested the system. The results indicate that KMAAS has high potential for succeeding and high practical value in the ICT-based educational assessment domain. Furthermore, the results show definitely that this method can assist teachers with assessment development.

In Chapter 13, the operational IKMAAS uses knowledge maps to show the weights and to provide teachers with comprehensive knowledge during the arrangement and construction phase of their assessments. Because of its power to collect teachers' assessment knowledge and organize it into concrete knowledge maps, the IKMAAS assists teachers in constructing assessments with great confidence. For veteran teachers, knowledge maps provide a visual overview of the distribution of concepts among the test items, thereby helping them to avoid neglecting important concepts on an assessment. For those teachers without much experience, knowledge maps and the accumulation of the experience and knowledge of veteran teachers help them to realize the relative importance of the concepts to be tested. Furthermore, the knowledge maps help them to arrange test items with a proper ratio reflective of the relative importance of the concepts. Finally, in the last stage of our study, we added clustering technology for the teachers' assessment preferences and an item recommendation approach, and integrated both into the IKMAAS. Some appropriate candidate items could be recommended to teachers by IKMAAS according to different teachers' assessment preferences. Finally, IKMAAS reduces the time that teachers spend on item selection, identifying the most appropriate items based on the individual teacher's specifications.

In Chapter 14, we persistently described an item-recommendation that utilizes clusters of teachers' assessment knowledge to provide appropriate items and facilitate to primary school teachers' assessment construction. The personalized item-recommendation mechanism was built out and integrated in the IKMAAS. A two round assessment activity was designed in this chapter. The first-round activity's historic assessment portfolio is being used to as the predefined data format, by clustering teachers' assessment behaviors and find out these similar item selection behaviors. A series of item recommendation policies are carried out in the second-round assessment activity. The effectiveness of item recommendation is evaluated by examining the system usage logs and user questionnaire responses. The results indicate that the item recommendation based on clustering teacher assessment knowledge indeed benefit to help primary school teachers on assessment construction. Therefore, the item recommendation served on the IKMAAS by the cluster algorithm to gathering teacher assessment information, generate the "friends" group, and then retrieve the item recommendation. The IKMAAS was initially designed to promote assessment collaboration and knowledge-sharing among different teachers. The IKMAAS has a small-grained focus on items sharing and provide teachers a convenient assessment environment they can construct, especially emphasize assessment knowledge sharing among teachers. In certain extent it allows teachers to work "together apart" by sharing their assessment knowledge and allows instructors to share "craft wisdom" in a professional online assessment culture.

Although the present study used the IKMAAS to evaluate science and technology curricula found with its related items or assessments in elementary school in Taiwan, China it is possible to use the system for other subjects and curricula without making any changes other than uploading different assessment files and test items. The IKMAAS uses only well-developed methodologies and technologies, which makes it domain-independent and highly flexible for transfer to another course domains. For other subject course material, test items, and test sheets, using KMAAS would require no further labor work than download/upload and creating files. In the near future, we will extend the depth and breadth of the IKMAAS in several technical ways, such as increasing the volume of test items, covering diverse course materials to cater for different teachers' requirements, improving the user interface to make the system more appealing to teachers is also an urgent work. Furthermore, on-going improvements to the IKMAAS include providing suitable item recommendations in compliance with the teachers' personal needs, calculating an algorithm that can leverage the acceptance of the recommendations, establishing incentive policies to encourage teachers to contribute their assessment experience and knowledge, and improving the design of the item repository and the recommendation engine to increase the desire to contribute. Future research will also investigate clustering procedures should examine larger samples of teachers, different assessment topics and obtain more extensive teacher assessment profiles. In particular, other data-mining algorithms, clustering algorithms that do not require teachers to specify any parameters could also be examined to assist educational assessment construction.

Reference

Abecker, A., Bernardi, A., Hinkelmann, K., Kühn, O., & Sintek, M. (1997). *Towards a well-founded technology for organizational memories.* In Proceedings of the AAAI Spring Symposium on Artificial Intelligence in Knowledge Management.

Abel, R., &Kulhavy, R. (1986). Maps, mode of text presentation, and children's prose learning. *American Educational Research Journal, 23*(2), 263-274.

Agarwal, R., Edwards, S. H., & Perez-Quinones, M. A. (2006). Designing an adaptive learning module to teach software testing. *ACM SIGCSE Bulletin, 38*(1), 259-263.

Agor, W. H. (1987). The logic of intuition: How top executives make important decisions. *Organizational Dynamics, 14*(3), 5-18.

Ainsworth, S. (2006). DeFT: A conceptual framework for considering learning with multiple representations. *Learning and Instruction, 16*(3), 183-198.

Airasian, P. W., & Russell, M. K. (2001). *Classroom Assessment: Concepts and Applications*. Boston: McGraw-Hill.

Al-Smadi, M., & Gütl, C. (2008). Past, present and future of e-assessment: Towards a flexible e-assessment system. Paper presented at the proceedings of ICL 2008, Liuach.

Alavi, M., & Haley, B. (1999). Knowledge management systems: Implications and opportunities for data warehousing. *Journal of Data Warehousing, 4*(1), 2-7.

Alavi, M., & Leidner, D. E. (1999). Knowledge management systems:

issues, challenges, and benefits. *Communications of the AIS, 1*(2), 1.

Alavi, M., & Leidner, D. E. (2001). Review: Knowledge management and knowledge management systems: Conceptual foundations and research issues. *MIS Quarterly, 25*(1), 107-136.

Alshawi, H. (1992). *The core language engine.* Cambridge, MA: The MIT Press.

Amer, A. A. (1994). The effect of knowledge-map and underlining training on the reading comprehension of scientific texts. *English for Specific Purposes, 13*(1), 35-45.

Anderson, L. W., Krathwohl, D. R., & Bloom, B. S. (2001). A taxonomy for learning, teaching, and assessing: A revision of bloom's taxonomy of educational objectives. Boston: Allyn & Bacon.

Anderson, T. H., & Armbruster, B. B. (1985). Studying strategies and their implications for textbook design. *Designing Usable Texts*, 159-177.

Arkoudis, S., & O'Loughlin, K. (2004). Tensions between validity and outcomes: teacher assessment of written work of recently arrived immigrant ESL students. *Language Testing, 21*(3), 284-304.

Ashton, H. S., Beevers, C. E., Korabinski, A. A., & Youngson, M. A. (2006). Incorporating partial credit in computer-aided assessment of Mathematics in secondary education. *British Journal of Educational Technology, 37*(1), 93-119.

Ausubel, D. (1968). *Educational Psychology: A Cognitive Approach.* New York: Holt, Rinehart and Winston.

Böhm, K., Heyer, G., Quasthoff, U., & Wolff, C. (2002). Topic map generation using text mining. *Jaurud of Universal sctence, 8*(6), 623-643.

Baartman, L. K. J., Bastiaens, T. J., Kirschner, P. A., & Van der Vleuten, C. P. M. (2007). Teachers' opinions on quality criteria for Competency Assessment Programs. *Teaching and Teacher Education, 23*(6), 857-867.

Balabanović, M., & Shoham, Y. (1997). Fab: content-based, collaborative recommendation. *Communications of the ACM, 40*(3), 66-72.

Baniulis, K., & Rĕklaitis, V. (2002). Testtool: web-based testing, assessment, learning. *Informatics in Education-An International*, 17-30.

Barak, M., & Rafaeli, S. (2004). On-line question-posing and peer-assessment as means for web-based knowledge sharing in learning. *International Journal of Human-Computer Studies, 61*(1), 84-103.

Barki, H., Rivard, S., & Talbot, J. (1993). A keyword classification scheme for IS research literature: An update. *MIS Quarterly*, 209-226.

Basili, R., &Pazienza, M. (1997). Lexical acquisition for information extraction. *Lecture Notes in Computer Science*, 44-72.

Basilico, J., & Hofmann, T. (2004). *Unifying collaborative and content-based filtering*. In Proceedings of the twenty-first international conference on Machine learning.

Baumard, P. (1999). *Tacit Knowledge in Organizations*. London: Sage.

Bennett, R. E. (2004). How the Internet will help large-scale assessment reinvent itself. In M.Rbinowitz, F.C. Blumberg, H.T. Everson (ed.), *The Design of Instruction and Evaluation: Affordances of Using Media and Technology*, 101-108.

Bergendahl, C., & Tibell, L. (2005). Boosting complex learning by strategic assessment and course design. *Journal of Chemical Education, 82*(4), 645.

Bergmann, R. (2002). *Experience management: Foundations, development methodology, and internet-based applications*. Berlin: Springer-Verlag.

Black, P., & Wiliam, D. (1998). Assessment and classroom learning. *Assessment in Education, 5*(1), 7-74.

Blair, D. C. (2002). Knowledge management: hype, hope, or help? *Journal of the American Society for Information Science and Technology, 53*(12), 1019-1028.

Bloom, B. S., Engelhart, M., Furst, E. J., Hill, W. H., & Krathwohl, D. R. (1956). *Taxonomy of educational objectives*. Handbook I: Cognitive Domain. New York: David McKay.

Bloom, B. S., & Krathwohl, D. R. (1956). *Taxonomy of educational objectives: The classification of educational goals*. Handbook I: Cognitive Domain. New York: David Mckay.

Bloom, B. S., Madaus, G. F., & Hastings, J. T. (1981). *Evaluation to improve learning*. New York: Mc Graw-Hill.

Bonham, S. W., Beichner, R. J., Titus, A., & Martin, L. (2000). Education research using web-based assessment systems. *Journal of Research on Computing in Education, 33*(1), 28-45.

Bowden, J. A., Bowden, J., & Marton, F. (1998). *The university of learning*. New York: Psychology Press.

Bransford, J., Brown, A., & Cocking, R. (2000). How *people learn*: *Mind, brain, experience and school, expanded edition*. Washington DC: The National Academy Press.

Breese, J. S., Heckerman, D., & Kadie, C. (1998). *Empirical analysis of predictive algorithms for collaborative filtering*. In Proceedings of the Fourteenth Conference on Uncertainty in Artificial Intelligence.

Bridgeman, B. (2009). Experiences from large-scale computer-based testing in the USA. In F. Scheuermann & J. Björnsson (Ed.), *The Transition to Computer-Based Assessment*, 39-44.

Brown, G. A., Bull, J., & Pendlebury, M. (2013). *Assessing student learning in higher education*. New York: Routledge.

Brown, J., Hinze, S., & Pellegrino, J. W. (2008). Technology and formative assessment. *21st Century Education, 2*, 246-255.

Brown, S. A., & Glasner, A. (1999). Assessment matters in higher *education: Choosing and using diverse approaches*. New York McGraw-Hill International.

Browne, G. J., Curley, S. P., & Benson, P. G. (1997). Evoking information in probability assessment: knowledge maps and reasoning-based directed questions. *Management Science, 43*(1), 1-14.

Brusilovsky, P. (1999). Adaptive and intelligent technologies for web-based eduction. In: C. Rollinger and C. Peylo (Ed.) *Künstliche lntelligent, Special lssue on lutelligent Systerns and Teleteaching*, *4*, 19-25.

Burgess, G. A. (2005). Introduction to programming: blooming in America. *Journal of Computing Sciences in Colleges, 21*(1), 19-28.

Burke, R. (2002). Hybrid recommender systems: Survey and experiments. *User Modeling and User-adapted Interaction, 12*(4), 331-370.

Burkhard, R. A. (2005). Towards a framework and a model for knowledge visualization: synergies between information and knowledge visualization. *Knowledge and Information Visualization*. Berlin: Springer.

Burkhard, R. A., & Meier, M. (2005). Tube Map Visualization: Evaluation of a Novel Knowledge Visualization Application for the Transfer of Knowledge in Long-Term Projects." *Journal of Universal Computer Science.11*(4), 473-494.

Burkhardt, H., & Pead, D. (2003). Computer-based assessment: a platform for better tests. In C. Richardson (Ed.), Whither assessment. London: Qualifications and Curriculum Authority.

Buzan, T., & Buzan, B. (1993). *The mind map book.* New Delhi: Rajpal & Sons.

Cañas, A. J., Carff, R., Hill, G., Carvalho, M., Arguedas, M., Eskridge, T. C., & Carvajal, R. (2005). Concept maps: Integrating knowledge and information visualization. *Knowledge and information visualization.* Berlin: Springer.

Cañas, A., Coffey, J., Carnot, M. J, Feltovich, P. J, Hoffman, R. R., & Novak, J. (2003). A summary of literature pertaining to the use of concept mapping techniques and technologies for education and performance support. Technical Report submitted to the US Navy Chief of Naval Education and Training. Pensacola, FL: Institute for Human and Machine Cognition.

Carrell, P. L., Pharis, B. G., & Liberto, J. C. (1989). Metacognitive strategy training for ESL reading. *Tesol Quarterly, 23*(4), 647-678.

Carroll, T., & Moody, L. (2006). Teacher-made tests. *Science Scope*, 66-67.

Carvalho, M., Hewett, R., & Cañas, A. J. (2001). Enhancing web searches from concept map-based knowledge models. In Proceedings of the SCI 2001 Conference. Orlando, FL: AAAI Press.

Chamoso, J. M., &Ca'ceres, M. J. (2009). Analysis of the reflections of student-teachers of mathematics when working with learning portfolios in Spanish university classrooms. *Teaching and Teacher Education, 25*(1), 198-206.

Chang, C.-C., Tseng, K.-H., & Lou, S.-J. (2012). A comparative analysis of the consistency and difference among teacher-assessment, student self-assessment and peer-assessment in a web-based portfolio assessment environment for high school students. *Computers & Education, 58*(1), 303-320.

Chang, J. C., Chiu, Y. P., Lin, Y. Y., & Heh, J. S. (2003). *Learning diagnosis process with SCORM Compatible learning materials.* Paper presented at the conference of WISCS 2003.

Chartrand, G., & Oellermann, O. R. (1993). Applied and algorithmic graph theory. New York. McGraw-Hill.

Chen, C.-h. (2010). The implementation and evaluation of a mobile self- and peer-assessment system. *Computers & Education, 55*(1), 229-236.

Chen, C. M., & Chen, M. C. (2009). Mobile formative assessment tool based on data mining techniques for supporting web-based learning. *Computers & Education, 52*(1), 256-273.

Chen, K.-J., & Ma, W.-Y. (2002). *Unknown word extraction for Chinese documents.* Paper presented at the Proceedings of the 19th International Conference on Computational Linguistics - Volume 1.

Chen, M. S., Han, J., & Yu, P. S. (1996). Data mining: An overview from a database perspective. *IEEE Transactions on Knowledge and data Engineering, 8*(6), 866-883.

Chen, N.-S., Wei C.-W., & Chen, H.-J. (2008). Mining e-Learning domain concept map from academic articles. *Computers & Education, 50*(3), 1009-1021.

Chen, Y.-L., Cheng, L.-C., & Chuang, C.-N. (2008). A group recommendation system with consideration of interactions among group members. Expert Systems with Applications, *34*(3), 2082-2090.

Chen, Y. Y., & Xia, H. S. (2009). Research on the Auto-construction Methods of Concept Map. Paper presented at the Intelligent Human-Machine Systems and Cybernetics, 2009.

Cheng, S.-Y., Lin, C.-S. Chen, H.-H., & Heh, J.-S. (2005). Learning and diagnosis of individual and class conceptual perspectives: an intelligent systems approach using clustering techniques. *Computers & Education, 44*(3), 257-283. doi: http://dx.doi.org/10.1016/j.compedu.2004.02.005

Chetty, M. (2000). A scheme for on-line Web-based assessment. *Engineering Science & Education Journal, 9*(1), 27-32.

Cheung, K.-W., Kwok, J. T., Law, M. H., & Tsui, K.-C. (2003). Mining customer product ratings for personalized marketing. *Decision Support Systems, 35*(2), 231-243.

Chiasson, T., Hawkey, K., McAllister, M., & Slonim, J. (2002). An architecture in support of universal access to electronic commerce. *Information and Software Technology, 44*(5), 279-289.

Chien, L.-F. (1997). *PAT-tree-based keyword extraction for Chinese information retrieval.* Paper presented at the ACM SIGIR Forum.

Cho, Y. H., & Kim, J. K. (2004). Application of web usage mining and product taxonomy to collaborative recommendations in e-commerce. *Expert Systems with Applications, 26*(2), 233-246.

Cho, Y. H., Kim, J. K., & Kim, S. H. (2002). A personalized recommender system based on web usage mining and decision tree induction. *Expert Systems with Applications,* 23(3), 329-342.

Choren, R., Blois, M., & Fuks, H. (1998). *Quest: an assessment tool for web-based learning*. In proceedings of Webnet' 98 World Conference of the WWW, lnternet and lntranet. Orlando, EUA.

Chou, C., & Lin, H. (1998). The effect of navigation map types and cognitive styles on learners' performance in a computer-networked hypertext learning system. *Journal of Educational Multimedia and Hypermedia, 7*(2-3), 151-176.

Chou, S. W., & Liu, C. H. (2005). Learning Effectiveness in A Web based virtual learning Environment: A Learner Control perspective. *Journal of Computer Assisted Learning, 21*(1): 65-76.

Chu, K.-K., Lee, C.-I., & Tsai, R.-S. (2011). Ontology technology to assist learners' navigation in the concept map learning system. *Expert Systems with Applications, 38*(9), 11293-11299.

Chung, W., Chen, H., & Nunamaker Jr, J. F. (2003). Business intelligence explorer: a knowledge map framework for discovering business intelligence on the Web. ln Proceedings of the 36th Annual Hawaii lnternational Conference on System Science (HICSS' 03).

Cizek, G., Fitzgerald, S., &Rachor, R. (1995). Teachers' assessment practices: preparation, isolation, and the kitchen sink. *Educational Assessment, 3*(2), 159-179.

Cizek, G. J. (1997). Learning, achievement, and assessment: Constructs at a crossroads. *Handbook of classroom assessment: learning, achievement, and adjustment*, 1-32. Salt Lake City : Academic Press.

Clark, H. H., & Wasow, T. (1998). Repeating words in spontaneous speech. *Cognitive Psychology, 37*(3), 201-242.

Clifton, C., Cooley, R., & Rennie, J. (2004). TopCat: data mining for topic identification in a text corpus. *IEEE Transactions on Knowledge and Data Engineering, 16*(8), 949-964.

Cluster Analysis (n. d.). In Wikipedia. Retrieved February 4, 2014, from http://en. wikipedia. org/wiki/Cluster. analysis.

Conca, L., Schechter, C., & Castle, S. (2004). Challenges teachers face as they work to connect Assessment and instruction. *Techners and Teaching, 10*(1), 59-75.

Conole, G., & Warburton, B. (2005). A review of computer-assisted assessment. *Journal of the Association for Learning Technology, 13*(1): 17-31.

Costa, A. L., &Garmston, R. J. (2002). *Cognitive coaching: A foundation for renaissance schools*. Norwood, MA: Christopher-Gordon Publishers, Inc.

Crampes, M., Ranwez, S., Villerd, J., Velickovski, F., Mooney, C., Emery, A., & Mille, N. (2006). Concept maps for designing adaptive knowledge maps. *Information Visualization, 5*(3), 211-224.

Crespo, R. G., Martínez, O. S., Lovelle, J. M. C., García-Bustelo, B. C. P., Gayo, J. E. L., & Pablos, P. O. d. (2011). Recommendation System based on user interaction data applied to intelligent electronic books. *Computers in Human Behavior, 27*, 1445-1449.

Csapó, B., Ainley, J., Bennett, R. E., Latour, T., & Law, N. (2012). Technological issues for computer-based assessment and teaching of 21st century skills. Berlin: Springer.

Czerniak, C. M., & Haney, J. J. (1998). The effect of collaborative concept mapping on elementary preservice teachers' anxiety, efficacy, and achievement in physical science. *Journal of Science Teacher Education, 9*(4), 303-320.

Davenport, T. H., & Prusak, L. (2000). *Working knowledge: How organizations manage what they know.* Watertown: Harvard Business Publishing.

Davison, C. (2004). The contradictory culture of teacher-based assessment: ESL teacher assessment practices in Australian and Hong Kong secondary schools. *Language Testing, 21*(3), 305-334.

Dhillon, I. S., & Modha, D. S. (2001). Concept decompositions for large sparse text data using clustering. *Machine Learning, 42*(1-2), 143-175.

Dicheva, D., & Dichev, C. (2006). TM4L: Creating and browsing educational topic maps. *British Journal of Educational Technology, 37*(3), 391-404.

Dodge, M. (2000). *News Maps: topographic mapping of information.* Atlas of Cyberspace. Upper saddle River, NJ: Addison-Wesley.

Doyle, L. B. (1961). Semantic road maps for literature searchers. *Journal of the ACM , 8*(4), 553-578.

Edwards, D., & Hardman, L. (1999). Lost in hyperspace. Cognitive Mapping and navigation in a hypertext environment. In R. McAleese. *Hypertext: Theory into Practice,* 90-105.

Eisenhardt, K. M. (1989). Making fast strategic decisions in high-velocity environments. *Academy of Management Journal, 32*(3), 543-576.

El-Alfy, E., & Abdel-Aal, R. (2008). Construction and analysis of educational tests using abductive machine learning. *Computers & Education, 51*(1), 1-16.

Ellson, J., Gansner, E., Koutsofios, E., North, S., & Woodhull, G. (2003). Graphviz and dynagraph-static and dynamic graph drawing tools. *Graph Drawing Software*, 127-148.

Eppler, M. J. (2001). *Making knowledge visible through intranet knowledge maps: concepts, elements, cases.* Paper presented at the System Sciences, 2001. In Proceedings of the 34th Annual Hawaii International Conference on Sytem Science.

Eppler, M. J. (2004). Knowledge visualization - Towards a new discipline and its fields of application. Working Paper, Wirtschaftsinformatik.

Firdausiah Mansur, A. B., & Yusof, N. (2013). Social learning network analysis model to identify learning patterns using ontology clustering techniques and meaningful learning. *Computers & Education, 63*, 73-86.

Fisher, K., Faletti, J., & Quinn, C. (1990). Exploring cognitive structure with semantic networks. *SemNet Research Group Technical Report*, c/o Fisher, San Diego State University.

Frey, B. B., Petersen, S., Edwards, L. M., Pedrotti, J. T., & Peyton, V. (2005). Item-writing rules: Collective wisdom. *Teaching and Teacher Education, 21*(4), 357-364.

Fu, X., Budzik, J., & Hammond, K. J. (2000). *Mining navigation history for recommendation.* Paper presented at the Proceedings of the 5th International Conference on Intelligent User Interfaces.

Gómez, A., Moreno, A., Pazos, J., & Sierra-Alonso, A. (2000). Knowledge maps: An essential technique for conceptualisation. *Data & Knowledge Engineering, 33*(2), 169-190.

Gaines, B. R., & Shaw, M. L. G. (1995). Concept maps as hypermedia components. *International Journal of Human-Computer Studies, 43*, 323-361.

Ghani, R., & Fano, A. (2002). Building recommender systems using a knowledge base of product semantics. Paper presented at the Proceedings of the Workshop on Recommendation and Personalization in E-Commerce at the 2nd International Conference on Adaptive Hypermedia and Adaptive Web based Systems.

Goldberg, D., Nichols, D., Oki, B. M., & Terry, D. (1992). Using collaborative filtering to weave an information tapestry. *Communications of the ACM, 35*(12), 61-70.

Gong, S. (2010). An Efficient Collaborative Recommendation Algorithm Based on Item Clustering. *Advances in Wireless Networks and Information Systems. 72*, 381-389.

Goodison, T. (2002). Learning with ICT at primary level: pupils' perceptions. *Journal of Computer Assisted Learning, 18*(3): 282-295.

Gordon, J. L. (2000). Creating knowledge maps by exploiting dependent relationships. *Knowledge-Based Systems, 13*(2): 71-79.

Gray Southon, F., Todd, R. J., & Seneque, M. (2002). Knowledge management in three organizations: an exploratory study. *Journal of the American Society for Information Science and Technology, 53*(12), 1047-1059.

Grey, D. (1999). *Knowledge mapping: a practical overview.* available at http://www.impactalliance.org/file_download.php?location=S_U&filename=1 0383546681Knowledge_Mapping.htm Retrieved 9.14, 2009.

Griffith, B. C., Small, H. G., Stonehill, J. A., & Dey, S. (1974). The structure of scientific literatures II: Toward a macro-and microstructure for science. *Social Studies of Science, 4*(4), 339-365.

Gunel, K., & Nuriyev, U. (2009). Relation extraction among learning concepts in intelligent tutoring systems. Paper presented at the conference of the Application of Information and Communication Technologies (AICT 2009)

Guri-Rozenblit, S. (1989). Effects of a tree diagram on students' comprehension of main ideas in an expository text with multiple themes. *Reading Research Quarterly. 24*(2), 236-247

Hall, R. H., Dansereau, D. F., & Skaggs, L. P. (1992). Knowledge maps and the presentation of related information domains. *The Journal of Experimental Education, 61*(1), 5-18.

Hall, R., Balestra, J., & Davis, M. (2000). *A navigational analysis of linear and non-linear hypermedia interfaces.* Paper presented at the the annual meeting of the American Educational Research Association, New Orelans, LA.

Hall, R. H., & O'Donnell, A. (1996). Cognitive and affective outcomes of learning from knowledge maps. *Contemporary Educational Psychology, 21*(1), 94-101.

Han, J., Lee, J.-G., & Kamber, M. (2009). An overview of clustering methods in geographic data analysis. *Geographic Data Mining and Knowledge Discovery, 2*, 149-170.

Han, J., Kamber, M., & Pei, J. (2011). *Data mining: Concepts and techniques*. New York: Morgan Kaufmann Publishers.

He, L. (2006). A novel web-based educational assessment system with Bloom's taxonomy. *Current Developments in Technology-Assisted Education*, Badajoz, Spain, 3, 1861-1865.

He, Q., & Tymms, P. (2005). A computer-assisted test design and diagnosis system for use by classroom teachers. *Journal of Computer Assisted Learning, 21*(6), 419-429.

Heard, S., Nicol, J., & Heath, S. (1997). *Setting effective objective tests* University of Aberdeen, Centre for Educational Development, CTI Centre for Land Use and Environmental Sciences and the Department of Geography.

Herl, H., O'Neil Jr, H., Chung, G., & Schacter, J. (1999). Reliability and validity of a computer-based knowledge mapping system to measure content understanding. *Computers in Human Behavior, 15*(3), 315-333.

Herlocker, J. L., & Konstan, J. A. (2001). Content-independent task-focused recommendation. *Journal of IEEE Internet Computing, 5*(6), 40-47.

Herlocker, J. L., Konstan, J. A., &Riedl, J. (2000). Explaining collaborative filtering recommendations. Paper presented at the ACM conference on Computer supported cooperative Work, 241-250.

Herschel, R. T., Nemati, H., & Steiger, D. (2001). Tacit to explicit knowledge conversion: knowledge exchange protocols. *Journal of Knowledge Management, 5*(1), 107-116.

Hill, W., Stead, L., Rosenstein, M., & Furnas, G. (1995). *Recommending and evaluating choices in a virtual community of use.* Paper presented at the Proceedings of the SIGCHI conference on Human factors in computing systems.

Holley, C. D., & Dansereau, D. F. (1984). *Spatial Learning Strategies: Techniques, Applications and Related Issues*. Salt Lake City: Academic Press.

Hou, X., Ong, S.-K., Nee, A. Y.-C., Zhang, X., & Liu, W. (2011).

GRAONTO: A graph-based approach for automatic construction of domain ontology. *Expert Systems with Applications, 38*(9), 11958-11975.

Hsieh, T.-C., Wang, T.-I., Su, C.-Y., & Lee, M.-C. (2011). A fuzzy logic-based personalized learning system for supporting adaptive English learning. *Educational Technology & Society, 15*(1), 273-288.

Hsu, C., Kuo, R., Chang, M., & Heh, J. (2002). *Implementing a problem solving system for physics based on knowledge map and four steps problem solving strategies.* Paper presented at the IEEE 2nd International Conference on Advanced Learning Technologies, Kazan, Russia.

Hsu, C.-N., & Chang, C.-C. (1999). *Finite-state transducers for semi-structured text mining.* Paper presented at the Proceedings of IJCAI-99 Workshop on Text Mining: Foundations, Techniques and Applications.

Huang, J., He, L., & Davidson-Shivers, G. V. (2011). Educational Assessment via a Web-Based Intelligent System. *8* (5), 666-674.

Huang, C.-J., Chen, C.-H., Luo, Y.-C., Chen, H.-X., & Chuang, Y.-T. (2008). Developing an intelligent diagnosis and assessment e-learning tool for introductory programming. *Educational Technology & Society, 11* (4), 139-157.

Huang, Y.-M., Lin, Y.-T., & Cheng, S.-C. (2009). An adaptive testing system for supporting versatile educational assessment. *Computers & Education, 52*(1), 53-67.

Hwang, G., Chu, H., Yin, P., & Lin, J. (2008). An innovative parallel test sheet composition approach to meet multiple assessment criteria for national tests. *Computers & Education, 51*(3), 1058-1072.

Hwang, G. J., Tseng, J. C. R., & Hwang, G. H. (2008). Diagnosing student learning problems based on historical assessment records. *Innovations in Education and Teaching International, 45*(1), 77-89.

Hull, D. (1994). *Improving text retrieval for the routing problem using latent semantic indexing.* Paper presented at the SIGIR'94.

Hung, L.-P. (2005). A personalized recommendation system based on product taxonomy for one-to-one marketing online. *Expert Systems with Applications, 29*(2), 383-392.

Ittycheriah, A., Franz, M., & Roukos, S. (2002). *IBM's Statistical Question Answering System-TREC-10*. In Proceedings of the Tenth Text Retrieval Confenence (TREC. 2011).

Ives, B., & Hoy, C. (2003). Graphic organizers applied to higher-level secondary mathematics. *Learning Disabilities Research & Practice, 18*(1), 36-51.

Jacobson, M. J. (2004). Cognitive visualisations and the design of learning technologies. *International Journal of Learning Technology, 1*(1), 40-62.

Jacobson, M. J., & Archodidou, A. (2000). The design of hypermedia tools for learning: Fostering conceptual change and transfer of complex scientific knowledge. *Journal of the Learning Sciences*, 145-199.

Jia, H., Wang, M., Ran, W., Yang, S. J., Liao, J., & Chiu, D. K. (2011). Design of a performance-oriented workplace e-learning system using ontology. *Expert Systems with Applications, 38*(4), 3372-3382.

Jiang, C., Coenen, F., Sanderson, R., & Zito, M. (2010). Text classification using graph mining-based feature extraction. *Knowledge-based* Systems, *23*(4), 302-308.

Johnson, R., &Wichern, D. (2002). *Applied Multivariate Statistical Analysis* (5th.). New York: Prentice Hall.

Kang, I., Park, Y., & Kim, Y. (2003). A framework for designing a workflow-based knowledge map. *Business Process Management Journal, 9*(3), 281-294.

Kaufman, L., & Rousseeuw, P. J. (1990). Partitioning around medoids (program pam). New York: Wiley.

Kaufman, L., & Rousseeuw, P. J. (2009). *Finding Groups in Data: An Introduction to Cluster Analysis*. New York: John Wiley & Sons.

Keim, D. A., & Kriegel, H.-P. (1994). *Using visualization to support data mining of large existing databases*. Berlin: Springer.

Khan, T. M., Clear, F., & Sajadi, S. S. (2012). *The relationship between educational performance and online access routines: analysis of students' access to an online discussion forum.* Paper presented at the Proceedings of the 2nd International Conference on Learning Analytics and Knowledge.

Kim, H.-G., Fillies, C., Smith, B., & Wikarski, D. (2002). *Visualizing a Dynamic Knowledge Map Using Semantic Web Technology Engineering and Deployment of Cooperative Information Systems.* Berlin: Springer.

Kim, S., Suh, E., & Hwang, H. (2003). Building the knowledge map: an industrial case study. *Journal of Knowledge Management, 7*(2), 34-45.

Kinnersley, N., Mayhew, S., & Hinton, H. S. (2001). *The design of a web-based computer proficiency examination.* Paper presented at the 31st Annual. Frontiers in Education Conference.

King, W., & He, J. (2006). A meta-analysis of the technology acceptance model. *Information & Management, 43*(6), 740-755.

Klosgen, & Zytkow. (2002). *Handbook of Data Mining and Knowledge Discovery.* New York: Oxford University Press.

Knight, K. (1999). Mining Online Text. *Communications of the ACM, 42*(11), 58-61.

Knorr, E. M., Ng, R. T., & Tucakov, V. (2000). Distance-based outliers: algorithms and applications. *The International Journal on Very Large Data Bases, 8* (3-4), 237-253.

Ko, C. C., & Cheng, C. D. (2008). Flexible and secure computer-based assessment using a single zip disk. *Computers & Education, 50*(3), 915-926.

Kohonen, T. (2001). *Self-organizing maps.* Berlin: Springer.

Konstan, J. A., Miller, B. N., Maltz, D., Herlocker, J. L., Gordon, L. R., & Riedl, J. (1997). GroupLens: applying collaborative filtering to Usenet news. *Communications of the ACM, 40*(3), 77-87.

Koong, C.-S., & Wu, C.-Y. (2010). An interactive item sharing website for creating and conducting on-line testing. *Computers & Education, 55*(1), 131-144.

Kozma, R. (2009). Transforming education: Assessing and teaching

21st century skills. In F. Scheuermann & J. Bjornsson (Eds.). *The Transition to Computer-Based Assessment.*

Kremer, R. (1998). *Visual languages for knowledge representation.* In Proceedings of 11th Workshop on Knowledge Acquisition, Modeling and Management (KAW' 98) Banff, Alberta, Canada.

Krishna, K., & NarasimhaMurty, M. (1999). Genetic K-means algorithm. *IEEE Transactions on Systems, Man, and Cybernetics, Part B: Cybernetics, 29*(3), 433-439.

Kuo, C.-Y., & Wu, H.-K. (2013). Toward an integrated model for designing assessment systems: an analysis of the current status of computer-based assessments in science. *Computers & Education. 68*, 388-403

Kuo, R., Lien, W., Chang, M., & Heh, J. (2004). Analyzing problem's difficulty based on neural networks and knowledge map. *Journal of Educational Technologyand Society, 7*, 42-50.

Kuwata, Y., &Yatsu, M. (1997). Managing knowledge using a semantic-network. *AAAI Technical Report, 2*(1), 94-98.

Kveton, P., Jelinek, M., Voboril, D., & Klimusova, H. (2007). Computer-based tests: the impact of test design and problem of equivalency. *Computers in Human Behavior, 23*(1), 32-51.

López-Cuadrado, J., Pérez, T. A., Vadillo, J. Á., & Gutiérrez, J. (2010). Calibration of an item bank for the assessment of Basque language knowledge. *Computers & Education*, *55*(3), 1044-1055.

Lai, J.-Y., Wang, C.-T., & Chou, C.-Y. (2009). How knowledge map fit and personalization affect success of KMS in high-tech firms. *Technovation*, *29*(4), 313-324.

Lambiotte, J. G., Dansereau, D. F., Cross, D. R., & Reynolds, S. B. (1989). Multirelational semantic maps. *Educational Psychology Review, 1*(4), 331-367.

Lang, K. (1995). Newsweeder: Learning to filter net news. In Proceedings of the Twelfth International Conference on Machine Learning.

Larkin, J., & Simon, H. (1987). Why a diagram is worth ten thousand words. *Cognitive Science*, *11*(1), 65-100.

Lazarinis, F., Green, S., & Pearson, E. (2010). Creating personalized assessments based on learner knowledge and objectives in a hypermedia Web testing application. *Computers & Education, 55*(4), 1732-1743.

Lee, H.-Y., & Ong, H.-L. (1996). Visualization support for data mining. *IEEE Intelligent Systems, 11*(5), 69-75.

Lee, J. H., & Segev, A. (2012). Knowledge maps for e-learning. *Computers & Education, 59*(2), 353-364.

Lee, W.-P., Liu, C.-H., & Lu, C.-C. (2002). Intelligent agent-based systems for personalized recommendations in Internet commerce. *Expert Systems with Applications, 22*(4), 275-284.

Leydesdorff, L., Cozzens, S., & Van den Besselaar, P. (1994). Tracking areas of strategic importance using scientometric journal mappings. *Research Policy, 23*(2), 217-229.

Leydesdorff, L., & Rafols, I. (2009). A global map of science based on the ISI subject categories. *Journal of the American Society for Information Science and Technology, 60*(2), 348-362.

Li, J.-J., & Choi, K.-S. (1997). Corpus-based Chinese-Korean abstracting translation system. Paper presented at the IJCAI (2).

Li, X., & Roth, D. (2002). Learning question classifiers. Paper presented at the Proceedings of the 19th International Conference on Computational Linguistics, Taipei, Taiwan, China.

Li, X., & Roth, D. (2006). Learning question classifiers: the role of semantic information. Natural Language Engineering, *12*(3), 229-249.

Li, Y., Chung, S. M., & Holt, J. D. (2008). Text document clustering based on frequent word meaning sequences. *Data & Knowledge Engineering, 64*(1), 381-404.

Li, Z., & Xing, L. (1998). *Search the Chinese Web-design and the operation of net-compass*. In Proceedings of the first Asia digital library workshop.

Liang, T.-P., Yang, Y.-F., Chen, D.-N., & Ku, Y.-C. (2008). A semantic-expansion approach to personalized knowledge recommendation. *Decision Support Systems, 45*(3), 401-412.

Liebowitz, J. (1999). *Knowledge management handbook.* Cleveland, OH:

CRC press.

Liebowitz, J. (2000). Building organizational intelligence: A knowledge management primer (Vol. 1). Cleveland, OH: CRC press.

Liebowitz, J. (2005). Linking social network analysis with the analytic hierarchy process for knowledge mapping in organizations. *Journal of Knowledge Management, 9*(1), 76-86.

Lin, F.-r., & Hsueh, C.-m. (2006). Knowledge map creation and maintenance for virtual communities of practice. *Information Processing & Management, 42*(2), 551-568.

Lin, Y.-C., & Tserng, H. P. (2003). Knowledge management and its application to Lean Construction. Paper presented at the Proceedings of Eleventh Annual Conference of the International Group for Lean Construction (IGLC-11).

Lin, Y.-C., Wang, L.-C., & Tserng, H. P. (2006). Enhancing knowledge exchange through web map-based knowledge management system in construction: Lessons learned in Taiwan. *Automation in Construction, 15*(6), 693-705.

Lippmann, R. P. (1987). An introduction to computing with neural nets. *IEEE Signal Processing Magzine, 4*(2), 4-22.

Liu, L., Li, J., &Lv, C. (2009). A Method for Enterprise Knowledge Map Construction Based on Social Classification. *Systems Research and Behavioral Science, 26*, 143-153.

Low, G. (2004). Graphviz - Graph Visualization Software. From http://www.graphviz.org/About.php.

Luhn, H. (1999). The automatic creation of literature abstracts. Advances in Automatic Text Summarization, 15.

Ma, W.-Y., & Chen, K.-J. (2003). Introduction to CKIP Chinese word segmentation system for the first international Chinese Word Segmentation Bakeoff. Paper presented at the Proceedings of the second SIGHAN workshop on Chinese language processing, *17*, 168-171.

Maclellan, E. (2004). Initial knowledge states about assessment: novice teachers' conceptualizations. *Teaching and Teacher Education*, *20*(5), 523-535.

Madaus, & Hastings (1981) Malhotra, Y. (2000). *Knowledge Management and Virtual Organizations*. Hershey: IGI Global.

Markman, A. B. (2013). *Knowledge Representation*. New York: Psychology Press.

McCagg, E. C., & Dansereau, D. F. (1991). A convergent paradigm for examining knowledge mapping as a learning strategy. *The Journal of Educational Research, 84*(6), 317-324.

McClure, J. R., Sonak, B., & Suen, H. K. (1999). Concept map assessment of classroom learning: Reliability, validity, and logistical practicality. *Journal of Research in Science Teaching*, 36(4), 475-492.

McDonald, A. S. (2002). The impact of individual differences on the equivalence of computer-based and-paper-and pencil educational assessments. *Computers & Education, 39*(3): 299-312.

McMillan, J. H., & Workman, D. J. (1998). *Classroom Assessment and Grading Practices: A Review of the Literature*. Refrieved from ERIC database (NO. ED' 453263).

Meng, A., Ye, L., Roy, D., & Padilla, P. (2007). Genetic algorithm based multi-agent system applied to test generation. *Computers & Education, 49*(4), 1205-1223.

Mertins, K., Heisig, P., &Vorbeck, J. (2003). *Knowledge management: Concepts and best practices*. Berlin: Springer-Verlag.

Michalski, R. S., & Stepp, R. E. (1983). Learning from Observation: *Conceptual Clustering Machine Learning*. Berlin: Springer.

Miller, H. J., & Han, J. (2009). *Geographic Data Mining and Knowledge Discovery*. Cleveland, OH: CRC Press.

Mitri, M. (2003). Applying tacit knowledge management techniques for performance assessment. *Computers & Education, 41*(2), 173-189.

Mirza, B. J. (2001). Jumping connections: A graph-theoretic model for recommender systems. Virginia Polytechnic Institute and State University.

Mobasher, B., Cooley, R., & Srivastava, J. (2000). Automatic personalization based on Web usage mining. *Communications of the ACM, 43*(8), 142-151.

Mobasher, B., Dai, H. Luo, T., & Nakagawa, M. (2002). Discovery and evaluation of aggregate usage profiles for web personalization. *Data Mining and Knowledge Discovery, 6*(1), 61-82.

Moldovan, D., Harabagiu, S., Pasca, M., Mihalcea, R., Girju, R., Goodrum, R., & Rus, V. (2000). The structure and performance of an open-domain question answering system. Paper presented at the 38th Annual Meeting of the Association for Computational Linguistics, Hong Kong, China.

Mulvenna, M. D., Anand, S. S., & Büchner, A. G. (2000). Personalization on the Net using Web mining: introduction. *Communications of the ACM, 43*(8), 122-125.

Myers, B. A. (1990). Taxonomies of visual programming and program visualization. *Journal of Visual Languages & Computing, 1*(1), 97-123.

Nesbit, J., & Adesope, O. (2005). Dynamic concept maps. Paper presented at the World Conference on Educational Multimedia, Hypermedia and Telecommunications.

Nesbit, J. C., & Adesope, O. O. (2006). Learning with Concept and Knowledge maps: A Meta-Analysis. *Review of Educational Research, 76*(3), 413-448.

Nevin, A., Thousand, J., & Villa, R. (2009). Collaborative teaching for teacher educators—What does the research say? *Teaching and Teacher Education, 25*(4), 569-574.

Noh, J., Lee, K., Kim, J., Lee, J., & Kim, S. (2000). A case-based reasoning approach to cognitive map-driven tacit knowledge management. *Expert Systems with Applications, 19*(4), 249-259.

Nonaka, I. (1991). The knowledge-creating company. *Harvard business review, 69*(6), 96-104.

Nonaka, I. (1994). A dynamic theory of organizational knowledge creation. *Organization science, 5*(1), 14-37.

Nonaka, I. (1995). *The knowledge-creating company: How Japanese companies create the Dynamics of Innovation.* Oxford: Oxford University Press.

Noorbehbahani, F., & Kardan, A. A. (2011). The automatic assessment of free text answers using a modified BLEU algorithm. *Computers & Education, 56*(2), 337-345.

Novak, J. (1979). The reception learning paradigm. *Journal of Research in Science Teaching, 16*(6), 481-488.

Novak, J. D. (1984). *Learning How to Learn*. Cambridge: Cambridge University Press.

Novak, J. D. (2010). *Learning, Creating, and Using Knowledge: Concept Maps as Facilitative Tools in Schools and Corporations*. New York: Routledge.

Novak, J. D., & Cañas, A. J. (2006). The theory underlying concept maps and how to construct them. *Florida Institute for Human and Machine Cognition, 1*.

Novak, J. D., & Gowin, D. B. (1984). *Learning How to Learn*. Cambridge: Cambridge University Press.

Novak, J. D., & Musonda, D. (1991). A twelve-year longitudinal study of science concept learning. *American Educational Research Journal*, 28(1), 117-153.

Nuntiyagul, A., Naruedomkul, K., Cercone, N., & Wongsawang, D. (2008). Adaptable learning assistant for item bank management. *Computers & Education, 50*(1), 357-370.

O'Donnell, A. M., Dansereau, D. F., & Hall, R. H. (2002). Knowledge maps as scaffolds for cognitive processing. *Educational Psychology Review, 14*(1), 71-86.

O'Donnell, A. M., & Dansereau, D. F. (1992). Scripted cooperation in student dyads: A method for analyzing and enhancing academic learning and performance. In R. Hertz Lazarowitz, & N. Miller.(Eds.), *Interaction in cooperative groups: The theoretical anatomy of group learning*. Cambringe: Cambridge University Press.

O'Leary, D., & Selfridge, P. (1999). Knowledge management for best practices. *Intelligence, 10*(4), 12-24.

Oard, D. W., & Kim, J. (1998). Implicit feedback for recommender systems. Paper presented at the Madison, WI: AAAI Workshop on

Recommender Systems.

Oliver, D., Dobele, T., Greber, M., & Roberts, T. (2004). This course has a Bloom Rating of 3.9. In Proceedings of the Sixth Australasian Conference on Computing Education 30.

Ong, T.-H., Chen, H., Sung, W.-k., & Zhu, B. (2005). Newsmap: a knowledge map for online news. *Decision Support Systems, 39*(4), 583-597.

Oosterhof, A. (2003). *Developing and Using classroom Assessments (3 ed.)*. Upper Saddle River, NJ: Merriu/Prentice Hall.

Page, L., Brin, S., Motwani, R., & Winograd, T. (1999). The PageRank citation ranking: Bringing order to the web. Techical Report, Standford Infolab.

Pahl, C. (2006). Data Mining for the Analysis of Content Interaction in Web-based Learning and Training Systems, *4*, 41-53. Billerica, MA: WIT Press.

Palmer, S. (1978). Fundamental aspects of cognitive representation. In Eleanor Rosch & Barbara Lloyd (Eds.), *Cognition and categorization.* Hillsdale, NJ : Erlbaum.

Panjaburee, P., Hwang, G.-J., Triampo, W., & Shih, B.-Y. (2010). A multi-expert approach for developing testing and diagnostic systems based on the concept-effect model. *Computers & Education*, *55*(2), 527-540.

Paolucci, R. (1998). The effects of cognitive style and knowledge structure on performance using a hypermedia learning system. *Journal of Educational Multimedia and Hypermedia, 7*, 123-150.

Papanikolaou, K. A., Grigoriadou, M., Magoulas, G. D., & Kornilakis, H. (2002). Towards new forms of knowledge communication: the adaptive dimension of a web-based learning environment. *Computers & Education, 39*(4), 333-360.

Parshall, C. G. (2002). Practical considerations in computer-based testing. Berlin: Springer.

Patterson, M. E., Dansereau, D. F., & Wiegmann, D. A. (1993). Receiving information during a cooperative episode: effects of communication aids and verbal ability. *Learning and Individual differences, 5*(1), 1-11.

Pazzani, M., Muramatsu, J., & Billsus, D. (1996). Syskill & Webert: Identifying interesting web sites, in AAI Spring Symposium on Machine Learning in Information Access, *Lecture Notes in Computer Science, 11*.

Peat, M. (2000). *Online assessment: The use of web based self assessment materials to support self directed learning*. Paper presented at the Flexible Futures in Tertiary Teaching. In Proceedings of the 9th Annual Teaching Learning Forum.

Pellegrino, J. W., Chudowsky, N., & Glaser, R. (2001). *Knowing what students know: The science and design of educational assessment.* Washington DC: The National Academies Press.

Pepper, S. (2000). The TAO of topic maps. In Proceedings of the of XML Europe 2000, Paris, France.

Phelps, J., & Reynolds, R. (1999). Formative evaluation of a web-based course in meteorology. *Computers & Education, 32*(2), 181-193.

Pirnay-Dummer, P., &Ifenthaler, D. (2010). Automated knowledge visualization and assessment. In D. Ifenthaler, P. Pirnay-Dummer, & N. M. Seel (Eds.), *Computer-Based Diagnostics and Systematic Analysis of Knowledge*, 77-115.

Polanyi, M. (1967). *The Tacit Dimension*. New York: Doubleday Press.

Polanyi, M. (1997). Tacit knowledge. *Knowledge in Organizations-Resources for the knowledge-based economy,* 135-146.Oxford: Butterworth-Heinemann.

Polanyi, M., & Sen, A. (2009). *The Tacit Dimension*. Chicago: University of Chicago Press.

Popham, W. J. (2000). *Modern Educational Measurement: Practical Guidelines for Educational Leaders*. Boston: Allyn and Bacon.

Porter, M. F. (1980). An algorithm for suffix stripping. Program: Electronic Library and Information Systems, *14*(3), 130-137.

Pritchard, A. (1969). Statistical bibliography or bibliometrics. *Journal of Documentation*, *25*(4), 348-349.

Procter, P., & Ayto, J. (1978). Longman dictionary of contemporary English. Harlow: Longman.

Prusak, L., & Davenport, T. (1998). *Working knowledge: How organizations manage what they know*. Boston: Harvard Business Publishing.

Punj, G., & Stewart, D. W. (1983). Cluster analysis in marketing research: review and suggestions for application. *Journal of Marketing Research, 20*(2), 134-148.

Pyo, S. (2005). Knowledge map for tourist destinations—needs and implications. *Tourism Management, 26*(4), 583-594.

Rafaeli, S., Barak, M., Dan-Gur, Y., & Toch, E. (2004). QSIA: a web-based environment for learning, assessing and knowledge sharing in communities. *Computers & Education, 43*(3), 273-289.

Rashid, A. M., Albert, I., Cosley, D., Lam, S. K., McNee, S. M., Konstan, J. A., & Riedl, J. (2002). Getting to know you: learning new user preferences in recommender systems. In Proceedings of the 7th International Conference on Intelligent User Interfaces.

Reed, D. (2006). Diagnostic Assessment in Language Teaching and Learning. Center for Language Education and Research, available at http://www. google. com/url.

Reimann, P., & Zumbach, J. (2003). Supporting virtual learning teams with dynamic feedback. In K. T. Lee & K. Mitchell (Eds.), *The "Second Wave" of ICT in Education: from Facilitating Teaching and Learning to Engendering Education Reform*, 424-430.

Resnick, P., & Varian, H. R. (1997). Recommender systems. *Communications of the ACM*, 40(3), 56-58.

Rewey, K. L., Dansereau, D. F., Dees, S. M. & Skaggs, L. P. (1992). Scripted cooperation and knowledge map supplements: effects on the recall of biological and statistical information. *Journal of Experimental Education. 60*(2), 93-101.

Rewey, K. L., Dansereau, D. F., & Peel, J. L. (1991). "Knowledge maps and information processing strategies. *Contemporary Educational Psychology, 16*(3), 203-214.

Rewey, K. L., Dansereau, D. F., Skaggs, L. P., Hall, R. H., & Pitre, U. (1989). Effects of scripted cooperation and knowledge maps on the processing of technical material. *Journal of Educational Psychology,*

81(4), 604.

Reynolds, S. B., Patterson, M. E., Skaggs, L. P., & Dansereau, D. F. (1991). Knowledge hypermaps and cooperative learning. *Computers & Education, 16*(2), 167-173.

Riecken, D. (2000). Personalized views of personalization. *Communications of the ACM, 43*(8), 27-28.

Romero, C., López, M.-I., Luna, J.-M., & Ventura, S. (2013). Predicting students' final performance from participation in on-line discussion forums. *Computers & Education, 68*(0), 458-472. doi: http://dx.doi.org/10.1016/j.compedu.2013.06.009.

Romero, C., & Ventura, S. (2013). Data mining in education. *Wiley Interdisciplinary Reviews: Data Mining and Knowledge Discovery. 3*(1), 12-27.

Roschelle, J. M., Pea, R. D., Hoadley, C. M., Gordin, D. N., & Means, B. M. (2000). Changing how and what children learn in school with computer-based technologies. *The Future of Children*, 76-101.

Rouse, W. B., Thomas, B. S., & Boff, K. R. (1998). Knowledge maps for knowledge mining, Application to R&D/technology management. *IEEE Transactions on, Systems, Man, and Cybernetics*, *Part C: Applications and Reviews, 28*(3), 309-317.

Ruiz-Martínez, J. M., Valencia-García, R., Fernández-Breis, J. T., García-Sánchez, F., & Martínez-Béjar, R. (2011). Ontology learning from biomedical natural language documents using UMLS. *Expert Systems with Applications, 38*(10), 12365-12378.

Sallis, E., & Jones, G. (2002). *Knowledge Management in Education: Enhancing Learning & Education*. New York: Psychology Press.

Salton, G., & Buckley, C. (1988). Term-weighting approaches in automatic text retrieval. *Information Processing & Management, 24*(5), 513-523.

Salton, G., & McGill, M. (1983). *Introduction to Modern Information Retrieval.* New York: McGraw-Hill.

Salton, G., Wong, A., & Yang, C.-S. (1975). A vector space model for automatic indexing. *Communications of the ACM, 18*(11), 613-620.

Sarkar, M., Yegnanarayana, B., &Khemani, D. (1997). A clustering algorithm using an evolutionary programming-based approach. *Pattern Recognition Letters, 18*(10), 975-986.

Sarwar, B., Karypis, G., Konstan, J., & Riedl, J. (2001). *Item-based collaborative filtering recommendation algorithms.* In Proceedings of the 10th international conference on World Wide Web.

Schafer, J. B., Frankowski, D., Herlocker, J., & Sen, S. (2007). Collaborative filtering recommender systems. *The Adaptive Web.* Berlin: Springer.

Schafer, J. B., Konstan, J. A., & Riedl, J. (2001). E-commerce recommendation applications. *Applications of Data Mining to Electronic Commerce*. Berlin: Springer.

Schwartz, D. G. (2006). *Encyclopedia of Knowledge Management*: San Francisco, CA: IGI Global.

Scott, T. (2003). Bloom's taxonomy applied to testing in computer science classes. *Journal of Computing Sciences in Colleges*, *19*(1), 267-274.

Scriven, M. (1966). *The methodology of evaluation.* Boulder, CO: Social Science Education Consortium.

Sebastiani, F. (2002). Machine learning in automated text categorization. *ACM Computing Surveys (CSUR), 34*(1), 1-47.

Shahabi, C., & Chen, Y.-S. (2003). An adaptive recommendation system without explicit acquisition of user relevance feedback. *Distributed and Parallel Databases, 14*(2), 173-192.

Shardanand, U., & Maes, P. (1995). Social information filtering: algorithms for automating "word of mouth". In Proceedings of the SIGCHI conference on Human factors in computing Systems.

Shaw, R.-S. (2010). A study of learning performance of e-learning materials design with knowledge maps. *Computers & Education, 54*(1), 253-264.

Shepard, L. (2000). The role of assessment in a learning culture. *Educational Researcher, 29*(7), 4-14.

Smith, M., Wood, W., & Knight, J. (2008). The genetics concept assessment: a new concept inventory for gauging student understanding of genetics. *CBE-Life Sciences Education, 7*(4), 422-430.

Snowden, D. (1999). A Framework for Creating A Sustainable Programme, in (Ed.) Rock, Stuart: Knowledge Management: A Real Guide. London: CBI/IBM., 7-17.

So, W. W., Pow, J. W., & Hung, V. H. (2009). The interactive use of a video database in teacher education: Creating a knowledge base for teaching through a learning community. *Computers & Education, 53*(3), 775-786.

Somech, A., & Bogler, R. (1999). Tacit knowledge in academia: its effects on student learning and achievement. *The Journal of Psychology, 133*(6), 605-616.

Song, W., Wenyin, L., Gu, N., Quan, X., & Hao, T. (2011). Automatic categorization of questions for user-interactive question answering. *Information Processing & Management, 47*(2), 147-156.

Speel, P., Shadbolt, N., Vries, W., Dam, P., & O'hara, K. (1999). Knowledge mapping for industrial purposes. In Proceedings of the 12th Workshop on Knowledge Acquisition, Modeling and Management, Alberta, Canada.

Stenmark, D. (2001). Leveraging Tacit Organizational Knowledge." *Journal of Management Information Systems, 17*(3), 9-24.

Sternberg, R. J. (2000). *Practical Intelligence in Everyday Life*. Cambridge: Cambridge University Press.

Stiggins, R. J., & Conklin, N. F. (1992). *In teachers' hands: Investigating the practices of classroom assessment*. New York: State University of New York Press.

Stoyanova, N., & Kommers, P. (2002). Concept mapping as a medium of shared cognition in computer-supported collaborative problem solving. *Journal of Interactive Learning Research, 13*(1), 111-133.

Su, C., & Wang, T. (2010). Construction and analysis of educational assessments using knowledge maps with weight appraisal of concepts. *Computers & Education, 55*(3), 1300-1311.

Sung, Y.-T., Chang, K.-E., Chiou, S.-K., &Hou, H.-T. (2005). The design and application of a web-based self- and peer-assessment system.

Computers & Education, 45(2), 187-202.

Sveiby, K. E. (1997). *The New Organizational Wealth: Managing & Measuring Knowledge-based Assets*. San Francisco: Berrett-Koehler Publishers.

Taft, D. (2000). Stopping knowledge overflow—knowledge management tools still in developmental phase. *Computer Reseller News*, 14-14.

Tang, T., & McCalla, G. (2006). Active, Context-dependent, Data-centered Techniques for E-learning: A Case Study of A Research Paper Recommender System: In C. Romero & S. Ventura (Eds.). *Data Mining in E-learning*. WIT Press, Computational Mechanics Inc.

Teece, D. J. (2004). Knowledge and Competence As Strategic Assets. *Handbook on Knowledge Management 1*. Berlin: Springer.

Teo, T., Lee, C. B., Chai, C. S., & Wong, S. L. (2009). Assessing the intention to use technology among pre-service teachers in Singapore and Malaysia: A multigroup invariance analysis of the Technology Acceptance Model (TAM). *Computers & Education, 53*, 1000-1009.

Thomas, A. (2009). Knowledge Mapping. From http://pmtips.net/knowledge-mapping/.

Ting, E. T. J. E. A., & Liang, P. (2005). *Decision Support Systems and Intelligent Systems*. Upper Saddle River, NJ: Prentice Hall.

Tiwana, A. (2000). *The Knowledge Management Toolkit: Practical Techniques for Building A Knowledge Management System*. Upper Saddle River, NJ: Prentice Hall.

Trucano, M. (2005). *Knowledge maps: ICTs in education: ICT and Education Series. Washington,* DC: infoDev/World Bank.

Tseng, S.-S., Sue, P.-C., Su, J.-M., Weng, J.-F., & Tsai, W.-N. (2007). A new approach for constructing the concept map. *Computers & Education, 49*(3), 691-707.

Tseng, Y.-H., Chang, C.-Y., Rundgren, S.-N. C., & Rundgren, C.-J. (2010). Mining concept maps from news stories for measuring civic scientific literacy in media. *Computers & Education, 55*(1), 165-177.

Tseng, Y.-H., Lin, C.-J., & Lin, Y.-I. (2007). Text mining techniques for patent analysis. *Information Processing & Management, 43*(5),

1216-1247.

Turban, E., Aronson, J., & Liang, T.-P. (2005). Decision Support Systems and Intelligent Systems 7th. Upper Saddle River, NJ: Pearson Prentice Hall.

Vail, E., & Andersen, A. (1999). Mapping organizational knowledge. *Knowledge Management Review, 8*, 10-15.

Venkatesh, V., & Davis, F. (2000). A theoretical extension of the technology acceptance model: Four longitudinal field studies. *Management Science, 46*(2), 186-204.

Verdi, M., &Kulhavy, R. (2002). Learning with maps and texts: An overview. *Educational Psychology Review, 14*(1), 27-46.

Wagner, R. K. (1987). Tacit knowledge in everyday intelligent behavior. *Journal of Personality and Social Psychology, 52*(6), 1236.

Wang, F. (2006). *On Using Data Mining for Browsing Log Analysis in Learning Environments. In Proceedings of World Conference on Educational Multimedia, Hypermedia and Telecommunications. 4,* 57-73. Billerica, MA: WIT Press, Computational Mechanics Inc.

Wang, F. H., & Shao, H. M. (2004). Effective personalized recommendation based on time-framed navigation clustering and association mining. *Expert Systems with Applications, 27*(3), 365-377.

Wang, H.-C., Chang, C.-Y., & Li, T.-Y. (2008). Assessing creative problem-solving with automated text grading. *Computers & Education, 51*, 1450-1466.

Wang, K. C. (2000). The research of teachers' teaching believes and teaching practice. *Educational Research & Information, 8*(2), 84-98.

Wang, M., & Jacobson, M. J. (2011). Guest editorial-knowledge visualization for learning and knowledge management. *Educational Technology & Society, 14*(3), 1-3.

Wang, M., Jia, H., Sugumaran, V., Ran, W., & Liao, J. (2011). A web-based learning system for software test professionals. *IEEE Transactions on Education, 54*(2), 263-272.

Wang, M., Ran, W., Liao, J., & Yang, S. J. H. (2010). A performance-oriented approach to e-learning in the workplace. *Subscription Prices and Ordering Information, 13*(4), 167-179.

Wang, S.-L., & Wu, C.-Y. (2011). Application of context-aware and personalized recommendation to implement an adaptive ubiquitous learning system. *Expert Systems with Applications, 38*(9), 10831-10838.

Wang, S. (2002). Knowledge maps for managing web-based business. *Industrial Management & Data Systems, 102*(7), 357-364.

Wang, T.-H. (2011). Implementation of Web-based dynamic assessment in facilitating junior high school students to learn mathematics. *Computers & Education, 56*(4), 1062-1071.

Wang, T.-H., Wang, K.-H., & Huang, S.-C. (2008). Designing a Web-based assessment environment for improving pre-service teacher assessment literacy. *Computers & Education, 51*(1), 448-462.

Wang, T.-I., Su, C.-Y., & Hsieh, T.-C. (2011). Accumulating and visualising tacit knowledge of teachers on educational assessments. *Computers & Education, 57*(4), 2212-2223.

Wang, Y.-h., & Liao, H.-C. (2011). Data mining for adaptive learning in a TESL-based e-learning system. *Expert Systems with Applications, 38*(6), 6480-6485.

Watthananon, J., & Mingkhwan, A. (2012). Optimizing knowledge management using knowledge map. *Procedia Engineering, 32*, 1169-1177.

Wexler, M. N. (2001). The who, what and why of knowledge mapping. *Journal of Knowledge Management, 5*(3), 249-264.

Wiegmann, D. A., Dansereau, D. F., McCagg, E. C., Rewey, K. L., & Pitre, U. (1992). Effects of knowledge map characteristics on information processing. *Contemporary Educational Psychology, 17*(2), 136-155.

Wielinga, B. J., Bredeweg, B., & Breuker, J. (1988). *Knowledge Acquisition for Expert Systems.* Berlin: Springer.

Wong, K., & Li, W.-j. (1998). *Intelligent Chinese information retrieval—Why is it so difficult*? In Proceedings of the first Asia digital library workshop.

Woo, J.-H., Clayton, M. J., Johnson, R. E., Flores, B. E., & Ellis, C. (2004). Dynamic knowledge map: reusing experts' tacit knowledge in the AEC industry. *Automation in Construction, 13*(2), 203-207.

Wu, X., Kumar, V., Quinlan, J. R., Ghosh, J., Yang, Q., Motoda, H., McLachlan, G. J., Angus, N., Liu, B., Philip, S. Y., Zhou, Z. H., Steinbach, M., Hand, D. J., & Steinberg, D. (2008). Top 10 algorithms in data mining. *Knowledge and Information Systems, 14*(1), 1-37.

Wu, Z., & Tseng, G. (1993). Chinese text segmentation for text retrieval: Achievements and problems. *Journal of the American Society for Information Science, 44*(9), 532-542.

Wu, Z., & Tseng, G. (1995). ACTS: An automatic Chinese text segmentation system for full text retrieval. *Journal of the American Society for Information Science, 46*(2), 83-96.

Xu, Y., & Liu, Y. (2009). Teacher assessment knowledge and practice: a narrative inquiry of a chinese college EFL teacher's experience. *TESOL Quarterly, 43*(3), 493-513.

Yang, H.-C., & Lee, C.-H. (2004). A text mining approach on automatic generation of web directories and hierarchies. *Expert Systems with Applications*, 27(4), 645-663.

Yang, J.-B. (2007). Developing a knowledge map for construction scheduling using a novel approach. *Automation in Construction*, 16(6), 806-815.

Yang, Q., Song, B., Lu, W., & Zhang, Y. (2007). *Integrating knowledge maps in design process configurations for concurrently engineered product development.* In Proceedings of the Institution of Mechanical Engineers.

Yang, Y., & Chan, C. (2008). Comprehensive evaluation criteria for English learning websites using expert validity surveys. *Computers & Education, 51*(1), 403-422.

Yin, P.-Y., Chang, K.-C., Hwang, G.-J., Hwang, G.-H., & Chan, Y. (2006). A particle swarm optimization approach to composing serial test sheets for multiple assessment criteria. *Educational Technology and Society, 9*(3), 3-15.

Yu, P., & Van de Sompel, H. (1965). Networks of scientific papers. *Science, 169*, 510-515.

Yu, P. S. (1999). *Data mining and personalization technologies.* In Proceedings of the 6th International Conference on Database Systems for Advanced Applications.

Zaliane, O. (2006). *Recommender Systems for E-learning: Towards Non-Intrusive Web Mining.* Billerica, MA: WIT Press.

Zenebe, A., & Norcio, A. F. (2009). Representation, similarity measures and aggregation methods using fuzzy sets for content-based recommender systems. *Fuzzy Sets and Systems*, *160*(1), 76-94.

Zhang, D., & Lee, W. S. (2003). *Question classification using support vector machines.* In Proceedings of the 26th annual international ACM SIGIR conference on research and development in information retrieval Toronto, Canada.

Zhang, Z.-K., Zhou, T., & Zhang, Y.-C. (2010). Personalized recommendation via integrated diffusion on user-item-tag tripartite graphs. *Physica A: Statistical Mechanics and its Applications, 389*(1), 179-186.

Zhangang, H. (2009). *Building text knowledge map for product development based on CSEP method.* Paper presented at the International Symposium on Computer Network and Multimedia Technology.

Zhao, J. (2010). School knowledge management framework and strategies: the new perspective on teacher professional development. *Computers in Human Behavior, 26*(2), 168-175.

Zumbach, J. (2009). The role of graphical and text based argumentation tools in hypermedia learning. *Computers in Human Behavior, 25*(4), 811-817.

Subject Index

图书在版编目（CIP）数据

可视化教师隐性知识之知识地图辅助评量系统 = The knowledge map assisting assessment system based on accumulating and visualizing tacit knowledge of teachers : 英文 / 苏建元著. — 杭州 : 浙江大学出版社，2014.9
ISBN 978-7-308-13921-2

Ⅰ. ①可… Ⅱ. ①苏… Ⅲ. ①计算机辅助教学—研究—英文 Ⅳ. ①G434

中国版本图书馆CIP数据核字(2014)第224513号
浙江省版权局著作权合同登记图字：11-2014-220号

The Knowledge Map Assisting Assessment System Based on Accumulating and Visualizing Tacit Knowledge of Teachers
Chien-Yuan Su / 苏建元　著

责任编辑　曾　熙（zxpeggy@zju.edu.cn）
封面设计　十木米
出版发行　浙江大学出版社
　　　　　（杭州市天目山路148号　邮政编码310007）
　　　　　（网址：http://www.zjupress.com）
排　　版　杭州林智广告有限公司
印　　刷　杭州杭新印务有限公司
开　　本　700mm×960mm　1/16
印　　张　14.25
字　　数　290千
版 印 次　2014年9月第1版　2014年9月第1次印刷
书　　号　ISBN 978-7-308-13921-2
定　　价　40.00元
